WOMEN OF COURAGE:
FIVE PLAYS BY JOANNA H. KRAUS

JANET E. RUBIN and JOANNA H. KRAUS

Foreword by Nellie McCaslin

Dramatic Publishing
Woodstock, Illinois • England • Australia • New Zealand

*** NOTICE ***

Published by The Dramatic Publishing Company
P.O. Box 129, Woodstock, IL 60098

ACKNOWLEDGMENTS

Gratitude is sincerely bestowed upon the following for their assistance and support:

Cheryl Hadsall
Tim Inman
Saun Strobel
Katherine Fehrman
Gayle Sergel
Kathy Krzys
Special Collections, Arizona State University Library
Jeannine Leslie
Saginaw Valley State University

To Margaret Merrion, who is a creative, caring and courageous friend.

J.E.R.

To my husband, Ted, and to our son, Tim, loyal supporters, who've given me love and candor. Thank you!

J.H.K.

CONTENTS

Foreword by Nellie McCaslin vii

CHAPTER ONE
Introduction.. 1
The Playwright: Joanna H. Kraus 2
Plays, Books and Articles by Joanna H. Kraus........ 7
Brief Bits to Begin 8
How to Use This Book 11

CHAPTER TWO — *The Ice Wolf*
The Playwright Speaks........................... 13
The Play 16
    Prologue 17
    Act One 19
    Act Two 32
    Act Three 46
Classroom Concepts 53

CHAPTER THREE — *Mean to be Free*
The Playwright Speaks........................... 63
"Runagate, Runagate"........................... 65
The Play 67
    Act One 68
    Act Two 88
Classroom Concepts 108

CHAPTER FOUR — *Remember My Name*
The Playwright Speaks........................ 120
The Play 123
    Act One 125
    Act Two 173
Classroom Concepts 198

CHAPTER FIVE — *Angel in the Night*
The Playwright Speaks........................ 207
The Play 212
    Prologue 214
    Act One 217
    Act Two 245
    Epilogue............................... 258
    Pronunciation Guide 260
Classroom Concepts 263

CHAPTER SIX — *Sunday Gold*
The Playwright Speaks........................ 274
The Play 278
    Act One 279
    Act Two............................... 303
Classroom Concepts 323

CHAPTER SEVEN
*A Unique Collaboration Between a History Museum and
   Community Theatre Strikes Gold in "Sunday Gold"*
   — Richard King 334

Permission Acknowledgments.................... 341
Bibliography 342

FOREWORD

It is a particular pleasure to write a foreword to this book, for I have followed the work of Joanna Halpert Kraus from the time of the production of her first published play, *The Ice Wolf*, in 1963. Many of us who saw the Equity Library production in New York sensed that it represented a turning point in children's theatre. The content, a legend that showed the tragic consequences of prejudice and an unhappy ending, defied the rules of traditional children's theatre fare. The reactions of those first audiences was predictable: enthusiasm, shock, confusion. Was it really a play for children? Though it would take several years for a consensus to be reached, *The Ice Wolf* has become one of America's finest and most popular children's plays. Furthermore, it established Joanna Halpert Kraus as a leading American dramatist for young audiences.

In the thirty-five years that have passed since that production, Kraus has moved in several directions but common threads run through all of them: compassion for the victims of discrimination, the plight of the outsider, recognition of the role of women in all cultures, and the endurance of the human spirit in the face of adversity. This is not to imply that she has repeated herself for she has not. Her material has varied from carefully researched history to folklore and original plots. Although the playwright has a strong social conscience, her work is neither didactic nor political, for the themes are rooted in the plots. Viewers take from them what they are ready and willing to receive.

During the eighties, the Holocaust was a preoccupation of many writers and artists, and Kraus' contribution to the literature for young viewers was both noteworthy and appropriate. Again, I had the opportunity of being in the audience at the Playwrights' Conference in Indianapolis where the script of *Remember My Name* was first performed. A spirited discussion followed the production, revealing the impact of the play on an audience of educators, playwrights, and children's theatre directors.

Angel in the Night is the true story of Marysia Pawlina Szul, a young Polish girl whose compassion and courage saved the lives of a little family of Jews during the Nazi occupation. Risking her own life, as did Harriet Tubman, she not only provided them with food and shelter but for two years refused to betray them. As a result, she was imprisoned and beaten. In the last scene of the play, we see her fifty years later on the day she is honored for her bravery. The fact that the story was scrupulously researched and documented adds a compelling dimension.

Mean to be Free, one of the earlier plays, is still among the most popular. The story of one of Harriet Tubman's trips north with two children and two young people, runaway slaves, is gripping as theatre, while at the same time imparting historical information on the Underground Railroad prior to the Civil War.

Sunday Gold, a play commissioned by the Raleigh Little Theatre and the North Carolina Museum of History, has an original plot set in a mining town in the 1840s. Here the victims of discrimination on the basis of gender are a poor white girl of twelve and a slave girl her age. Poverty, race, and the attitude toward women stand in the way of their dreams to attend school and make something of themselves. In this play, as in all of Kraus' work, we are left with hope at the end of the struggle, though we know that a happy ending will be a long time coming.

The five plays in this collection are representative of the work of one of America's most distinguished children's playwrights, in main because there is a balance between entertainment and substance. Young audiences leave the theatre challenged by the material while at the same time they are held by the story. Every play stands alone as dramatic literature, and every play also has within it exciting workshop possibilities for classroom use afterward. I am honored to have been asked to write the foreword to this book.

Nellie McCaslin
New York University

CHAPTER ONE

Introduction

The presentation of the Chorpenning Cup today reminds all of us of the innovative scripting and pioneer work in Children's Theatre of Charlotte Chorpenning at nearby Goodman Theatre.

This year's recipient of this award fully sustains the spirit of its namesake.

It is a pleasure to announce that the 1971 Chorpenning Cup is presented to Joanna H. Kraus. Joanna's plays: The Voyage of the Seven Seas, The Ice Wolf, Mean to be Free: A Flight North on the Underground Railroad *are truly creative contributions to the American and world repertoire of children's plays. In a time of non-form, she has brought theatrical form and artistry to the popular terms of "relevance" and "culture-gap." She has provided an imaginative (gift) to young audiences of today and to young audiences to come.*

(Presentation of the 1971 Chorpenning Cup by Orlin Corey at the CTC Awards Luncheon-Art Institute of Chicago, August 16, 1971. Courtesy of Special Collections, Arizona State University.)

The importance of Ms. Kraus in the history of children's theatre in the United States is recognized by everyone in the field and is documented in two histories of the movement written by Nellie McCaslin, as well as by the appearance of her plays in anthologies of the last three decades. In advancing themes of prejudice, in areas of cultural, physical and gender differences, Ms. Kraus has broadened the scope of serious theatre for youth.

(Dr. Lowell Swortzell, Director, Program in Educational Theatre, New York University, 1996.)

The Playwright: Joanna H. Kraus

As the heroes in this anthology, Joanna Halpert Kraus has been a stellar example of courage and commitment as she moved youth theatre artistry forward. From *The Ice Wolf* to *Sunday Gold*, Kraus has composed a succession of plays unparalleled in their ability to combine theatricality, intelligent writing, and sensitivity to subject and audience. As a playwright and teacher, her work truly enhances the discipline of child drama.

Since her seminal work, *The Ice Wolf*, Kraus has provided youth theatre with plays that challenge young people. She has been a leader in broadening the scope of subject matter considered appropriate for young audiences. Her work has helped theatre artists and educators to recognize that young people could both enjoy and learn from plays which were not fairy or folk tales but which, indeed, considered far weightier matters. Always respectful of her audience, Kraus has crafted a body of work that examines social issues and serious subjects. Through plays that deal with diverse topics such as intolerance, the Holocaust, and adoption, she has challenged both adults and children to examine their own thoughts, feelings, and sense of belonging. Always, she has done so with interesting characters, solid stories, truthful dialogue, and honest dramatic action.

What has drawn so many for so long to this respected playwright's important works? The reasons are obvious, as readers of the plays in this anthology will soon discover. Her gift for creating characters with whom young people can identify is unquestionable. Further, her plays partner effectively with curricular content areas such as history. The breadth of subject matter offers further appeal. Kraus' plays treat themes and life experiences of special interest to older children, an audience that is sometimes overlooked and difficult to reach. The plays which constitute her body of work are useful vehicles for performance and for study, making them practical tools for educating and entertaining.

Born in Portland, Maine, in 1937, Kraus began writing plays as a teenager. When she was thirteen, she joined the Children's Theatre of Portland, under the direction of Marghi Dutton, and worked with them from 1951 to 1955, the year in which she graduated from Portland's Deering High School. One year prior to graduation, Kraus received the Best Actress Award (CT) and Scholarship to the Manhattan Theatre Colony at the Ogunquit Playhouse in Ogunquit, Maine, where she appeared with Rudy Vallee and Lee Remick in *Jenny Kissed Me*.

As a freshman at Sarah Lawrence College, she saw her first children's theatre play, *The Ticklish Harp* (unpublished) produced on a bill that included poetry by Dame Edith Sitwell. Henry Hewes, drama critic of the *Saturday Review of Literature* encouraged the young playwright to see as much theatre as possible. She took his words to heart. Several more of her plays were subsequently produced and one, *The Voyage of the Seven Seas*, was published by the Association of Junior Leagues of America. Kraus spent her junior year abroad at Westfield College, University of London. She then returned to Sarah Lawrence to complete her B.A. and graduated in 1959.

During the period from 1960 through 1961, Kraus assumed the role of associate director of the Children's Theatre Association in Baltimore, Maryland, where she worked with Isabel B. Burger. From there, she went to the University of California for her Master of Arts degree, which she received in 1963. *The Ice Wolf* was written as her master's thesis in theatre. Samuel Selden and George Savage guided the young playwright in this effort to dramatically tell a story she first heard orally in reference to an Eskimo print. This play launched her career and redefined the boundaries regarding acceptable subject matter in theatre for young audiences.

The decade from 1966 to 1976 was filled with personal and professional triumphs for Joanna Halpert. In 1966, she married drama critic Ted Kraus in New York City. In 1971, she won the prestigious Charlotte B. Chorpenning Cup for Achievement in Playwriting given by the American Alliance for Theatre and Education (formerly the Children's Theatre Conference). The following year (1972), she received her Ed.D. from Columbia University, having written, "A History of the Children's Theatre Association of Baltimore, Maryland, from 1943 1966," as her dissertation. In 1976, she and her husband adopted a child from Korea. (Her play, *Kimchi Kid*, was a 1987 finalist at the IUPUI National Playwriting Competition[1] and is dedicated to her adopted son, Tim, who inspired the story.) Also in 1976, Kraus earned a Creative Artists Public Service Fellowship (CAPS) in playwriting from the New York State Council on the Arts and the National Endowment for the Arts.

Kraus began a distinguished teaching career at the State University of New York College at New Paltz in 1972 and left there in 1979 for a post at the State University of New York College at Brockport. There, she served for fifteen years as coordinator of the Undergraduate and Graduate Interdisciplinary Arts for Children Program and earned the rank of full professor in 1986. As a professor, Kraus' disciplinary areas

---

1 Now called the Waldo M. and Grace C. Bonderman Youth Theatre Playwriting Workshop.

of specialization included child drama, playwriting, and improvisation. Kraus retired from SUNY Brockport with emeritus status in 1995 and, in that same year, received the Lifetime Achievement Award from the New York State Theatre Education Association. She now lives in California and teaches part-time classes in drama and writing in the East Bay area and is a correspondent for *The Sunday Times*, a Knight Ridder newspaper.

In addition to the honors already noted, her play *For the Glory* was a winner at the American Voices, New Play Reading Series at GeVa Theatre located in Rochester, New York. Earlier in her career (1983), Kraus earned the first Millay Colony for the Arts—Empire State Institute for the Performing Arts Playwriting Award. Her commissions include those from the Raleigh Little Theatre and the North Carolina Museum of History for *Sunday Gold*, the Honor of Humanity Project under the direction of National-Louis University in affiliation with the Avenue of the Righteous in Evanston, Illinois, for *Angel in the Night*, and Arizona State University for *The Last Baron of Arizona*. For several years, she received grants from the State University of New York for research. In addition, Kraus has held residencies at Humboldt State University at Arcata, California, at the University of Texas at Austin, at the California Theatre Center, Alfred University Summer Place, and at the William G. Enloe High School in Raleigh, North Carolina. She also has been involved in invitational conferences such as the Getty funded "Informing the Future of Theatre Education" conference held in Chattanooga, Tennessee, in 1996, visiting professorships and faculty exchanges. Her associations with professional artists' colonies include YADDO at Saratoga Springs, New York, and Leighton Studios, Banff Centre for the Arts in Alberta, Canada.

Kraus has made significant contributions to theatre education and professional theatre practices through her articles, books, and plays. These are listed in the following pages. She is a member of the Dramatists Guild, the American Alliance for Theatre and Education, the California Writers Club, the Society for Children's Book Writers and Illustrators, and the International Association of Theatre for Children and Young People (ASSITEJ). She is listed in *Contemporary Authors, the World Who's Who of Women, The Writers Directory, Twentieth Century Children's Writers, International Authors and Writer's Who's Who, Who's Who in America,* and *Who's Who in Entertainment.*

The plays in this anthology exemplify not only Kraus' long and illustrious career, but also a dedication, curiosity, and passion inherited by her protagonists. Two of her plays, *The Ice Wolf* and *Mean to be Free*, earned her the prestigious Chorpenning Cup. *The Devil's Orphan*, later retitled *Remember My Name*, earned her first prize at the IUPUI National Playwriting Competition in 1989. She was again honored by the American Alliance for Theatre and Education (formerly the Children's Theatre Conference) in 1996 when *Angel in the Night*, competing with scripts for students in upper and secondary school grades, was named the winner of the Distinguished Play Award in Category A. In 1997, *Sunday Gold* won AATE's Unpublished Play Reading Project honors. Without a doubt, Kraus has indelibly marked theatre for young audiences throughout her distinguished career by creating thoughtful, skillfully crafted, and artistically enduring works for the stage. The respect and recognition she has earned is no less than that with which she has infused every character in her plays. Joanna Halpert Kraus, playwright, author, and teacher, is herself a talented and esteemed woman of courage.

Plays, Books, and Articles by Joanna H. Kraus

Plays

Voyage of the Seven Seas
The Ice Wolf
Mean to be Free
Vasalisa
Circus Home
The Last Baron of Arizona
Tenure Track (co-author Greer Woodward)
Kimchi Kid
The Shaggy Dog Murder Trial
Remember My Name
Angel in the Night
Sunday Gold
For the Glory (with Hobart Brown)

Books

Ms. Courageous: Women of Science
Tall Boy's Journey
The Last Baron of Arizona
Mean to be Free: Plays Plus
Sound and Motion Stories
The Dragon Hammer and The Tale of Oniroku
The Great American Train Ride
"The Night the Elephants Marched on New York," included
    in *Creative Drama in the Classroom*, 5th ed.
    Edited by Nellie McCaslin.
"The First Night of Sleep," included in *Creative Drama in
    the Primary Grades*. Edited by Nellie McCaslin.

Articles

Correspondent, The Sunday Times (a Knight Ridder newspaper)
Reviewer, *TYA Today* (ASSITEJ publication)
"Isabel Burger" in *Notable Women in American Theatre*
"Mary Coyle Chase" in *Women in World History*
"Taking Children's Theatre to the Moon" in *Players*
"Children's Theatre Baltimore Style," in *Players*
Reviewer, *Critical Digest*
Reviewer, *Children's Theatre Review*
Reviewer, *Times Herald Record* (Middleton, N.Y.)
"Dramatizing History" in *Children and Drama*
Theatre Critic, *Quarante*

Brief Bits to Begin

Bits of production and publication information about
each of the five plays in this anthology are briefly offered
to whet the reader's appetite for what is to come in the
following pages. Little more need be said. As these brief
histories attest, the broad scope of productions and diversity of audiences and readers confirm the consistent quality
and appeal found in Kraus' work. The scripts are universal
in appeal and stand proudly on their own as stories of humanity. Each is rich with suspense and conflict, tantalizing
characters, historical detail or legend, deep and sincere
emotions, an intriguing plot and, of course, women of
courage!

The Ice Wolf

First produced by Davey Marlin-Jones at the Equity Library Theatre for Children Off-Broadway in 1963, this play has been produced by professional companies as well as community and educational theatres throughout the world. Representative productions include those at the Alley Theatre in Houston, Texas; the National Technical Institute for the Deaf, Rochester, New York; Army Entertainment in Frankfort, Germany; the Rochester, Minnesota Community Playhouse; California State University at Hayward; Indiana University at Bloomington; the American Conservatory Theatre in San Francisco; the People's Theatre in Cambridge, Massachusetts; the Bastion Theatre Company and the Carousel Theatre, both in British Columbia, Canada; Actors Repertory Theatre in Portland, Oregon; Temple University in Philadelphia; Asolo Touring Theatre in Florida; University of Hawaii at Manoa, Oahu; and Theatre Calgary, Canada. The play has been translated into Spanish and American sign language and has been shown on Cablevision, British Columbia, Canada. Published by New Plays, *The Ice Wolf* appears in several anthologies.

Mean to be Free

Mean to be Free was first produced at Hunter College Playhouse in New York in 1967. In 1970, Cleveland, Ohio's, Karamu House used Title III funds and enlisted the board of education to assist in bringing students to see the play as staged by the Karamu Youth Theatre in honor of Black History Month. Other representative productions include those by Washington, D.C. Parks and Recreation; South Carolina Arts Commission Tour; Texas A&M University; University of Texas at Austin; U.S. Army base at Schweinfurt, Germany; and the Brussels American School in Belgium. Published by New Plays, it also appears in the British series *Plays Plus* edited by Cecily O'Neill.

Remember My Name

The Jerusalem Group Theatre gave this play a professional New York premiere in 1992. Prior to that, the play was the first prize winner at the IUPUI National Playwriting Competition in 1989, and it premiered at Indiana University/Purdue University at Indianapolis that same year. This script also was a finalist for honors at the Cleveland Jewish Community Center and a semi-finalist in the Forest Roberts Playwriting Competition, both in 1988. Representative productions include those at the Rochester Academy of Performing Arts in New York; Duquesne University in Pittsburgh, Pennsylvania; and Northwestern University of Evanston, Illinois. Excerpts from the play appear in the anthology, *Images from the Holocaust*, published by National Textbook Company and the entire script has been published by Samuel French.

Angel in the Night

Angel in the Night is the winner of the 1996 Distinguished Play Award given by the American Alliance for Theatre and Education. Published by Dramatic Publishing, the play was commissioned by the Honor of Humanity Project under the direction of National-Louis University, located in Evanston, Illinois. The project was done in affiliation with the Avenue of the Righteous and the play premiered at National-Louis in 1991. A regional tour followed in 1992. Other representative productions include those at Prime Stage in Pittsburgh, Pennsylvania, De La Salle High School in Concord, California, and the Cardinal Gibbons High School in Raleigh, North Carolina.

Sunday Gold

Sunday Gold is a result of a collaboration between the North Carolina Museum of History and the Raleigh Little Theatre whose Youth Theatre Program wished to commission a play for young audiences. Funding for the project was secured through the United Arts Council of Raleigh and Wake County with additional support from the North Carolina Department of Cultural Resources and the North Carolina Arts Council. The world premiere of the play, in 1995, was followed by a tour of North Carolina schools and museum sites. Other representative productions include that given at the University of North Carolina at Asheville. *Sunday Gold* was a winner in 1997 of the Unpublished Play Reading Project from the American Alliance for Theatre and Education. In 1998, Dramatic Publishing brought out the acting edition of the script.

How To Use This Book

This anthology brings together five of Joanna Kraus' best scripts. These plays represent the challenging subject matter, dramatic diversity, and the breadth of content for which she is known. It begins with her first important play, *The Ice Wolf*, and ends with the recent work, *Sunday Gold*.

The plays follow this introductory chapter. Each is preceded by a section entitled, "The Playwright Speaks."

Here, Kraus provides background information on the play, such as why it is important and what inspired its writing. The play itself then follows. "Classroom Concepts," a section offering strategies and activities for teaching and learning about the play, concludes each chapter.

This anthology brings together, for the first time, both important plays and personal insights from this award-winning playwright. Because of the quality of these scripts and the variety of topics and themes treated therein, the reputation of the playwright, and the teaching activities included, content is useful for both study and performance, making this book a practical tool for educating as well as entertaining.

CHAPTER TWO

The Ice Wolf

The Playwright Speaks

Ideas don't come when you want them to come. In fact the reverse is often true. It's why writers spend an inordinate amount of time staring out the window!

The Ice Wolf began one summer, when I was Drama Director at an arts camp outside of Ottawa. One of my staff created an improvisation with his group based on Inuit material. The scene lasted about five minutes; but I couldn't forget the young girl ostracized because she was different. The next year, looking for a subject for my thesis at the University of California at Los Angeles, I wrote the student requesting a written reference. He wrote back that there was none. The improvisation had been based on a brief explanation of an Inuit drawing from a Catholic Mission in Povungnetuk, Quebec. The drawing concerned a transformation, a popular motif in many cultures.

The source of this play was neither traditional folk tale nor literary. The idea that generated the artist's rice paper print was the starting point of my play. (That's why if you try to find the original source, you can't!) However, as a play for young audiences, I tried to structure the drama in the traditional form of the time honored folk tale. But as I went through dozens of Inuit folk tales, I found most of them to be too raw and gritty for *TYA*. I decided that the protagonist, Anatou, mustn't die accepting evil as the strongest force in her life. Rather she should understand the power of hatred and conquer it. In the explanation of the drawing, the girl sought revenge and killed countless hunters. While this is psychologically valid, it made her seem, not only full of fury, but incapable of love. So I had her flee to the forest, "a place where" her friend Tarto warns, "Eskimos never go." When she exchanges her human skin for a wolf skin, she is trying to escape the unbearable anguish within.

When her short-lived tranquility passes and the hatred is reawakened, she retaliates. But it's only when the Wood God accuses her of killing "out of hate. Men do that, not the animals!" that she realizes she's become even more brutal than the villagers. At the end, it is her courage and her compassion for Tarto that awakens the villager's remorse.

I had a terrible time getting the play produced in the sixties. Up to then, no American children's theatre production ever had the hero die. So I had offers, *if* I would change the ending, which I adamantly refused. I'd done exhaustive research on various aspects of Inuit life and folklore, had trained in theatre, had grown up in children's theatre, and I firmly believed the play was aesthetically valid. But I was discouraged.

It was Davey Marlin-Jones at Equity Library Theatre who said, "We like your play and want to do it. But—"

"I know," I said in frustration, "You want to change the ending."

"No." He looked surprised. "I like the ending. But we'll do a production of *Red Shoes* and run them both in repertory, so we don't lose money."

They didn't.

And it was Pat Whitton, who was just starting New Plays, who took the script others feared.

It's had productions every single year since that time.

Though many adults have questioned the brutality of the play and "sad" ending, children are moved by the story, recognize Anatou's growth and change, and comprehend the dramatic justice of her death. (After all, she did kill villagers.)

The play was not meant to negate life but to affirm it, to suggest that goodness requires greater strength than evil, and to argue that both forces coexist within us.

The Play

CHARACTERS

STORYTELLER

ANATOU, a girl born to Eskimo parents. Her skin is pale and her hair blond; a phenomenon in the village

KARVIK, her father

ARNARQIK, her mother

TARTO, her best friend, a village boy

KIVIOG, Tarto's father

ATATA, an old man of the village but a good hunter

SHIKIKANAQ, a village girl

MOTOMIAK, a village boy

VILLAGER 1, a woman

VILLAGER 2, a man

WOOD GOD, the God of the Forest

A BEAVER

A FOX

An ERMINE

SETTING

The entire action of the play takes place in a small, isolated Eskimo village, Little Whale River, and the forest, a few days inland. It is located in the Hudson Bay area of Canada.

TIME

The time is long before the missionaries established their settlements, long before white man had been seen, a time when the spirits and the Shaman, or the Wise Man, ruled.

Prologue

SCENE: *It is the end of January. In the foreground we see an expanse of white spread out. It is broken in a few places by hillocks which rise up like seal's heads from the plains. There is an atmosphere of cold beauty and awesome space.*

The STORYTELLER enters on the apron of the stage. He is dressed, as all the Eskimos, in the attire of the Hudson Bay Eskimos, but somehow there is the quality about him of excitement. He is no ordinary hunter.

STORYTELLER. Far beyond the world you know—
    Of sun, rushing rivers, and trees
    Is the Northland
    Where the winter snow is gray,
    There is no sound of birds
    Nothing but the stillness of space
    Of endless snow
    And endless cold.
    There, the child Anatou was born
    In the village of Little Whale River.
    It was small, beside the sea.
    But the search for food never ended.

(Lights up on igloo. Eskimos in circle, one beating drum, chanting.)

Aja, I remember. It was one of the coldest nights of the year, so cold the dog team had buried themselves in the snow.

ATATA. And the seal-oil lamps trembled before the Great North wind.

KARVIK. Just before dawn, when the baby came, Karvik had to go out and repair their home. His fingers seemed to freeze at once. Never had there been such a storm in Little Whale River.

(Lights up on KARVIK cutting a snow block and fitting it into dome.)

ARNARQIK. Inside Arnarqik sewed the caribou skins she had chewed. She was making new clothes for Karvik. Only once did she dare to look at the small child beside her wrapped in skins. It was strangely still, strangely quiet. It was unlike any child Arnarqik had ever seen.

STORYTELLER. Atata was at the seal's breathing hole...

(Lights up on ATATA crouched by breathing hole, poised, ready with harpoon.)

...waiting...waiting until the seal came up for air. For days there had been no food in Little Whale River. He thought the birth of a new child might bring him luck! Then...he struck with his harpoon! *(ATATA harpoons seal.)*

ATATA. Aja, Nuliayuk, now everyone will eat!

STORYTELLER. He took the choice bit of meat, the seal's liver, to return to the seal goddess, Nuliayuk. The Shaman, the wise man, had told him to do this so she would feast on it and then remember to send more seals to the hunters of Little Whale River. Atata rushed back. Now there was something to celebrate. A new child, a fresh caught seal. There would be drum chants and dancing and stories in the long white night. *(Drum chants begin. They break off abruptly.)* But there was no singing or dancing.

KARVIK. It was long ago...

ARNARQIK. Just about this time.

STORYTELLER. It was a pale dawn...

ATATA. Like this one...

STORYTELLER. When Anatou was born.

ACT ONE
Scene One

SCENE: *The interior of KARVIK and ARNARQIK's home in Little Whale River. Masses of thick, heavy caribou skins are spread about. Seal-oil lamps, made of soapstone, light the home.*

AT RISE: *The sound of Eskimo dogs howling. A strong wind is blowing. Villagers come in from all sides dressed in their habitual furs. They crawl through the passageway and lights come up in the interior of the igloo. KARVIK and ARNARQIK are seated. Their new child is beside ARNARQIK on a caribou skin not visible from the entrance.*

KARVIK. Welcome! Welcome all of you!

VILLAGER 2. Aja! Your first child. Of course we'd come. *(To others.)* We must sing many songs to welcome it.

KIVIOG. And if it's a man child, Karvik will already have made him a harpoon, a sled, and a whip.

VILLAGER 1. By the next moon he will be able to use them. Wait and see! (*They laugh.*)

VILLAGER 2. Good, he can hunt a seal with us this winter and the caribou next fall. If he's as good a hunter as Karvik, we'll get twice as much.

KIVIOG. And he'll be a companion for my son, Tarto, born under the same moon. (*They all laugh except KARVIK and ARNARQIK, who are strangely quiet.*)

VILLAGER 1. Karvik! Arnarqik! You are silent. Show us the man child. We've come a long way to see him. (*ARNARQIK moves slowly.*)

ARNARQIK. It is a girl child... but we are glad.

KARVIK. She will be good.

ARNARQIK. It is true. There is joy in feeling new life come to the great world.

VILLAGER 1. A girl! Ah-ah. That means more care.

VILLAGER 2. And more attention.

KIVIOG. She cannot hunt.

VILLAGER 2 (*politely*). But let us see her anyway. (*AR-NARQIK moves away troubled, then points to the caribou skin.*)

ARNARQIK. There, look for yourself. (*KARVIK has turned away. Villagers crowd around the child, move back abruptly, and whirl on KARVIK and ARNARQIK.*)

VILLAGER 1 (*in low horror*). Her hair is white!

VILLAGER 2. Her face is pale.

KIVIOG. She cannot be an Eskimo.

VILLAGER 1. She cannot be one of us!

KARVIK. Of course she is. Her hair will get darker. Wait.

VILLAGER 2. But her face. Look at it. No Eskimo child was ever born as pale as that.

VILLAGER 1. She's a devil.

ARNARQIK. No!

VILLAGER 1. She will not live one moon.

ARNARQIK. She will live.

VILLAGER 1. She will bring bad luck.

ARNARQIK. She's only a baby.

KIVIOG. Put her out in the snow now, before she turns the gods against us.

VILLAGER 2. And our stomachs shrink.

VILLAGER 1. And our dishes are empty.

VILLAGER 2. It's happened before. We all know it. Get rid of the child before it's too late.

KIVIOG. She will offend Nuliayuk, the goddess of the seals. Nuliayuk will stay at the bottom of the sea, and keep the seals beside her, and we will all go hungry. Put the child out into the snow or we will die of famine!

ARNARQIK. No! She will be a good Eskimo.

VILLAGER 2. Then let her grow up in another village. We don't want her here.

KIVIOG. She doesn't look like us. She won't think like us.

VILLAGER 1. She doesn't belong here.

KARVIK. Then where does she belong? Where should she go?

VILLAGER 1. Put her out in the snow. *(Starts to grab her.)*

ARNARQIK. No! No! No, I can't. Don't you understand? She is our child.

VILLAGER 2. Then leave our village in peace. Don't anger the spirits of Little Whale River.

KARVIK. But this is our village and you are our people. How can we leave it? Wait! She will be like the others. You'll see. She'll sew and cook just as well as any Eskimo girl. Better! Arnarqik will teach her.

KIVIOG *(holds up his hands)*. Very well. We will watch and wait. Perhaps you are right, and we will see her hair and cheeks grow darker. But we have not gifts or good wishes to welcome a white-faced child—a white-faced girl child! (*Villagers exit. ARNARQIK tries to run after them.*)

ARNARQIK. Come back! Please wait. Don't go yet. Oh, Karvik, what will we do?

KARVIK (*slowly*). Her hair should be as dark as the raven's wing.

ARNARQIK. It is as white as the caribou's belly. Karvik, what if they are right? She is different. Karvik, why is her hair pale? Why doesn't she cry? She is so still! It's not natural.

KARVIK. She is frightened already. The Fair One will have a hard journey. (*Looks out the passageway.*) Arnarqik, the villagers spoke wisely. (*Looks for a long time at his wife.*) She would never know. It would not hurt if we put her in the snow now.

ARNARQIK. No, Karvik! You mustn't ask me to.

KARVIK. But if we leave, will the next village think she looks more like an Eskimo?

ARNARQIK (*shakes her head*). No, she is Anatou, the Fair One—she will not change. But I will teach her, Karvik. She will be a good Eskimo girl!

KARVIK. But will they ever think she is like the others?

ARNARQIK. Yes. Yes. Of course they will. Let us stay here. Who knows what is beyond the snow?

KARVIK. Then we must be strong. We must teach Anatou to be strong. Only then will our home be her home and our friends her friends. It won't be easy, Arnarqik. (*AR-NARQIK is beside the baby.*)

ARNARQIK. Oh Karvik, I couldn't leave her. Not like that! (*Abruptly she changes.*) Look, Karvik...she is smiling. (*Picks her up.*) Oh, Karvik, we mustn't let them hurt her. We must protect her.

KARVIK. Sing, Arnarqik, sing the morning song. Bring Anatou luck. She will have a hard journey.

ARNARQIK (*sits, sings or chants*). I rise up from rest
    moving swiftly as the raven's wing
    I rise up to greet the day
    Wo-wa
    My face is turned from dark of night
    My gaze toward the dawn
    Toward the whitening dawn. (*Lights fade.*)

STORYTELLER. But her hair did not grow dark as the raven's wing. Instead, each day she grew fairer. They called her the "different one," and when the blinding snow swept across the North or when the hunters returned with empty sleds, the villagers whispered, "It's Anatou. She's the one."

Scene Two

SCENE: *The village, TARTO, SHIKIKANAQ and MO-TOMIAK are playing an Eskimo game, a combination of Hide-and-Seek and Touch. MOTOMIAK is just dashing for the goal pursued by SHIKIKANAQ. TARTO is at the goal watching and laughing.*

TARTO. Hurry up, Motomiak. She's right behind you. Shikikanaq is right behind you!

(*MOTOMIAK turns to look, still running. ANATOU enters. She sees the race but moves out of the way too late and they collide. MOTOMIAK falls and SHIKIKANAQ tags him.*)

SHIKIKANAQ. There! I won!

MOTOMIAK. That wasn't fair. You made me lose the game, Anatou. I've never lost before—not to a girl! See what you made me do. Clumsy!

ANATOU. I'm sorry. I tried to get out of the way. I didn't see you in time.

SHIKIKANAQ *(whispering).* You better not say anything more, Motomiak, or Anatou will put a spell on you— the way she did the seals.

TARTO. What are you talking about? You know that isn't true.

ANATOU. Oh, I'm sorry I spoiled your game, Motomiak, but couldn't you start again?

SHIKIKANAQ. No. I won. Tarto saw. Didn't you, Tarto? *(He nods.)*

MOTOMIAK. Beside, we don't want to play in front of a freak. *(ANATOU gasps.)*

TARTO. Who's a freak?

MOTOMIAK. She is. The whole village says so.

ANATOU *(furious).* No, I'm not! I'm an Eskimo just like you.

SHIKIKANAQ *(doubtfully).* Ohh...

MOTOMIAK. Well, her face is different enough. *(ANA-TOU touches it.)*

TARTO. Why, what's wrong with it? It has two eyes, a nose and a mouth just like everyone else's.

SHIKIKANAQ. But it's white, Tarto—like snow. I bet if you put her in the sun she'll melt and that's why she stays inside all the time.

TARTO. You're just jealous because she's prettier than you, Shikikanaq.

ANATOU. Stop it. Stop it, all of you. *(She is crying.)* Leave me alone. *(Starts to go.)*

TARTO (*furious*). Now see what you've done. If she were made of snow, Shikikanaq, she couldn't cry. (*Crosses to her.*) Come on, Anatou. They didn't mean it. Please come back. (*To others.*) Let's have another game—all four of us.

SHIKIKANAQ. Well...all right...if she'll tell us why she looks that way.

TARTO (*sharply*). What way?

SHIKIKANAQ. I mean her eyes and her hair. They're such funny colors. There must be a reason.

ANATOU (*desperate*). I don't know. Each time you've asked me I said I didn't know.

SHIKIKANAQ. I bet if you asked your mother and father they'd know. It must be something terrible or they'd tell you.

MOTOMIAK. Maybe the Wood God from the forest put a spell on an animal and sent it back here. No one else in Little Whale River looks like you. Maybe that's why you look so funny. They say he has the power to make an animal appear like a human.

SHIKIKANAQ. And he can make people look like animals too...just by saying a spell! My father says that's why no Eskimo should go into the forest.

ANATOU. No! No! It's not true. I'm just like you are!

MOTOMIAK. Then, maybe, some devil spirit looked at you and took all the color away.

SHIKIKANAQ. Yes, that's it. And why do you always sit inside and sew?

ANATOU (*lying*). There's a lot of work. It has to get done.

TARTO (*quickly*). She can sew better than any woman in the whole village! Show them, Anatou. (*He points to her dress which is carefully and beautifully stitched. SHIKIKANAQ examines it.*)

SHIKIKANAQ. It is beautiful. There aren't any mistakes at all.

ANATOU (*can't believe her praise*). My mother taught me and she is very good and careful.

SHIKIKANAQ. Can you make anything else?

ANATOU. Two snows ago, I made warm boots for my father. Very special boots and he's worn them ever since.

MOTOMIAK. Then how come he's lost in the snow right now, if the boots you made were so special.

ANATOU. He went to look for food. Both my mother and father did. That's all I know.

MOTOMIAK. There's barely any food left in the village. For three days the hunters have returned with empty sleds.

ANATOU. Famine is everywhere. Not just here. I heard my father say so before he left. That is why he said he was going far away to look.

MOTOMIAK. You made those boots your father wore. I bet you put a charm on them. Shikikanaq and I saw you talking to them once and blowing on them.

ANATOU. That's not true. I was cleaning them.

MOTOMIAK. But you were talking too. You were putting a charm on them, weren't you?

ANATOU. Don't you see? If I did have any magic powers, I'd bring them back. They're my parents. I love them. They're the only ones who've been good to me. (*Softly.*) I couldn't stay in Little Whale River if it weren't for them.

SHIKIKANAQ (*cruelly*). Well, they're gone now. So you can go too.

ANATOU. What do you mean? They're coming back. I know they are.

MOTOMIAK. Maybe. But my father says you killed your own parents.

ANATOU *(with a cry)*. No!

TARTO *(challenging him and pinning his arm back)*. Take that back or else!

MOTOMIAK *(stubbornly)*. That's what my father said.

TARTO *(knocking him down)*. Well, he's wrong.

(A fight starts. SHIKIKANAQ shrieks and ANATOU watches horrified. THREE VILLAGERS rush in.)

SHIKIKANAQ *(quickly)*. She started it. It's all her fault. Anatou's fault!

KIVIOG *(to ANATOU)*. Get away from our children. *(VILLAGER 2 has separated the boys.)*

TARTO. Anatou wasn't doing anything.

KIVIOG. Be still!

VILLAGER 1. She's brought nothing but trouble since the day she was born.

TARTO *(to KIVIOG)*. But it's not fair, Father, she ...

KIVIOG. Silence! For days we have searched for Karvik and Arnarqik. They are good people. Karvik was the best hunter we had. But no man can fight off charmed boots.

VILLAGER 2. No wonder they got lost in the blizzard.

VILLAGER 1. Look at her. She doesn't care her parents are gone.

ANATOU *(suddenly)*. I don't understand. Do you mean they're ... they're dead? *(KIVIOG nods.)* How can you be sure?

KIVIOG. If they haven't frozen, they have starved. We cannot find them anywhere.

VILLAGER 1. You're to blame. You and your witchcraft.

VILLAGER 2. Look, she doesn't even care.

ANATOU. Don't you think I want them here? Don't you think the fire is colder without my mother's face and lonesome without my father's singing? They went to look for food...for all of us. I'm hungry too...just like the rest of you.

VILLAGER 1. Then why do you anger the Seal Goddess? We used to have days of feasting.

VILLAGER 2. Pots boiling...

KIVIOG. But since the same day you were born, the hunters have had to work twice as hard—twice as hard for the same amount!

VILLAGER 2. We used to thank the Seal Goddess, bow down to her and give her seal liver. Now there is none to give her and she is angry—at the bottom of the sea. Our harpoons break in our hands.

ANATOU. It is the bitter cold.

VILLAGER 2. Why is there blizzard after blizzard if the gods aren't angry?

VILLAGER 1. Why is there a famine if the gods aren't angry?

KIVIOG. It's your fault.

VILLAGER 2. You're to blame.

KIVIOG. We have kept silent for the sake of Karvik and Arnarqik, but now they are no longer here.

VILLAGER 1. They took care of you and see what it brought them to!

ANATOU *(sobbing)*. But I am all alone too.

VILLAGER 2. There is no more to eat.

VILLAGER 1. No oil to burn.

VILLAGER 2. We fear sickness.

KIVIOG. And the souls of the dead.

VILLAGER 1. The souls of animals and men.

VILLAGER 2. We know the spirits of the earth and the air are angry with us.

ANATOU. What am I to do? What do you want of me?

KIVIOG. Leave here. Leave us!

ANATOU. But I haven't done anything. Where will I go? I'll never find my way alone.

KIVIOG. If you stay, you will get no help or protection from us, Anatou. From now on, find your own food and eat with the dogs. No one else will eat with you.

VILLAGER 2. And from now on, speak to yourself. No one else will listen. *(Adults start off.)*

VILLAGER 1. Go home, children, all of you. Go home quickly.

KIVIOG. Don't talk to that one. That one is evil. Leave her alone. *(They leave. ANATOU has turned away. TARTO looks back before exiting but she doesn't see it. ANATOU sinks down, unable to bear it.)*

ANATOU. It isn't true! I loved my parents. Even Tarto believed them. He didn't say a word—he didn't even say good-bye. Oh, Moon God, is there nothing I can do?

(She is crying. TARTO reappears, puts his hand out to touch her hair, then in fear withdraws it.)

TARTO *(gently)*. What are you going to do? Where will you go?

ANATOU *(jerks her head up abruptly but doesn't turn around)*. All right! All right! I'm leaving. Are you satisfied now?

TARTO. But it's me, Anatou—Tarto. I wanted to say good-bye.

ANATOU *(turns around)*. Tarto, you came back!

TARTO. But I can't stay. If they catch me ... I'll ... get into trouble. I brought you some food, Anatou. It's just a little, but I thought ...

ANATOU. Thank you, Tarto. *(Suddenly she takes off an amulet that she is wearing.)* Tarto, you're the only friend I have now. I want you to keep this to remember me. The Shaman gave it to my mother before I was born. It's to bring good luck, but it was really always meant for a boy child, not a girl. *(He takes it.)* Tarto, I wish I had something special to give you, but it's all I have.

TARTO. Then it is special, Anatou. I'll always keep it. I won't forget you. I promise. And when I am older, Anatou, I'll harpoon my own seal. I'll be the best hunter in the village and the men will do anything I say because I'll know all the hiding places of the seals. Then they'll listen to me and ... *(Breaks off and slowly asks what he has always wondered.)* Anatou, why is your hair so light?

ANATOU *(pierced by the question)*. Tarto, why is the sky gray in the winter? I don't know. All I want is to be like the others, to play with you and sing with you, and I want to see my mother and father again. I love them. Do you believe me? *(He nods.)* I want to be friends with the villagers, but they won't let me. You're the only one who tried to understand. I used to wake up and say, "Today will be different." My mother said, "Anatou, every day is the beginning of some new wonderful thing." But it wasn't true! Each day ended the same way and each dawn I was frightened again. And then today ... today was the worst of all.

TARTO. I'm sorry, Anatou.

ANATOU. Tarto, you were brave to come back here. You know they'll be angry if they find you here.

TARTO. I know.

ANATOU. You will be a fine hunter, Tarto...the finest of the whole village one day. Tarto, why did you come back?

TARTO. I am your friend, Anatou. I always will be even if...

ANATOU. Even if what, Tarto?

TARTO. Anatou, listen. My father said...that...well, he said... (*Gulps.*) He said you put spells on the seals so they couldn't come out of the water. Anatou, couldn't you say another spell so we could all eat? Then it would be all right again, Anatou.

ANATOU (*horrified*). Do you believe that, Tarto?

TARTO (*miserably*). Well, first I said it wasn't true! But today...

ANATOU. Tarto, listen. There's nothing I can do. I can't make a spell like a shaman, like the wise man. I'm hungry, too, just like you. Even if I wanted to, there is nothing I can do.

TARTO (*slowly*). Don't you want to? Don't you want to help us, Anatou?

ANATOU. Don't you believe me either, Tarto? Doesn't anyone? I'm not any different. I don't have any magic powers. I'm just like anyone else.

TARTO. Your skin is white, mine is brown. Your hair is pale like the dawn, mine is dark like the night. (*He is colder now.*) You're not like anyone I've seen. (*A long pause.*)

ANATOU. I've never heard you say that before. Everyone else, but not you! You never seemed to care. You made up for all the others. (*Sound of Eskimo dogs.*)

TARTO (*uncomfortably*). I have to go, Anatou...it's late. What will you do?

ANATOU *(with a horrible realization)*. I know I can't stay here now. Tarto, when you lose everything at once, your choice has been made. You can only follow it.

TARTO. But where will you go? What will you do?

ANATOU *(pauses, makes difficult decision)*. The forest, Tarto. It's only a few days from here. I've heard about it from the old men and the Shaman.

TARTO *(impulsively)*. But you can't. Don't you know about it? It's a place of whispers in the night, of strange whines. They say the trees are living beings but they can't speak. It's not safe for an Eskimo to spend a night in the forest. What if the Wood God changes you into a wolf or another animal?

ANATOU *(slowly)*. Yes... what if he changes me into a wolf?

TARTO *(continuing without hearing her)*. It's dark and mysterious, Anatou. It's a place where Eskimos never go.

ANATOU. But, don't you see? That's just why. There is no place else! *(Pauses.)* Maybe the Wood God won't care if my hair is pale... like the dawn!

ACT TWO
Scene One

SCENE: *Outside the forest at night. Late March. The opening of this scene is mimed and the audience only sees ANATOU's silhouette.*

STORYTELLER. Anatou ran. It was dark and frightening. The only sound she heard was the wind whipping the snow around her. *(ANATOU drops from exhaustion. She is crying but she must continue.)*

ANATOU. Where shall I go?

STORYTELLER. No one could hear her cry. There was no one but the wind. Anatou knew if she stopped too long she would freeze in the fierce cold. Then suddenly she saw the place where no one had ever been.

(Part of the forest appears stage right. ANATOU stops stage left.)

ANATOU. The forest! I remember the old men used to tell each other tales by the fire. What did they say? No Eskimo must ever go into the forest. You must never spend the night there. But that's where the Wood God lives. *(She starts to move toward the forest.)* I must go. I must ask him.

(Rest of forest scrim appears as ANATOU runs first to stage right, then stage left, stopping at center stage. Exhausted, she sinks to the ground. She is trembling with fear and slowly rises to her knees.)

(Softly.) Wood God! *(Louder.)* Wood God! *(Looks all around her.)* Wood God... help me.

(The WOOD GOD enters. He appears, as the spirits are reputed to, in the shape of an animal. He has chosen the shape of an awesome owl which is white in color.)

WOOD GOD. Who dares to come into my forest where the wind and snow cry into the darkness?

ANATOU *(draws back)*. Are you the Wood God?

WOOD GOD. I am! And will be till the end of time! Who said you could enter my forest?

ANATOU *(terrified)*. No one.

WOOD GOD. Where do you come from?

ANATOU. I come from Little Whale River.

WOOD GOD. Are you an Eskimo? *(She nods.)* Then why did you come here? Don't you know no Eskimo comes into the middle of the forest and dares to disturb my sleep? Leave my kingdom now and be glad you still have your life.

ANATOU *(pleading)*. No! You don't understand. Please don't send me away. *(Crying. The WOOD GOD comes closer and as he approaches, moonlight shines around them both.)*

WOOD GOD. Ah-ah. Even in the darkness your hair shines. Is it the moon, child?

ANATOU *(desperate)*. Wood God. Wood God, can't you see? Even hidden here it shines and glitters. If I were to crawl into a cave it would be the same.

WOOD GOD *(lifts her face and peers into it)*. Your face is as pale as ice. *(Softer.)* And your eyes are red from crying. *(Shakes his head.)* That's too bad. It means you're human.

ANATOU. I am an Eskimo. But they don't believe me. Nobody does. Help me. Wood God, help me!

WOOD GOD. How can I help you? Are you hungry, child? Is that why you came here?

ANATOU *(nods)*. We all are...no one has eaten in days. But it is not my fault...they blame me because my hair shines, because it isn't like the raven's wing. But I am hungry too. I can't go any further...I can't.

WOOD GOD. We have no food to give you, child. You must leave. Your people will be worried. *(He starts to exit.)*

ANATOU. Wait! Wait and hear me, Wood God. It is not food I want. It is not food that made me wake the great spirit of the Wood God.

WOOD GOD. What then?

ANATOU *(slowly)*. I want what only your powers can grant. But first, Wood God, hear my story.

WOOD GOD. Begin. Quickly, child. You mustn't savor what tastes bitter.

ANATOU. Aja. It is true. You do see much.

WOOD GOD. Begin from the beginning; when you were born.

ANATOU. Even though I was a girl, my parents were happy, or a least they seemed to be. Even though I couldn't hunt...even though...even though I was different.

WOOD GOD. Why? You have two arms, two legs, and a face with two eyes and a mouth.

ANATOU. But a face that people were afraid of and hair that grew lighter instead of darker. They named me Anatou, the Fair One.

WOOD GOD. So you are Anatou. Then not all the spirits of the earth and air can help you. You are as you are.

ANATOU. But you can help me, Wood God. Please. You must.

WOOD GOD. Go home, fair child. I can do nothing. I cannot turn your pale hair to the dark of night or your fair skin brown. I cannot teach them to like you. You must do that yourself. Go home to your parents. Go home where you belong.

ANATOU *(blurts out)*. I can't. They'll kill me if I do.

WOOD GOD *(puzzled)*. Who will? Your parents, too?

ANATOU. No, they are spirits now. They were the only good people I ever knew. I did love them, Wood God. Some people say that I am a witch and that I cursed my parents, that the Seal Goddess is angry with me. They say that is why there is no food. But it isn't true. Wood God! It isn't true!

WOOD GOD. My power would only hurt you, Anatou. You are young. Go back.

ANATOU. I've heard you can make a seal seem like a man or a girl seem like a wolf. Is that true?

WOOD GOD. I can.

ANATOU. Then, Wood God...

WOOD GOD *(interrupts)*. Think, Anatou. Is it so terrible to be an Eskimo girl, to learn to laugh and sing, or sew or cook?

ANATOU. Wood God, my father and mother taught me to sew and cook, but not to laugh and sing. I don't know what that is.

WOOD GOD. But what about the villagers?

ANATOU. They only taught me one thing—to hate. When my parents were gone, they wanted me to eat in the passageway with the dogs. They would not give me a skin to sew. Everywhere I went they turned away. *(Softly.)* Even Tarto.

WOOD GOD. Tarto?

ANATOU. My best friend.

WOOD GOD. Where is he?

ANATOU. Wood God, they all say I'm planning evil, and now even Tarto thinks so, too. Wood God, Wood God, there are more ways of killing than with a harpoon!

WOOD GOD *(pauses before he speaks)*. What do you wish, Anatou?

ANATOU. I don't want to be human any more. It hurts too much. I want you to turn me into a wolf. Then they'll be afraid of me. Then they'll leave me alone.

WOOD GOD. Think, Anatou, think! An animal cannot...

ANATOU. Is a wolf's face white like mine?

WOOD GOD. You know it is not.

ANATOU. Then quickly change me into a beast.

WOOD GOD. An animal is hungry.

ANATOU. I am used to that.

WOOD GOD. He tears with his teeth to eat. A wolf is alone.

ANATOU. I am alone now.

WOOD GOD. Anatou, there is no return. What if you miss your village?

ANATOU. Miss them! When you take a thorn out of an animal's paw, does it miss it? When you fill an empty stomach, does it miss the ache? When you cannot remember pain, do you miss the tears? What would I miss, Wood God, but all of these things?

WOOD GOD. Once it is done, you cannot change your mind.

ANATOU. I will not want to.

WOOD GOD. You will never be an Eskimo girl again, not until you are about to die. Not till then. Are you sure? Are you sure, Anatou?

ANATOU. Will I forget everything? I want to forget everything. Now.

WOOD GOD. No, Anatou. Not at first. As time goes by, you'll forget more and more and only remember your life here.

ANATOU. No! I want to forget everything now. Everything, Wood God. I want to forget I was ever Anatou, the Fair One.

WOOD GOD. But you can't escape pain, Anatou. Even a
wolf can't escape that. *(She pauses to think; she looks
up. He watches her closely.)* Are you ready?

ANATOU. Yes. *(Suddenly frightened.)* Wood God, will it
hurt much?

WOOD GOD. Listen to my words. Hear them well. *(Lifts
his arms so it appears as though his spirit, in the shape
of a white owl, were commanding the universe. Drum
beat begins.)* Come spirits of earth and sky.

Rise through the snow.
Speed over the ice.
Encircle this child in a coat of thick fur.

*(Three forest animals appear, a FOX, a BEAVER, and
an ERMINE—and form a circle around ANATOU.)*

FOX. Night protect it.

BEAVER. Forest watch it.

ERMINE. Nothing harm it.

WOOD GOD. As long as it remembers...

FOX. As long as it remembers...

BEAVER. As long as it remembers...

WOOD GOD. To stay in the forest far from man.

ERMINE. Far from man.

FOX *(echoes)*. ...from man.

*(There is more dancing. Animals close in. Their move-
ments become more intense, then with a cry, they disappear and we see the wolf. Note: This should not be a
realistic representation, but rather done with masks in
a costume, lean and sleek, that would be worn under
the Eskimo dress, removed and disposed of at the end
of the enchantment with a momentary darkening of the*

stage and more intense beating of the drum. There should be a marked difference in the movement once ANATOU has been changed into a wolf.)

FOX. It is done!
ERMINE. Now you are a wolf!
BEAVER. A wolf! *(Curtain.)*

Scene Two

STORYTELLER. All that winter Anatou lived with the animals enjoying the forest. She made friends with the beaver, fox, and ermine. She forgot she had ever been Anatou, the Fair One—an Eskimo. Then one morning she woke up to a spring sun. It warmed the air and touched her fur.

(Spring in the forest. Early dawn. ANATOU wakes, stretches, and smells the air with curiosity.)

ANATOU. Whorl berries. That's what I smell. And sunlight! Even the forest can't shut it out. *(She puts a paw down on a patch of melting snow.)* Beaver! Fox! Wake up. The snow's melting.

(They enter.)

FOX. Did you have to wake me up to tell me that? It happens every spring.
ANATOU *(with growing excitement).* But there are at least a thousand things to see and smell and hear. Come on.

I'll race you through the forest and we'll explore the other side.

BEAVER *(slowly)*. What do you mean by the other side? We've never gone beyond the edge.

ANATOU. Oh, that was all right in the winter time. But now it's Spring. I want to leave the forest today, see what else there is.

FOX *(sharply)*. No, Anatou.

BEAVER. I thought you liked it here in the forest.

ANATOU. Of course I do, but... *(Reluctant to speak of it.)* But last night I had a strange dream. I can't remember it now. But it was something out there. There's something I have to see.

BEAVER. Outside the forest?

FOX. Don't go there, Anatou.

ANATOU. Why not?

FOX. Don't go, or you'll be sorry.

ANATOU. I just want to look. It's a beautiful day. I want to run in the sunlight and explore.

FOX. If you leave, the Wood God will be furious.

ANATOU. The Wood God? Why? I'll be back tonight, I promise. What's there to be afraid of?

FOX *(quietly)*. Danger.

BEAVER. Danger.

ANATOU. Maybe there's something dangerous for little animals like you, but I'm strong. I've got sharp teeth and claws. *(Boasting.)* Nothing can hurt me.

FOX. You're a fool!

ANATOU *(angry)*. Wait and see. I'll be back without a scratch on me. I'm not afraid like the rest of you.

BEAVER. Listen to her! We'll let her go if she wants to.

FOX. For the last time. We're warning you. Don't go. There'll be trouble if you do.

ANATOU. I must go. I don't know why, but I must. Don't try to stop me.

FOX. Remember, we warned you!

BEAVER. You wouldn't listen.

ANATOU. I can't help it. It's something inside.

(Lights fade, animals exit. Forest scrim rises and ANA-TOU mimes her journey through the forest. She stops at the edge. The hilltops are brown, and there are black willow twigs with new buds.)

Willow trees! And sunlight everywhere. Wood God, what a beautiful world outside your forest. *(Her journey continues in dance movement. The lights fade to indicate twilight. She stops, worn out.)* Loons on the water. It's so peaceful here. *(Enjoying it.)* I'm all alone in the world.

(She prepares to settle down when lights begin to come up on a summer village tent and we hear the sharp sound of an Eskimo dog howling. ANATOU peers at the tent and moves in cautiously, closer and closer. The tent should be a movable unit that glides on. As ANA-TOU gets closer, we hear the sound of Eskimo singing or chanting. ANATOU realizes what it is and cries out.)

ANATOU. Eskimos! Wood God! Wood God! I'd forgotten. Oh, I should never have left the forest.

(As she watches, KIVIOG and TARTO cross stage to tent.)

Tarto. And he still has the charm I gave him. He still has it.

KIVIOG. Tarto, we'll never have to worry with you as a hunter. All the pots of the village will boil this Spring. Aja, since Anatou left, there's been plenty to eat.

TARTO. There'd be enough for her, too, if she were here.

KIVIOG. Forget about her, Tarto. *(They go inside.)*

ANATOU *(creeping closer)*. Look at them eating, laughing, and singing. "Let her die in the snow." That's what they said. I'll show them. I'm strong now. I'll get even. If it's the last thing I do, I'll get even. *(She moves nearer the tent and sees a piece of meat outside.)* I'll take some back to the forest.

(But the dogs hear her and they start howling. The singing stops and a VILLAGER runs out with his bow and arrow. ANATOU sees him and runs, but not before he shoots an arrow at her. ANATOU is hurt but gets up, limping to the side of the tent.)

That one! That one used to call me names. He hurt my mother and father. *(In pain.)* I'm remembering. His arrow cut through my heart! *(VILLAGER comes out to check whether the animal is dead or not, and he carries another weapon. He looks about.)* He'll kill me! Unless... *(ANATOU springs. There is a short struggle and the man falls without a sound.)* Who is stronger now, Eskimo? Who's stronger now? *(ANATOU leaves. Curtain.)*

Scene Three

SCENE: *In the forest. ANATOU goes toward FOX. FOX retreats. ANATOU approaches BEAVER. He moves away in fear.*

WOOD GOD. You must leave man alone.

ANATOU. He did not leave me alone. Why should I?

WOOD GOD. Man has a bow, harpoons, knives, spears. You will see, Anatou. He will hunt you out. Stay away! Do not hurt another human.

ANATOU. But he wounded me.

FOX. You shouldn't have gone near his tent.

BEAVER. You don't deserve to stay in the forest with us.

ANATOU. But the wound hurt. *(Softly.)* And then...I saw his face. I remembered. I remembered everything before then!

WOOD GOD. That wound will heal, Anatou. But will this new wound heal? Your hatred is more chilling than the ice caves near the sea. It will grow if you don't kill it now, Anatou. It will grow and freeze your heart.

FOX. You are a disgrace to the animals.

BEAVER. Animals kill because they must eat.

FOX. They must survive.

WOOD GOD. It's the law of the forest. But you, Anatou, killed out of hate. Men do that, not the animals!

ANATOU *(with awful realization)*. Wood God...when I saw him, and I saw the tent, and I remembered how they made me leave the village, and the arrow pierced me...I felt something...something I had forgotten. I had to get even!

WOOD GOD *(sternly)*. Live in peace with man, Anatou, or leave the forest forever. *(He sweeps off with the animals. Curtain.)*

Scene Four

SCENE: *The interior of a snow house. Drums are beating. Three village hunters are assembled in a circle. In the distance there is the piercing cry of a wolf. They shudder.*

KIVIOG *(rises)*. We must try again. The wolf must be stopped.

ATATA. Never was a wolf spirit so hungry for men's souls.

VILLAGER. Hunter after hunter has gone and not returned. What can we do?

ATATA. Aja! But what good is a bow and arrow?

VILLAGER 2. What good are knives if we live in terror in our own houses?

KIVIOG. The great North is no longer safe. We mustn't let the wolf escape this time. Since Spring, he has not let us alone. At night he always disappears into the forest... where no Eskimo ever goes.

VILLAGER 2. Even if it does go into the forest, we must find it and put an end to this.

ATATA. But if we go into the forest, we'll be trapped.

KIVIOG. We are trapped in our own homes now!

ALL. Aja! Aja!

ATATA. Never has there been a wolf like this. Its howl makes the fire die and the seal-oil lamp tremble.

VILLAGER 2. We must hunt till we find it.

ATATA. We have lost many good hunters.

VILLAGER 2. They have all failed.

KIVIOG. But we must find it.

TARTO *(has been sitting there all the time unnoticed by the others)*. I have hunted before. Let me go, Father.

KIVIOG. Tarto! This is a council for our best hunters. Go outside. You should not be here. You're too young.

VILLAGER 2. He is so small that we don't notice him. It's all right, Kiviog.

ATATA. Perhaps he is so small that he could creep up on the wolf and he wouldn't notice him either. *(They all laugh.)*

TARTO. Please, Father. Please, I'm strong.

KIVIOG. No. We go too far. You will be tired.

TARTO. I won't. Wait and see.

KIVIOG. The men of Little Whale River are going to the forest, Tarto. It's dangerous.

TARTO. Then I will find the wolf's hiding place.

VILLAGER 2. He is swift, Kiviog. His eyes are sharp. He is as good a hunter as the men. If he wishes, let him come. *(KIVIOG thinks, then nods to TARTO. TARTO beams.)*

KIVIOG. We must cover the great North and not stop till the snow is free of the wolf's tracks.

VILLAGERS. Aja! Aja!

VILLAGER 2. We must hunt toward the great plains.

KIVIOG. And hunt towards the forest.

ATATA. And by the caves along the sea.

KIVIOG. We've no time to waste. Harness the dogs! *(Drums increase. Men leave to get dog teams and begin the hunt. Interior fades.)*

ACT THREE

SCENE: *The forest. There is snow on the ground and a rock unit has been added left center. There is a group of tangled trees that have been blown down in the winter. ANATOU sleepily comes from behind the rock. She sniffs the air casually, then her body tenses.*

ANATOU *(calling with increasing alarm)*. Wood God! Wood God! Wood God! I smell danger.

(BEAVER and FOX appear.)

FOX. The hunters are here.
BEAVER. The hunters.
ANATOU. But the Eskimos are afraid of the forest. Why do they come here?
FOX. They hunt the wolf.
BEAVER. They hunt you.
FOX. Anatou.

(WOOD GOD enters.)

WOOD GOD. I warned you, Anatou. You have hurt too many of them. They are angry, angry enough to enter the forest and to hunt you out.
ANATOU. I'm frightened, Wood God. Please help me.
WOOD GOD. You hate and so you killed. You deliberately disobeyed me after I first sheltered you. I cannot protect you now.

46

ANATOU. Was I wrong to defend myself, Wood God, to wound when I was wounded?

WOOD GOD. You've been cruel, Anatou, and hate is like a disease spreading through your heart. If you strike an Eskimo, how does the Beaver know that you won't strike him too, when he sleeps in the night?

ANATOU. No! I'd never do that. You know that, Wood God.

WOOD GOD. How do I know? I only see what you do. That speaks for itself.

ANATOU (*ashamed*). I won't leave the forest again, Wood God. I have been wrong.

WOOD GOD (*angry*). It's too late for that, Anatou. The hunters are here.

FOX. They're coming closer.

BEAVER. Closer.

ANATOU (*panicked*). Wood God, what should I do?

WOOD GOD (*harshly*). Replace the hunters you made them lose. Erase the terror you've caused them. Anatou, even the animals have been frightened of you.

ANATOU. But I didn't mean them. They've been good to me. I didn't want to hurt the animals.

WOOD GOD (*watching her intently*). If you cannot live in peace with man, Anatou, then one day you will have to face his bow and arrow. There is no law of the forest that can protect you from that time.

ANATOU. Wood God, why didn't you warn me? Why didn't you stop me? I have worn a coat of thick hate— so thick it stopped my feeling or seeing anything else.

WOOD GOD. We tried, Anatou, but before, you weren't ready to hear our words.

ANATOU. I am now, Wood God. Please, please, animals.

FOX. Hurry, Anatou. They are closer.

ANATOU. What should I do?

WOOD GOD. Run, Anatou. There is no time. If the hunters find you...

ANATOU. I know.

WOOD GOD. But remember this: if you are truly sorry, if you know what understanding means, if you can show me your heart is empty of all its dark hate and cruelty, no matter what happens, your spirit will not die. It will live forever and teach others. Remember that.

ANATOU. Thank you, Wood God.

WOOD GOD. Now run, Anatou.

ANIMALS. Run, Anatou, run.

(ANATOU exits across the stage. Village hunters enter. They are frightened. Suddenly a wind comes up.)

VILLAGER 2. Aja! The wind is alive.

ATATA. Let's leave. No Eskimo should be here.

KIVIOG. No! We have promised our village.

TARTO. We cannot return 'till the wolf is found.

KIVIOG. Look! His tracks are here.

VILLAGER 2. Follow them!

KIVIOG. Sh-h-h-h. Fresh tracks. Quickly, carefully.
(There is silence as they begin the serious search.)

ANIMALS *(whispering)*. Hurry, Anatou. Hurry.

(ANATOU streaks across the stage. They see her.)

VILLAGER 1. Follow it! Follow it! *(They rush off left. TARTO, who is behind them, gets trapped in the fallen trees; his bow and arrow fly to the side. TARTO tries to escape, but is caught fast.)*

TARTO. I can't get out! *(Trying to free himself.)* I'm trapped! *(There is deathly silence around him.)* Where did they go? I can't even hear them. *(Shouting.)* Father! Father, come back. Hurry!

(Sees his bow and arrow, but he can't reach it. ANATOU runs on right. She stumbles on bow and arrow and in so doing kicks it to other side. TARTO is terrified. He whispers horrified.)

The wolf. What'll I do? *(He tries to struggle out, but he can't. ANATOU comes closer. TARTO is wearing the charm she gave him. She half turns away.)*

ANATOU. It's Tarto! I've got to help him. *(ANATOU moves in. TARTO thinks she is going to attack him. He becomes more and more terrified.)*
TARTO. No! No! Father! Help! Help! *(He covers his face instinctively, afraid to watch, but then forces himself to look. She pushes with all her might and finally the pressure is released and TARTO is out of the trap. He is amazed and does not understand what happened. As soon as TARTO is free, ANATOU starts to run, but it is too late. Just as she is passing the rock unit, we hear the whiz of an arrow and ANATOU falls behind the rock unit.)* No! He set me free. Don't kill him. He set me free.

(KIVIOG, ATATA and VILLAGER 2 rush in.)

KIVIOG. Tarto, what happened?
TARTO. I got trapped over there in the logs... and then the wolf... he set me free.

KIVIOG. What?

TARTO. The wolf, Father, the wolf. That's the truth. He pulled the log away so I could get out. I thought he was going to kill me.

KIVIOG. Where is your bow and arrow?

TARTO. There! I couldn't reach them. But Father, he saved my life. He pushed the log away.

ATATA. Aja. The forest is alive with things we can't understand.

KIVIOG. Where is he now?

TARTO. The arrow hit him near the rock...but... *(They look. She is not there.)* He's not there. Where did he go?

ATATA. It may be a trick.

VILLAGER 2 *(advancing cautiously)*. Here's a fresh footprint.

ATATA. Watch out. *(They move cautiously.)*

TARTO *(with a cry)*. It's... *(Turns to KIVIOG.)* Anatou. It's Anatou. We've hurt her.

(They all stare amazed by the sight of the girl. TARTO kneels down by the rock unit. ANATOU's spirit appears above. This can be done by seeing her through a scrim on a higher level so that she looks the same but paler, as though in a dream.)

ANATOU. Tarto...don't cry.

TARTO *(to himself)*. Anatou. You were my best friend. *(To her.)* I didn't mean to hurt you. Do you understand? We didn't mean... *(He can't say it. TARTO tries to hold back the anguish inside.)*

ANATOU. I do, Tarto, I do. Oh, Wood God, they can't hear me.

TARTO. She could have killed me, Father, but she didn't. She saved my life instead.

VILLAGER 2. Aja. She was brave.

KIVIOG. Braver than all the hunters of Little Whale River. None of us would have done what she did. *(He puts his hand on TARTO's shoulder, but he can't say what he'd like to.)*

VILLAGER. But why did she run into the forest?

TARTO. Don't you see? She had no place else to go. We chased her here. *(This is the most painful of all.)* Anatou, even I chased you away.

KIVIOG. We would not speak or smile at the different one, remember. Our silence was worse than a hundred harpoons.

TARTO. Will she forgive me, Father?

KIVIOG. The spirits of the dead know our hearts, Tarto. You cannot keep a secret from them.

TARTO. But will she forgive me?

KIVIOG. We are all to blame.

TARTO. But I want to know! I have to know! She saved me, Father, and then the hunters shot an arrow when she finished.

KIVIOG. She had a bigger heart than you or I, Tarto, but if she is angry we'll be trapped by the snow and the wind and lose our way. No Eskimo should ever enter the realm of the forest. If she forgives us, our way will be safe.

ANATOU. Wood God! Please let me help them.

WOOD GOD *(pleased)*. 'Till the end of the forest and then I will guide them.

ANATOU. Do they understand, Wood God? How will they remember?

WOOD GOD. Tarto will tell your story tonight, the first time, and they will tell it for many nights. They will remember, for someone will always tell the story of Anatou, the Fair One.

VILLAGER 2 *(goes over slowly and picks up the arrow, holds it thoughtfully)*. I shot it! I killed her!

KIVIOG. No, we all killed her. But when? Today or long ago?

THE END

Classroom Concepts

⤳ *The Ice Wolf* is based upon an Inuit tale. Researching more Inuit stories can be the first step in developing other dramatizations. Divide students into groups and ask each group to adapt a story using one of the following techniques. Three ways for students to stage these stories in a classroom or in a theatre are offered.

Story Theatre

In this format, a narrator tells the story as the performers enact it, either pantomiming the action or combining action and dialogue. Actors each play one or more of the characters, functioning in role and sometimes offering narration related to their parts. In story theatre, actors also might comment to the audience about the thoughts, feelings, and actions of their characters. Costumes and settings are very basic or suggested through costume or set pieces. Props are simple or mimed.

Narrative Pantomime

Write the story so that it can be played solely through pantomime. One student serves as a narrator and tells the story. Other students are cast as the characters and pantomime their roles. In this format, dialogue is omitted. The story should be adapted so that it is action based. In other words, there should always be something physical or emotional for the character to do or show. Using this approach, individual students can each be cast in a particular role. The story also can be written for unison play, in which everyone plays Anatou, or for paired play, casting both the roles of Anatou and Tarto. In unison or paired play, all students can enact the story at the same time, following the cues of the narrator.

Story Dramatization

This technique requires students to be very familiar with the story. The teacher will want to use discussion and questions to check their level of comprehension. Emerging from this review should be a consensus as to what scenes are needed to tell the story, where these begin and end, and what actions and characters are essential to each.

Beginning with the first scene, identify the major characters. Invite students to envision each of these characters engaged in some action found in the story or one that would be appropriate for that character to perform. Have each student then try-on the character performing this action. Generally, this is done first in pantomime and next as a paired play which combines characters and to which dialogue is added.

After asking for ideas about what characters might say and do in the first scene, cast and play it. Follow this with an evaluative discussion. What was effective in the performance? What might be improved? Replay and continue to evaluate the scene until the class is satisfied with the outcome. In replay, the cast may either change or remain the same. In evaluating, talk about characters rather than individual actors. Continue staging the story by following this pattern. All scenes can then be put together for a complete staging of the story.

ꞔ꒱ The prologue suggests images of life in her village on the day that Anatou was born. Students can use their bodies to make a living picture that shows these common events.

Living Pictures

Bodies are the medium used to create living pictures. Either individually or with others, students take a position which produces one of the required visual images and then freeze. Others join, adding to the composition, until it is complete. The living pictures created should contain at least the vignettes below. Classmates may wish to add others.

Atata poised to strike at the seal's breathing hole.

Arnarqik sewing clothes inside her home.

Karvik repairing the outside of the igloo.

Arnarqik showing her new child to the neighbors.

⤷ The exercise below affords students an opportunity to empathize with Anatou's feelings of being left out by others. After playing, be certain to talk about how the students felt as they tried to gain entry to the center of the circle. What did it feel like when others worked together to keep them away?

Excluded

With the exception of one person, students form a circle with classmates and hold each other's hands. The objective of those making the circle is to keep the remaining person from finding an opening and gaining entry to the center of the ring. That student stands outside of the circle. He or she can move freely about the exterior looking for a way to break through and doing so if possible. Those making the circle can raise or lower hands, move their bodies to compact or expand the space, or use similar non-violent techniques to keep the ring secure from access. Each student should have a chance to try to successfully reach the inside of the circle.

ஒ♫♩ In *The Ice Wolf*, others accuse Anatou of having magical powers and unleashing ills upon the village. The following exercise uses choral reading to explore cause and effect, superstition and logic.

Accusations and Responses

Divide the students into three groups, with each becoming a chorus in this vocal recital. The first group should analyze the script and identify the accusations the villagers thrust upon Anatou. The second group should ascertain her responses to these allegations. While these will not be found in the script, the third group should suggest logical reasons why these misfortunes may have occurred. A choral reading should then be created which uses an accusation/response pattern among the three groups. How can the students construct and contrast these perceptions, defenses, emotions, and rationales through oral interpretation?

Group 1: There is no food.

Group 2: I'm hungry, too.

Group 3: Harsh environmental conditions make food hard to find for all the Eskimo villages.

ஒ♫♩ Transformations are a part of this play. The Wood God, for example, appears as an owl and Anatou changes from human to wolf. For *Transformations*, ask students to find a personal space which allows them freedom of mobility. Guide them to think about the movements necessary to effect their new forms. Using a hand drum, give the students a preparatory eight count. The ninth beat is their signal to execute their conversion.

Transformations

With eyes closed, students imagine that each is a character in this play and select a villager, a forest creature, or one of the major characters to begin. Next, each imagines that this character changes into something or someone else. (This may or may not actually happen in the play.) After envisioning the movements necessary to execute this transformation, they open their eyes. Eight drum beats afford time for mental and physical preparation. On the ninth beat, each person should use as much space, time, and steps as needed and carry out this transformation.

    ≋ A costume designer for a production of *The Ice Wolf* also would, most likely, be responsible for creating faces for the animals in the story. This activity invites students to do this in two different ways. When the faces have been completed, discuss the advantages and disadvantages associated with both ways of achieving desired creature features.

Masks and Make-up

Selecting either the fox, ermine, owl, or beaver, students should design a mask that an actor portraying that animal might wear. This can be a full or partial facial mask made from something as simple as a paper plate or from more challenging materials such as plaster of Paris.

Next, they are to create the animal's face using stage make-up. Students may work in pairs for this and serve as models for each other.

֍ In terms of genre, *The Ice Wolf* can be classified as a tragedy written for young audiences. Thematically, it is like the other plays in this anthology in that it addresses the need for tolerance. Students will need adequate time for group work as they undertake this project related to genre and theme.

Tragic Intolerance

Students should form groups who then identify a situation in which intolerance is a key element. This may be taken from historical, current, or local events. Gang fights or a bully picking on other children at school may serve as examples. Each group should create a story which stems from their chosen situation and which has a tragic outcome. Members should clearly identify the protagonist, antagonist, setting, conflict, and steps taken by the protagonist that produce dire results. The story should be scripted, cast, rehearsed, and staged for classmates. Following each performance, classmates should engage in a "talk back" with the cast that addresses (1) how the concept of intolerance is addressed in the story; (2) alternative actions that would have produced a more positive resolution; and, (3) how intolerance in this story compares and/or contrasts with that found in *The Ice Wolf*.

֍ In this play, Anatou goes into the forest to become a wolf. She later leaves the forest in spring to explore the changed landscape. Here, students have an opportunity to creatively replicate these ventures.

Journeys

Provide an opportunity for students, working in groups, to design a creative movement piece which illustrates both of these journeys. Encourage each group to select or compose music which supports their movements. Students may wish to incorporate typical Inuit instruments, such as drums, into this activity and may even make some of these as a class or group project.

In Act Two, Scene Two (p. 40), Anatou says that she had a strange dream but cannot remember it. At the end of the play, the Wood God tells Anatou that "someone will always tell the story of Anatou, the Fair One." This activity gives students an opportunity to imagine her dream and to share it with others.

Anatou's Dream

Working in small groups, students conceive a dream for Anatou. Stipulate that this dream must be one that can be fashioned into a tale which keeps alive her legend. When each group has completed this part of the assignment, all students should sit in a circle and imagine themselves as Inuit villagers listening to stories on a cold winter night. Groups should then orally share their story of Anatou's dream.

In the play, feelings of isolation and abandonment, acts of cruelty resulting in greater cruelty, and the acceptance and importance of friendship are prevalent, as is an underlying compassion for human rights and dignity. To begin this next activity, the teacher may wish to have students orally recall their personal scenes in detail or may instead offer them an opportunity to process their feelings by writing in a journal. (Given the nature of these responses, it may be desirable to preview content before it is shared with other students.) Adequate space should be available in the classroom for visual conversion of these memories.

Relating to Anatou's Feelings

Students should recall a personal experience related to one of the feelings, actions, or beliefs just described. One might, for example, recall a childhood experience of becoming separated from parents at an amusement park and the accompanying fears and feeling of abandonment. Another student may focus upon an incident involving teasing gone too far. After calling these episodes from memory in as much detail as possible, each student should use classmates to create a living picture or tableau of the event or a body sculpture that depicts the dominant emotional content inherent in it. Each student then should give a title to his or her piece and be prepared to speak to classmates about the incident and emotions it represents.

❧ Challenge students to imagine what happens after the final scene of the play. Their ideas are the basis for *What Happens Next.*

What Happens Next

Working in small groups, students envision and enact a scene which would follow the final one found in the script. What happens in the village after Anatou's death? Does her spirit reappear? How might her spirit influence the villagers? How do the people live now that she has died? What happens to Tarto? These questions and the students' own ideas will inspire new scenes for this story.

Looking at alternatives is at the heart of this next activity. At its conclusion, students should be more cognizant of problem-solving options.

An Alternative Course of Action

Working in groups, students select or are assigned one of the situations which follows. They are to brainstorm ideas as to how the encounter might be positively resolved. Stipulate that they cannot replicate what happens in the script. From their brainstorming, they are to choose one idea for improvisational development. Their concept, expanded upon and polished if necessary, should be dramatized for classmates.

The villagers' reaction to the baby when they first come to see the newborn Anatou and her parents.

The children keeping Anatou from playing with them.

The villagers blaming Anatou for her parents' death, the lack of food, and the other ills they suffer.

Anatou, as a wolf, venturing back to the village and avenging herself.

Anatou's fatal wounding as she helps Tarto.

In preparation for playing, students should be asked to think about an important friendship. What do they most value about this relationship? Next, they should remember a time in which they were afraid and a friend comforted them, i.e., perhaps a parent or sibling was ill and confiding about one's fears to a friend made the student feel better. These need not be shared with classmates but are used to focus students' thoughts and feelings for the following improvisation.

Fears and Friendship

Cast pairs of players. Give each twosome the following scenario based upon action found in *The Ice Wolf.*

Who: Anatou, Tarto

What: Anatou frees Tarto but is mortally wounded

Where: The forest

Before beginning to enact the scene, ask students to think about what the characters might say to each other and how they could express their feelings of fear and friendship.

Playing this scenario twice and reversing roles gives students a fuller opportunity to understand the characters' fears and the value of their friendship. When each pair has completed play, as a class discuss the ideas that emerged from their dramas. What did they learn about Tarto's feelings? About Anatou's? How might the feelings of the characters be similar to their own?

CHAPTER THREE

Mean to be Free

The Playwright Speaks

In the mid-sixties, I had several part-time teaching jobs in New York City—at a community college, at a Y, and as a substitute teacher in K-12 classrooms all over the city.

But the materials I used failed to reflect the variety of faces I saw daily. Multiculturalism was a banner yet to be waved. I wanted to expand my own knowledge so I could include heroes and folklore based on Hispanic, African American, and Asian heritages in my teaching.

One day, a school named after Harriet Tubman called me, and I began to wonder about her life.

She was a strong, determined woman overcoming physical dangers and the indignities of prejudice. But her story is also one of rejection. Tubman was a short, plain woman prone to paralyzing headaches because of a brick thrown at her by a slave owner. The first time Tubman a.k.a. Moses escaped, she bravely returned for her husband. She was eager for him to go north, too. But in the intervening months, he'd found someone else. Reports were she was uncommonly pretty. He refused Harriet's offer.

Harriet may have felt like weeping or screaming at him. We'll never know. What we do know is that the stinging hurt altered her life; and she became determined to help all those she could.

In total, Tubman made nineteen trips north. In defiance of the Fugitive Slave Law, she brought her passengers as far as Canada and said truthfully, "I never run my train off the track, and I never lost a single passenger."

I'd heard of the Underground Railroad (which was neither underground nor a railroad), had seen an historic station stop and knew that the Quakers, without any fanfare, had historically helped those in need. But who were these people who risked life and property to help the runaways that Moses led across swamps and rivers to the cold crisp air of freedom?

Thomas and Sarah Garrett were a Quaker couple who, over time, hid hundreds of escaping slaves. When Garrett was threatened with jail, he commented, "If this be a crime for which one goes to prison, then there must be some excellent people there." Their kindness and their staunch belief in the rights and innate dignity of each individual put into practice what most religions only preach.

Moses had a powerful motivation to escape from her insufferable life. But then she risked her own safety to go back, again and again, to help others. The Garretts had a perfectly pleasant life, which they chose to risk so that others could be free.

That is courage.

I chose to use two fictionalized children from whose point of view the journey is traveled. They are not lesser heroes. Each step they took toward the unknown was an act of courage; for whether out of desperation or hope, the danger was the same.

It was my belief then, and still is, that life is an opportunity—not to be wasted. Because of Moses, because of the Garretts, because of the Underground Railroad, Hedy and Tom learn what it means "to stand tall."

"Runagate, Runagate"

Rises from their anguish and their power,

Harriet Tubman,

woman of earth, whipscarred,
a summoning, a shining

Mean to be free

> And this was the way of it, brethren brethren,
> way we journeyed from Can't to Can.
> Moon so bright and no place to hide,
> the cry up and the patterollers riding,
> hound dogs belling in bladed air.
> And fear starts a-murbling, Never make it,
> we'll never make it. *Hush that now,*
> and she's turned upon us, levelled pistol
> glinting in the moonlight:
> Dead folks can't jaybird-talk, she says;
> you keep on going now or die, she says.

Wanted Harriet Tubman alias The General
alias Moses Stealer of Slaves

In league with Garrison Alcott Emerson
Garrett Douglass Thoreau John Brown

Armed and known to be Dangerous

Wanted Reward Dead or Alive

Tell me, Ezekiel, oh tell me do you see
mailed Jehovah coming to deliver me?

Hoot-owl calling in the ghosted air,
five times calling to the hands in the air.
Shadow of a face in the scary leaves,
shadow of a voice in the talking leaves:

Comes ride-a my train

Oh that train, ghost-story train
through swamp and savanna movering movering,
over trestles of dew, through caves of the wish,
Midnight Special on a sabre track movering movering
first stop Mercy and the last Hallelujah.

Come ride-a my train

Mean mean mean to be free.

The Play

CHARACTERS

HEDY, age 9

TOM, age 11

MISS NANCY, wife of the owner of the Tidewater, a Maryland plantation. She is quick-tempered, self-centered, and determined to have her own way on all plantation matters.

MOSES, (Harriet Tubman), a former slave in her mid-30s, short and plain in appearance. Now she is a conductor on the Underground Railroad. She is deeply religious.

LINDA, age 17, formerly a lady's maid on a plantation. She is delicate and spoiled.

JOE, in his mid-30; a former overseer of a plantation. He is handsome, hardworking, and has an innate sense of dignity.

THOMAS GARRETT and SARAH GARRETT, devout Quakers whose house has become one of the stops on the Underground Railroad.

TWO MEN, pursuers of fugitive slaves.

TWO BRICKLAYERS

POLICEMAN

OLIVER JOHNSON, head of the Anti-Slavery Office in New York City.

RAILROAD CONDUCTOR

ACT ONE
Scene One

SCENE: *Tidewater, a Maryland plantation, just before the Civil War, 1857. A backdrop, if used, would suggest fields of hay and stacked cornfields. On stage there is a windowless log cabin, its chinks filled with mud, which serves as the laundry cabin. The entrance to it is merely an opening in the wall. Inside there are huge washtubs, scrubbing boards, and so on. It is an autumn, Saturday afternoon. HEDY, age nine, drags a heavy washtub over to a pile of sheets. She kneels and begins the laborious chore of scrubbing the sheets clean. TOM enters, terrified. He sinks on the floor beside HEDY. His shirt is bloody and torn. He is half crying.*

TOM. Hedy!

HEDY. Tom! *(Stops her work.)* What happened?

TOM. Hedy, it hurts bad. You gotta help me. He used the whip.

HEDY. How many times?

TOM. Plenty!

HEDY *(lifts his shirt gingerly)*. Here, I'll wash it off for you. *(During the next few speeches, she cleans the wound.)* Tom, you get into any more trouble and they're gonna sell you down river...tie your hands and feet to a big rope, the way they did Old Jim. Who beat you?

TOM. Master Ed.

HEDY. Master Ed! What'd you do?

TOM. All I done was take a peach. It was there hangin' on the bough. Big and juicy. Just waitin' to be 'et. I was

68

hungry. Real hungry. There it was. Wasn't anyone around. Oh, I know I shouldn't have done it.

HEDY *(shocked)*. You mean that peach tree near the big house window? *(TOM nods.)* But that's Miss Nancy's own tree. She planted it herself. I heard Mama say so.

TOM. It was quiet. All the white folks were having lunch. I could smell the food. Didn't think no one could see me. But Miss Nancy, she looked out the window and screamed, 'Robber! Robber!' And Master Ed came out with his whip... with his whip, Hedy.

HEDY. Mama told you not to go near the big house. And you shouldn't steal, Tom. Mama told you that. *(HEDY finishes wiping the wound.)* Does it feel better, Tom?

TOM *(nods)*. Thanks, Hedy.

(MISS NANCY sweeps in. TOM moves away. HEDY conceals the cloth.)

MISS NANCY. I thought I heard a *boy's* voice down here. A familiar boy's voice. *(To HEDY.)* Looks to me like there's plenty of work to do, Hedy. And talking doesn't get it done.

HEDY. Yes, Miss Nancy. *(HEDY begins scrubbing again.)*

MISS NANCY *(to TOM)*. So this is the way you repay Master Ed for feeding and clothing you year after year. First, you steal. Now, you stop Hedy from doing her work. You should be ashamed of yourself. *(TOM doesn't answer.)* But I can see you're not. Well, I'll see to it, Tom, that you get another lesson from Master Ed, one you won't forget so easily! *(Her anger mounts.)* A boy like you should be sold! *(Pause, says to herself.)* I'll tell him this afternoon. *(To HEDY.)* Hedy, remember those sheets have to dry in the *sunlight.* You'll have to work a lot faster than you are now. Meanwhile, Tom, get a washbasin and help your sister until I get back. You've made her lose enough time already. *(MISS NANCY exits. HEDY gets a washbasin for TOM.)*

HEDY. Oh, Tom. *Sold!* Then, we'd never ever see you again. She couldn't mean that. Maybe if you work real hard this afternoon and help me finish, she'll forget about talkin' to Master Ed.

TOM. No, Hedy. She ain't the kind to forget. and I ain't doin' no laundry either. That's women's work. Miss Nancy knows no man does that kind of work. She knows that, but she told me to do it, just the same. She's just a ...

HEDY. *Sh-h-h,* Tom! She might come back and hear you! *(Sound of whippoorwill.)*

TOM *(excited).* Hedy, do you know what that is?

HEDY. Sure. A bird down by the river.

MISS NANCY *(offstage).* Hedy, I better not find you talking instead of washing. *(HEDY quickly continues to scrub the sheets.)*

HEDY. C'mon, Tom. Won't you help me finish?

TOM *(looks around to make sure they're alone).* That's a whippoorwill, Hedy.

HEDY *(scared).* Mama says that sound means death, 'cause a whippoorwill doesn't ever sing down by the river.

TOM. That sound ain't no bird, Hedy. *(Whispers.)* That's Moses calling.

HEDY. Who? Moses! Moses in the Bible. Mama taught me that. You're just trying to fool me. Moses lived some hundred and thousands of years ago.

TOM. Not that one, Hedy. And don't say the name so loud. She's a woman livin' now. And she takes people North, underground, and when they come up, they're all free and safe and happy.

HEDY. You're crazy, Tom.

TOM. No, I ain't. Listen, Hedy. (*Comes close to HEDY to tell her the amazing tale.*) I hear the old men talking, late at night. They say Moses is tall, tallest woman in the world. They say she can see things a l-o-n-g way off, even in the dark, just like a bat. They say she can run faster than rabbits, climb trees like a possum, jump over fences, and fly over streams...and that she can hear a patroller sneeze twenty miles away. There's a price on her head...but ain't no one can catch her. (*Sound of whippoorwill. TOM gets the idea.*) And Hedy ...listen, Hedy, I'm gonna run away with her...tonight!

HEDY (*looks around to see if they were overheard*). Tom, if you run away, they'll send the dogs after you and they'll find you and eat you.

TOM. They won't catch me. Not with Moses.

HEDY. But Master Ed says the people up North fatten up runaway slaves and then they eat them.

TOM. He just says that to keep us all from runnin' away. Hedy, do you want to scrub sheets all your life? (*HEDY shakes her head.*) Then, come with me. We could make it together.

HEDY (*looks around again*). Ain't it dangerous, Tom, to run away? Besides there's Mama and Papa. Anyway, how you gonna get past Miss Nancy? She'll be back any minute.

TOM. If they're gonna sell me anyway, Hedy, I ain't got nothin' to lose. If they sell me down river, I'll never get away...ever. Now's my only chance. (*Tries to persuade her.)* Hedy...Hedy, don't you want to make Mama and Papa proud of you? Do somethin' beside scrubbin' sheets?

HEDY *(gently).* Oh, Tom, what could I do?

TOM. You could go to school, Hedy. And then you could send Mama and Papa a letter and tell 'em we're fine. And then...

HEDY *(interrupts, laughing).* They can't read, and we can't write. Who you foolin'?

TOM. But we could learn. Oh, Hedy, come with me. Up North all the children go to school...girls too. *(Sound of whippoorwill. TOM tries to persuade HEDY.)* Hedy, it's Saturday. That's the day Moses always starts. They can't print no poster about us on a Sunday, so we'd get at least one day's start. *(Convincing her.)* And Hedy, when we're free, then we could help Mama and Papa and we could all have a nice little house together. *(She puts the sheets down thoughtfully.)*

HEDY *(rises).* Could we really help Mama and Papa come North? Really? And all have a nice house together?

TOM *(confident).* Sure we can. Besides there'll be people up there to help us.

HEDY. And could I really learn to read and write, Tom?

TOM. Sure you could, Hedy. But you'll never get a chance to learn down here. *(HEDY stands uncertainly.)* Hedy...Hedy, if you don't come with me, now, I might never see you. Never! Never again! *(TOM crosses to entrance to see if MISS NANCY is in sight. Whispers.)* Hedy, now's my chance. Miss Nancy's just gone inside the big house. I gotta go now. If they see me goin' I'm as good as dead. *(TOM starts out.)*

HEDY. Wait. Wait for me, Tom. I'm comin' too. *(Softly.)* Goodbye, old sheets. Goodbye, forever!

TOM. Quick, Hedy. *Now!*

(TOM grabs her hand. The curtains close.

The escape is choreographed. Their movements are tense, punctuated with the sound of the whippoorwill. Several times they think they are being followed. Finally they reach their destination and collapse near the river bank. There are clumps of bushes along the bank.)

HEDY. You go on alone, Tom. I can't. I've got to stop and rest. I bet Moses went on. We've walked for hours.
TOM. You can't stop now, Hedy.
HEDY. Sh. Down there. Who's that?

(They crouch down. Slowly a shape comes towards them. MOSES enters. She has a deep scar on her forehead, like a dent, and old scars on the back of her neck. She is thirty-seven years old, five feet tall and has a rich, husky voice. She calls like a whippoorwill.)

TOM *(whispers)*. Are you Moses?
MOSES *(nods)*. What are you children doing down here? Down here by the river bank this time of night. It's dangerous. Your mama and papa gonna be mighty worried.
TOM *(rises)*. We wanna go with you.
MOSES. Go? Where, child? Just where do you think I'm plannin' on going?
HEDY. Oh, Tom, she's not gonna take us. You said she was the tallest woman in the world and she'd take us North, and you were wrong the whole time. *(She starts to cry.)*

MOSES *(bends down. Sees HEDY's feet are torn and bleeding. Lifts them).* You done come a long way, child, to find me.

TOM. We been looking for you all night. We ran away from home. You gotta take us.

MOSES. Is that any way to ask a question? Why'd you run away? *(TOM looks embarrassed.)*

HEDY. Tom stole a peach. That's why, and Master Ed beat him!

MOSES *(notices wound, says gently).* You won't get far stealin', Tom.

TOM *(humbly).* I know.

HEDY. And then, Miss Nancy said she was gonna *sell* Tom!

TOM *(pleading).* Moses, please take us with you! We want a chance to grow up free. If I go back to Master Ed now, he'll sell me down river, and I'll never have another chance to get away. We mean to be free, Hedy and me.

MOSES. And once you get free, what do you mean to do?

TOM. I mean to be somebody... Not like Master Ed neither. But somebody I'm proud of... inside. And Hedy's gonna be a lady. A fine lady. And she's gonna learn to read and write along with me, and...

MOSES *(interrupts laughing).* Well, now before you two children turn into the finest lady and the smartest gentleman that this world ever seen, we gotta get North first. *(Looks at the two small figures before her, uncertain that they can make the hard journey.)* But this freedom train is goin' a long way. And the road ain't easy. You've got to sleep by day, walk by night. And never let folks know you're about. Watch me. You'll learn to hide as well as I can. You gotta walk so quiet that there's not even a sound of your bare feet on the earth. When you sleep, you gotta be so quiet that there's not a sound of breathing. Not a cough or a sneeze. Once this train starts, ain't no turning back.

TOM. Don't want to go back...ever!

HEDY. Ever.

MOSES. You're sure?

TOM. We're sure. *(HEDY nods.)*

MOSES *(looks up at sky)*. It's near daylight. We'll wait right here. There'll be two coming to meet me here. *(Thoughtfully takes out pistol.)* And I reckon there'll be a heavy price on the man's head.

TOM. Is that why you got a pistol?

MOSES. To protect us all, Tom. So no one falls off this train. *(Points to North Star.)* Got to follow that star, and it's a long way off yet. *(She crouches in the bushes, so she can barely be seen. HEDY crouches down beside her.)*

HEDY. How can you tell if you're looking at the right one?

MOSES. That's easy. The star up there never moves. It doesn't rise in the East or set in the West as the other stars seem to. Anyone walking towards it could use it as a guide, because it never moves. *(To TOM and HEDY.)* Come on, children. You've got to melt in with the bushes.

TOM. Then you will take us?

HEDY. *Please!*

MOSES. I never said 'No,' yet. *(They hug each other, then exit.)*

Scene Two

SCENE: *A grass swamp area. There is an oak tree with Spanish moss in the center. There are the noises of the swamp at night and the swish of the river against the bank. JOE enters, followed by LINDA. JOE is in his mid-thirties, handsome, muscular, and a former overseer of a plantation. LINDA is seventeen, delicate, spoiled, and a former lady's maid on a large plantation.*

LINDA (*sits down*). Joe, I'm not walkin' another step. I'm tired. We been walkin' and hidin' for a week now, since we met up with Moses and the two children. If she's so good at gettin' people North, how come there ain't no more along? And how come we ain't there yet? I think the old woman's crazy.

JOE. She ain't crazy, Linda, so none of that foolish talk. Why, a week's nothing. Sometimes it takes months. (*Sits beside her.*) Nothing's happened to us yet either, Linda, remember that. You and me gotta be careful. Remember we run away. I was hired out to be overseer of a plantation, and you were right there in the big house as a lady's maid. They're gonna be looking for us— soon—if they ain't looking already. There's no turning back just 'cause your feet's sore. It's a miracle we ain't dead, Linda. If it weren't for Moses, we would be. She sure do know where to hide out.

LINDA (*sarcastically*). Strange houses where we hide in secret rooms, or in potato holes in cabins, or sleeping all day in a hollowed out haystack in the fields. I thought I was gonna die from chokin' in that stuff. I've had enough.

JOE. But you didn't die. She knows what she's doing.

LINDA. Joe, it ain't a woman's job to lead us, it don't make no sense.

(MOSES enters with TOM and HEDY.)

MOSES. Nobody asked whether I was man or woman when they put an axe in my hand and tied me by the waist to a mule. I been doing man's work all my life. I'm not afraid. *(Gives TOM and HEDY a scarf from her neck.)* Here, fill this with all the berries you can find. *(TOM and HEDY work nearby throughout scene.)*

LINDA. Joe, I never should have listened to you. It's all your fault with your talk about a better life. Well, if this is the life, I don't like it. I don't see no tables lined with food or people welcomin' us. My dress is nearly torn off from briars pokin' at it, and my feet are covered with blisters and sores. As far as I can see, I ain't no better off than I was two weeks ago when I was still a lady's maid. I don't want to suffer like this for some fool notion in your head about freedom. All I want now is just to eat and sleep regular.

JOE *(angry)*. Just some fool notion? Do you think your mistress would welcome you back if you went and said that to her? Do you think she'd throw her arms around you and say, 'Linda, honey, we sure did miss you'? *(JOE takes out a bowie knife and sharpens it on rock throughout scene.)*

MOSES. It's too late, Linda. You're a runaway, remember that. You can't go back. You're wanted dead or alive and you're another man's property until you cross that line further north. If you don't want to go with us, then you'll die right here. I won't let you talk to anyone...

anyone, you hear, about our plans. Too many lives are at stake, and one scared, skinny young miss is not gonna stop my Underground Railroad, and the chance of Joe here and Tom and Hedy to go free!

JOE. And your chance too, Linda, if you'd think a minute.

LINDA *(subdued, but still complaining)*. I don't want to think. I'm tired. None of us wanna go further. It ain't worth this travellin', footsore, backs achin', bellies achin'.

TOM *(realizing how tired he is)*. When will we get there, Moses?

HEDY *(joining in)*. I don't reckon I can walk much further.

MOSES. Yes, you can!

LINDA *(bitter)*. Besides, what makes you so sure it'll be any better when we get North? At least we were alive in Maryland. Where's this Canada we're heading for? I never heard of it before. This crazy talk about a North Star. There are as many stars in the sky as grains of sand on the earth. It says so in the Bible. So how do you know which one's the North Star for sure? Have you got a special message from up above? We may be heading right back for Maryland.

MOSES *(firmly)*. We're headin' for WILMINGTON, Delaware, and when you get there you'll be fed.

LINDA *(skeptical)*. Fed?

MOSES *(the time has come to boost their spirits)*. Listen to me. There's a man in Wilmington, a Quaker with a wide brimmed hat. He calls himself Thomas Garrett. He don't dress like us or look like us...face as pale as cow's milk, but he's our friend and he's gonna give each one of you a pair of shoes to wear North and fresh milk and bread to eat soon as we get there.

HEDY. A pair of shoes? Honest? Real shoes?

MOSES. New shoes.

TOM *(uncertain)*. Milk? Bread? Do you mean it? Or are you just sayin' it to make us feel better?

MOSES. No. It's true. Thomas Garrett keeps a pail of milk and a loaf of bread always ready, always fresh, for God's poor that come to his door.

LINDA. God's poor. That sure is us alright.

MOSES. He's got a shoe store and one side wall of this shoe store swings open. Behind it is a whole room for us where we can be safe and sleep before goin' on.

LINDA *(sarcastically to JOE)*. In our new shoes. Sure. Well, I don't believe it. It sounds like crazy talk. Stories. I want to know where she's really takin' us?

MOSES. For the last time, we're goin' to Wilmington. I've made this trip eight times, and we've made it safely. Some folks say it can't be done. But it can be done. It's been done. And it's gonna be done once more. And at the end of the ride you're gonna stand tall—be proud of who you are—be proud of what you done.

LINDA. Proud, nothin'. As I see it, it still amounts to the same thing. You can work from sunup to sundown for someone else.

JOE. Don't you understand nothing? You can work for yourself. Up there in Canada, I hear folks like us go to school and some do the teaching in the school. Ain't that something? Something to live up to? *(Laughs softly.)* Maybe to tell my grandchildren.

HEDY. The way Tom talks about it, it's like there's nothing between you and the sun.

LINDA *(to MOSES)*. Is that why you do it? Make all these trips?

MOSES. We all God's children, ain't we? Every time I go home there's more to come back for. When I was Tom's and Hedy's age, I used to see half-starved runaways brought back. I cried when I saw some of them whipped, some sent South with a chain gang to work in the rice fields or in the hot sun of the sugar and cotton plantations. I began to wonder about the other runaways I didn't see come back. Master said he'd sold them or, to frighten us, he'd say that the dogs ate them. But I didn't believe it. So I began to wonder how come none of them didn't come back? How come no one ever said, 'You can do it, too'? That's why I keep goin' back. I tell 'em...and I take 'em.

LINDA. Well, I ain't no hero like you. I'm goin back. No one treated me bad at the big house. I ate regular anyhow, and I slept at night instead of creepin' through swamps.

MOSES (*takes out pistol, points it at LINDA's shoulder blades, calmly*). No, Linda, there's no goin' back on this road. Move ahead, or die here.

TOM. I don't see what she came for in the first place.

LINDA. It was Joe. He came to me talkin' about freedom, and I got to thinkin' about what he said. The folks in the big house treated me alright. But after that, every time I went to eat the food burned with master ownin' it. And I knew Joe was right. I was just another piece of property. And I got to thinkin' how plantation air could never be sweet—no matter how many flowers were bloomin' there.

HEDY. If you feel like that, what are you fussin' about?

LINDA. I didn't know walkin' to freedom was goin' to be like this. I know I can't walk clear to another country.

JOE *(pleading)*. C'mon Linda. Don't ruin everything. Come with us. Please. I'll help you. Moses will help you. Ain't no better conductor in the whole Underground Railroad. You'll see. We'll make it.

LINDA *(turns, slowly joining them)*. I'll try.

MOSES *(happy at LINDA's decision)*. Now, no more stops tonight. If you're tired, keep goin'. If you're scared, keep goin'. If you're hungry, keep goin'. If you want to taste freedom, keep goin'. *(They begin walking. There is the sound of hoofbeats. The sound is low at first but it increases in volume as the scene progresses.)*

JOE *(in a panic, freezes)*. They're coming for me, Moses. Hear 'em. *(There is the sound of dogs in the distance.)*

HEDY *(frightened)*. Oh, is Miss Nancy comin' after us?

LINDA *(starts to cry)*. I told you. I told you. Oh, we're all gonna die.

MOSES. Sh. All of you. Break off some pine branches.

TOM. What for?

MOSES *(ignores him)*. Linda, tear up your petticoat. We're gonna fool those dogs... *(TOM brings over pine branches and LINDA and HEDY give her strips of petticoat. MOSES works as she talks. She distributes pine boughs and rags to each.)* Take this pine bough and take this rag and tie a tail on yourself that will brush behind you the whole way. That's all the hounds is ever gonna smell is plain old pine trees. This freedom train is just startin'. It ain't got up its high speed. And fears gotta ride on this train. Right up front with us. Make friends with it. Shake its hand. It's one of the angels that's ridin' with us, protectin' you, remindin' you to be steady, silent and careful. It's gonna get a lot colder as we get on—and you're all gonna go hungry. But at the end of the ride, God willin', we're gonna be free.

We're gonna be free and safe and happy. *(They tie them on. HEDY starts to laugh at TOM.)*

HEDY. You look funny, Tom.

MOSES. Hush, child. Not a sound. Take your brother's hand, Hedy. Joe, take Linda's hand. *(MOSES takes HEDY's hand.)* We're gonna make a chain for the next few miles. When I stop, you stop. If I fall to the ground, you fall to the ground. Don't breathe a word. *(The children start as if it's a game.)* Now, listen. Any old body can go through the woods crashing and mashing things down like a cow. That's easy. You gotta move like an Injun. So quiet, even a bird in the nest don't hear you—and fly up. So quiet, not even a leaf makes a rustle. Not even a twig cracks back on itself when you come through them. *(Points to the star, and they begin.)* Remember that's where this train is goin'.

(This section can be choreographed. As they walk, MOSES stops dead. They all freeze. She listens. They continue. Behind it all, there is the steady rhythm of horses' hoofbeats and the sound of hounds in pursuit. At one point MOSES drops to the ground, and they drop too. The tension and weariness mount. Suddenly, MOSES points to the sky and in the distance a rooster is heard announcing dawn. There is now silence around them, and they realize they are safe for the moment. The sky is visibly lighter.)

We've lost them. We're safe for a while. Joe, see if you can get us a swamp rabbit. The rest of you sleep while you can. *(Silently they find spots to hide and sleep amongst the bushes and undergrowth. MOSES kneels*

and prays. HEDY crawls to her and tugs at her sleeve.
MOSES goes on praying. HEDY tugs again.)

HEDY *(whining)*. I'm hungry.

MOSES. Go to sleep. *(She goes on praying.)*

HEDY *(doesn't budge)*. I'm hungry. Ain't had nothin' to eat since yesterday.

MOSES *(firmly)*. When you wake up, we'll eat.

HEDY. But I'm hungry now.

MOSES. Well, I reckon we could all do with a good meal, Hedy; but there isn't enough food for that. Maybe later tonight Joe will catch us a swamp rabbit.

HEDY. I could eat a whole one myself. Right now. Without cooking it first, even. Moses, when we go underground, will there be food then?

MOSES *(laughing gently)*. What are you talking about, Hedy?

HEDY. Tom said you led people underground and when they got there, everything was fine and beautiful—and when they came up, they were free, just like that. *(She starts to cry from exhaustion, hunger and fear.)*

MOSES *(holds her in her arms)*. Oh, honey, it ain't gonna be like that. It's gonna be on this real earth and we're gonna be creepin' North in the night through trees and swamps, because we've got plenty of enemies around us by daylight.

HEDY *(fresh outburst of sobs)*. I wanna go home. I wanna go home. I miss Mama and Papa.

MOSES *(comforting her)*. Sure you do, honey. And I'll bet they're thinking of you too. Right now. Hedy, can you see that star up there? *(HEDY looks up and nods.)* It's almost mornin'! You can barely see it now. But it's traveled millions of miles so you could see its light every night. And it's tellin' you to be brave, not to give up now. Millions of miles just to tell you that.

HEDY *(slowly, questioningly)*. I guess if that star can go all that way, I guess I can go a little further, maybe. Only when we gonna get there, Moses, when?

MOSES. Why, honey, we only been walking a little more than a week. I reckon we'll be in Wilmington soon. But then we gotta go clear to Canada.

HEDY. Why we gotta go all that way? Why can't we just stay with the man who's gonna give us all new shoes? Can I pick any colour I want?

MOSES. Them shoes is to help you walk and the colour does not matter. Anymore of that lazy girl talk, and you won't get any shoes at all, Miss Hedy.

HEDY *(subdued)*. Is Canada very far? Very cold?

MOSES. Yes, it is.

HEDY. Why do we have to go so far?

MOSES. Didn't used to, Hedy. But seven years ago in 1850...

HEDY. What happened then?

MOSES. Now child, if you'd stop askin' so many questions and give me a chance to answer, I'd tell you. Seven years ago the government passed a law. Said runaway slaves couldn't have a trial by jury. Said they'd punish anyone tryin' to help us escape.

HEDY. Punish?

MOSES. If some people find out Mr. Garrett is helpin' us, they may just put him in jail.

HEDY. Why?

MOSES. Because the law says they can. Sometimes folks who are scared act like cowards and sometimes they pass laws to make them sound brave. They call the law the New Fugitive Slave law. Sounds important. But inside you know the men who passed it were just scared.

HEDY. Scared of what? Of me? What for? I wouldn't hurt no one. Neither would Tom. You just ask him.

MOSES. Scared that you and Tom and others like you really mean to be free ... to stand tall. *(Crisply.)* So, since I can't trust Uncle Sam with our people no longer, I gotta take 'em even further ... up to Canada. And when we get there, you gotta promise me you're gonna learn to read, Hedy, and write and you're gonna amount to somethin' and folks are gonna say, 'There goes Hedy. She's some fine brave girl.'

HEDY. I'm gonna try, Moses. I'm really gonna try. But I don't think I'll ever be as brave as you.

MOSES. Hush, now, honey. You sleep awhile. You gotta rest to grow up taller.

(She puts her shawl around her and sings softly a chorus of 'Go down, Moses.'

Lights come up softly and then fade to indicate the day has passed and it is now twilight. MOSES is asleep with HEDY in her arms. LINDA and TOM are asleep nearby. JOE enters, shakes MOSES urgently.)

JOE *(whispers)*. I went near the road. There wasn't anyone around. But it looked like a horse team had gone by— maybe a few hours ago. Looks like they lost this on the way.

MOSES *(picks up poster)*. A runaway poster. About you Joe? *(He nods.)* Read it to me.

JOE *(scans it)*. 'Reward, $1,000. Wanted alive. Valuable man.' Valuable man! First time I ever heard that.

MOSES. Does it go on to give your name and a description of you?

JOE (*nods, reads to himself, then aloud*). 'Believed to be heading North.'

TOM (*incredulous*). Joe! Can you read?

JOE. Enough to know we're in trouble.

TOM (*nudging HEDY*). Hedy, Joe can really read!

MOSES (*jumps to her feet, wakes LINDA*). Come on children. We're gonna have to leave this place...now...fast. We're still in danger. We're gonna wade in the water so no one will see our footprints. We gotta go a long way tonight, and even your breathin's gotta be soft. We're in trouble. Someone's lookin' for us and lookin' right around here, and if they find us, we'll never live to tell about it.

(*Lights dim to show passage of time. Lights up. They are making their way precariously along the river bank.*)

TOM (*whispers*). Moses, I'm cold.

MOSES. Sh. (*Clap of thunder. HEDY starts to scream and TOM covers her mouth. Lightning flashes in the sky.*)

LINDA. Storm comin'. We better stop and find shelter.

MOSES. No shelter tonight. We gotta keep movin'. If the heavens all open up, we gotta keep goin'. Only a few more miles and then we can stop. We've got to cross that line into Delaware or nothin' will matter again.

TOM. Moses, it's beginning to rain!

MOSES. I know, honey. Praise God there's no moon and there's a fog rollin' in. Ain't no one gonna see us tonight. You've been out before in the rain, Hedy. Didn't hurt you before. Won't hurt you now. You just follow me.

HEDY. How do you know we're even goin' in the right direction? We can't see the North Star now.

MOSES. Come here, and I'll show you. You feel the bark on the tree, this way. There, can you feel the side the moss is thickest on?

HEDY (*feels tree*). Yes!

TOM. What good does that do?

MOSES. The north side of the tree hardly ever gets sun. That means it's the north side where the moss grows thickest.

TOM. It's cold. I ain't never been so cold before, Moses.

MOSES (*lifts her head up, taking in the air. It is sharp and biting. She is jubilant*). There's a north wind, Tom. Come clear from Canada. There'll be frost on the ground tonight. Praise God! We're getting there! (*Stops.*) We cross the river there. It's the narrowest part. (*She steps into the river—on the side of the stage, so they will exit into the wings.*)

LINDA. You gonna wade that river?

MOSES. Runnin' water leaves no trace. And we gotta cross it here. We gotta cross that line.

LINDA. That does it. I'll wade no freezin' water for no crazy woman. (*JOE follows MOSES.*)

JOE. I'm coming, Moses.

LINDA. Joe, don't leave us.

TOM. Look, it's up to her knees.

LINDA. It's up to his waist.

HEDY. It's up to her chin. (*Pause. They watch, fearing the worst.*)

TOM, HEDY, LINDA. They made it!

LINDA. Joe's waving to us. C'mon children. He's coming back to help us cross.

HEDY. I'm scared, Linda. The water's high.

LINDA *(stronger)*. Now, remember what Moses said: 'If you're scared, keep going.' *(She takes TOM's and HEDY's hands and prepares to cross the river.)*

ACT TWO
Scene One

SCENE: *The interior of THOMAS GARRETT's Quaker home in Wilmington, Delaware. There is the front room, a shoe store with a front door up center. To the right is an old wooden desk and chair. Stage right on the diagonal is a wall lined with shoe boxes. A few boots and shoes are displayed. In front of the wall are chairs for customers. One panel of this wall leads to the secret room, stage left. The room is dark and windowless. On the floor are a few pallets and blankets to lie on. At the back of this room there is a water pitcher, basin, and a thick candle on a stand. It is just before dawn. There are three knocks in rapid succession. These are repeated a second time. THOMAS enters, wearing traditional Quaker garb, appropriate for the late hour. He opens the door slightly.*

THOMAS. Who goes there?

MOSES. Friend. *(She uses the secret code.)* I have four parcels with me.

THOMAS *(opens the door wide)*. Come in quickly, friends. I have room and thee are welcome.

(HEDY is half asleep. THOMAS carries her in. JOE carries LINDA, who is ill. MOSES and TOM enter.)

Sit down, my friends. Sit down. *(Carries over a pail of milk, ladle, and tin cups.)* I am glad to see thee, Moses. I was not sure if thee was alive or dead. *(He serves the milk.)*

MOSES. Alive, praise the Lord! But I have a risky cargo. Joe here has $1,000 on his head.

THOMAS *(takes a loaf of bread from desk and slices it).* Joe...yes...I think I saw the poster. We shall do our best to make sure no one gets that reward while you are here. *(Distributes bread.)* Is the girl ill?

JOE. Linda's been bad since yesterday.

THOMAS. Let us hope that rest will help, for I dare not call a doctor.

HEDY *(wakes up sleepily).* Moses, I'm hungry.

THOMAS *(with affection).* I see thee are hungry, child, and tired. Thee must have food and rest.

HEDY *(to TOM).* Why does he talk so funny?

TOM. Sh! Moses said he was a Quaker, and they all talk that way. *(Munching the bread.)* Everything's just like Moses said.

THOMAS. I see thee will need new shoes.

HEDY. It was all true. It really was!

THOMAS *(to MOSES).* Can thee rest here today? This evening I will send you on. There is more danger at present than before.

LINDA. More danger, Lord, I can't go on. I can't.

MOSES. She has been ill since yesterday, but we had to get to your house before we could risk stopping. *(THOMAS puts his hands on her forehead to see if she has a temperature.)*

LINDA *(shakes him away).* No! No! Go away.

THOMAS *(gently)*. Thee needs to rest and care. I will do what I can. Sit down for a moment, friend.

LINDA. So tired. So tired. *(She dozes off.)*

HEDY. Thank you for the bread, Mr. Garrett.

TOM. And the milk.

HEDY *(impatiently)*. And will we really get shoes? New shoes?

MOSES *(laughing)*. Hedy! Thomas Garrett, there are two North Stars, one in heaven, and one right here. We would be lost without your help.

THOMAS. Thee knows, I hope by now, that your knock will never go unanswered as long as I live in this house.

MOSES *(gratefully)*. Children, this is our greatest friend in the North.

THOMAS *(shakes his head)*. No. *(Humbly.)* It is He that inspires us to do the work He requires of our hands, and it is He that is your greatest friend. Moses, I am glad to see thee in good health and ready for action. *(Softly to her so children won't hear.)* The highway is not safe. Some slaves escaped nearby and there is great excitement. None of us are safe. They suspect I helped. *(To TOM and HEDY.)* Thee had better hide now and sleep out of sight.

TOM. Where? I don't see a place to hide. *(THOMAS pushes wall panel and panel springs open.)*

TOM. Look at that!

HEDY. A secret room!

THOMAS. Here thee will be safe. Rest now. Thee has a long journey ahead. I will call thee when it is time to leave, when it is safe. *(He carries in remainder of food and milk. JOE assists LINDA, puts her on pallet. MOSES, TOM, and HEDY walk in.)*

LINDA *(half asleep)*. Where am I? It looks like jail. *(She begins to cry.)*

THOMAS. I will light the candle, so thee will not be fearful. *(Lights candle.)* But thee must be silent. One sneeze, one cry, one cough, and thee will be found if there are unexpected visitors. Rest, my friends, and finish thy food, but in silence. *(Exits, closes panel. TOM and HEDY lie down. MOSES adjusts the blankets over them and JOE puts a blanket over LINDA. THOMAS sits at his desk in the front room, lights a lamp, takes a quill pen and dips it into the ink pot. He writes the following note:)* 'To William Still: Philadelphia. Respected friend, this evening I send to thee four of God's poor. May success attend them in their efforts to maintain themselves. Please send word whether or not these seven arrived safe I wrote thee of ten days ago. My wife and self are as ever thy friends, Thomas Garrett.' *(As he puts his pen down, there is a loud, sharp knock at the door. GARRETT looks surprised, snuffs out candle and hides letter. He opens the door slightly.)* Who goes there?

(Two men force their way in, one flourishing a pistol and the other a bowie knife. They look around briefly.)

FIRST MAN. Where are they?

SECOND MAN. Where are they hiding?

(In the secret room TOM wakes up. He listens terrified by the wall. MOSES and HEDY wake up. HEDY starts to ask a question. MOSES covers HEDY's mouth gently, hugs her, adjusts her blanket. MOSES and TOM listen intently while others sleep.)

THOMAS. Friend, thee has wakened me. Pray lower thy
voice.

FIRST MAN. We'll wake up the whole household if we
have to. Come on. Out with it. Where are they?

THOMAS. If you mean my wife, she is upstairs and I pray
not wakened by your loud noise. I am, as thee can see,
awake and in front of you, though thee knows God
meant for good men to sleep until the sun rose.

FIRST MAN. We know you've got slaves here, Garrett.
So you can cut out the holy talk. *(Flourishes knife.)*
Seems to me you lost all your property once before for
helping slaves and giving them breakfast! Heard you
lost all you owned. Did they thank you for it, Thomas
Garrett? Did they? *(Knife is near his throat.)* If you cooperate with us, Garrett, you'll live a lot longer.

THOMAS *(calmly pushes aside weapon. With disdain).*
No one but a coward resorts to such means to carry out
his ends.

SECOND MAN. We're after slaves, Tom Garrett. Not ser-
mons.

THOMAS. In my home, and despite what you may hear, it
is still my home, it is the word of God thee will hear,
and none other. If thee does not like its peaceful sound,
thee is free to leave!

FIRST MAN *(changing his tactics).* Garrett, we know
they're in here somewhere. Even if you can hide them
for three weeks, when they sneak out, we'll get them.
There's $1,000 on the man...he won't get away. Not
with that price on his head!

THOMAS *(tries to hide his concern).* Thee has strange information. How comes thee by it?

SECOND MAN. So they are here! By poster, Garrett, all
over the country. A good description, too. You can't

get away with it any longer. The law will catch up with you.

THOMAS. My law is God's law. If thee does not respect it, thee is not welcome in my home nor has thee a right to be here.

SECOND MAN. We'll catch you helping them soon enough, Garrett. We'll get you and put you out in the street with no place to go. See if your God protects you then. We're just waiting... and remember, the new law is on our side.

THOMAS. It's the Devil's law!

FIRST MAN. Call it what you will... 'Devil's law' or 'New Fugitive Slave law,' it was passed seven years ago and it hasn't been changed.

SECOND MAN. Let us refresh Mr. Garrett's memory. A man can lose all his property for giving food, shelter, and assistance to slaves. Or have you forgotten so quickly?

THOMAS. There are no slaves in my house. In the past, God's poor have passed through, but in His eyes we are all equal. *(Reflects.)* However, I am not sure what His opinion of thee would be.

FIRST MAN. I'm warning you, if you've got fugitive slaves in this house, now, they won't get past the Delaware border. There are police at both ends of the bridge and even at other crossing points.

THOMAS. Thank you for the warning, gentlemen. *(Firmly, ushering them out.).* I have only a few dollars left in the world, but if thee know a fugitive who needs breakfast, send him to me.

SECOND MAN. Garrett, you'll go to prison.

THOMAS. If this be a crime for which one goes to prison, then there must be some excellent people there. Now if thee will excuse me, I have work to do. The sun is up. An appropriate moment for a night call to end, I think.

(Opens door and firmly ushers them out. He stands there against the door for a moment to recover from the ordeal. His wife appears.)

SARAH. Again, Thomas?

THOMAS. Again.

SARAH. Will they not let us sleep?

THOMAS. They know.

SARAH. Who is here?

THOMAS. Moses and four others. They want the reward money.

SARAH *(angrily)*. They belong to the Devil.

THOMAS. And they will return to him, my dear, never fear.

SARAH. Oh, Thomas, it isn't fair. Some say women are weaker than men, but look at Moses. She's gone back eight times...alone, despite the danger, to free more slaves...a handful at a time. That's all she can take. And so she will go, again and again, until she dies or until the world comes to its senses. Is it right that such a woman should have to crawl along, tree by tree, and pray to pass unnoticed, while other men are free by law to hunt her down and be honoured for the deed?

THOMAS. My dear, be glad she goes unnoticed and yet I wish it were more unnoticed. And as for honour, that will come, someday. God chooses strong people to do His work, but He never promised any that it would be easy. Did the men wake thee?

SARAH. The noise did. Thomas, he had a gun. I saw it. It seemed to be the very shape of a devil.

THOMAS (*firm, calmly*). Yes, he had a gun. But we have reason and human kindness on our side.

SARAH. Oh, Thomas, is that any good against a knife and a gun?

THOMAS. Yes. (*Pause.*) Provided we know how to use them.

SARAH. How long will Moses stay?

THOMAS. I'll send them on tonight, but not by the way I planned. That way is too dangerous, now. There will be police at the entrance of the bridge. That much information I just received from the Devil's own aides.

SARAH. How, then?

THOMAS (*sits thinking*). A friend drives the bricklayers across the bridge to work...Yes, yes! That's a common enough sight. The men go over singing and shouting. No one stops them. And at nightfall they return. Still singing and shouting. Moses only brought four. Yes, they can lie on the bottom of the wagon and under the boards. Yes. Yes. We could do it. (*Jovial.*) Make a large breakfast, Mrs. Garrett. I'm hungry enough for six people this morning.

SARAH (*laughing*). Thomas Garrett, I'm glad I married thee.

THOMAS. Why?

SARAH. My mother always said a man with such a big appetite must have as big a heart as well. Eggs for them, Thomas!

THOMAS. Yes. Eggs, milk, bread. Two are children, Sarah. They are very thin...frightened.

SARAH. And eggs and milk for thee, Thomas. Thee looks thin, too.

THOMAS. Nonsense, with all those big breakfasts thee makes!

SARAH. They go to others, I know. Now, promise me, Thomas. Thee needs nourishment too, to go on with thy work. (*Exits.*)

THOMAS. If they escape this time, it will be God's miracle. If no one sees them, and if they don't suffocate... but it's the only way... the only chance... we've got to try it!

Scene Two

SCENE: *The outskirts of Wilmington. There is a bridge going from up center to down left. Down right there is a large bush. Several townspeople cross the bridge. SARAH crosses with a market basket. The two men are standing at the edge of the bridge watching each passerby. FIRST MAN smokes a cigar. SECOND MAN doffs his hat when he sees SARAH. A POLICEMAN stands on duty, watchful.*

SECOND MAN. Good morning, Ma'am. Fine day. Clear as can be. Can see for miles.

FIRST MAN. I was just saying it was nice weather to stand here and have a smoke.

SARAH (*coldly*). It's a fine day for work, gentlemen. I wonder that thee hast none to keep thee busy. (*Exits quickly.*)

FIRST MAN (*nudges the other*). No work, she says! By midnight you and I will be $1,500 richer.

SECOND MAN. $1,500?

FIRST MAN (*sorry he mentioned it*). Didn't you know? Reward's gone up. Five hundred dollars more.

SECOND MAN. How do you know we'll catch them by tonight? Maybe they got away already. We haven't seen anything.

FIRST MAN. Well now, you don't expect them to walk up and say, 'Here I am. Go get your reward.' The trouble with you is you're lazy. You better do your share of the work or you'll lose your share of the money.

SECOND MAN. You're the one who's standing here smoking a big, fancy cigar. Don't try to threaten me.

FIRST MAN. Take it easy. Maybe you should just look under the bridge. Maybe they're creeping along the river bank.

SECOND MAN. Why me? Why don't you go? Afraid to get mud on your shoes?

FIRST MAN. I got to stand here and watch the road.

SECOND MAN. Oh, alright. Anything coming? *(There are sounds of singing and shouting in distance.)*

FIRST MAN. Just the bricklayer's wagon coming up. Same as usual. They sure do make a racket. Go on, hurry up.

(SECOND MAN goes. A wagon makes its way across the bridge slowly. Two men are singing, walking beside it. They are stopped by the POLICEMAN. He checks the wagon wheels.)

POLICEMAN. Halt! Cargo?

BRICKLAYER. Bricks. Same as usual.

POLICEMAN. Oh, it's you two. Go ahead. No need to check your wagon.

(SECOND MAN reappears, reports to FIRST MAN.)

SECOND MAN. Nothing.

FIRST MAN. Let's go and check the other side of town. He's stopping all the traffic anyway, so they can't escape over this end of the bridge.

(They exit. Wagon turns off bridge and goes to bush. BRICKLAYER walks to back of wagon, knocks three times. Slowly, painfully, MOSES, HEDY, TOM, LINDA, and JOE creep out. All are wearing new shoes.)

BRICKLAYER. Run for it. I don't dare stop long. Good luck. *(They thank him.)* Run!

HEDY. C'mon, beautiful new shoes. We're going North.

MOSES. This way! Not a sound.

TOM. Ain't we free yet, Moses? I'm tired.

MOSES. Mean to be free, Tom. But we ain't free yet. Now, down on your bellies and crawl! *(They do so. The wagon moves on.)*

Scene Three

SCENE: *OLIVER JOHNSON's Anti-Slavery office, New York City, 1857. On the wall there is a large 'Wanted' poster which reads $1,500. In the upper left-hand corner is a black woodcut of a small running figure with a stick over his shoulder, a bundle tied to the end of a stick and another stick in his hand. This is the symbol of the runaway slave. The legend reads: 'Joe Bailey ran away from his subscriber on Saturday night, October 12, 1857. He is about 5 ft. 10 in. tall, chestnut colour, bald head with a remarkable skin. $1,500 to anyone* *who will apprehend said Joe Bailey and lodge him safely in jail at Aston Talbot County, Maryland.' OLIVER JOHNSON is at his desk. MOSES, HEDY, TOM, LINDA, and JOE enter. MOSES is dressed in a man's suit. There are briars clinging to it. It is old, worn, and snagged. She wears a felt hat and men's shoes on her feet.*

OLIVER JOHNSON. Harriet Tubman! We just had word from William Still in Philadelphia that you were on your way. *(Glances at poster on wall and studies JOE.)* And this is Joe Bailey, if I'm not mistaken. I am glad to see the man who is worth $1,500 to his master.

JOE *(trembling)*. Mr. Johnson, how did you know me?

OLIVER *(points to poster)*. The poster's right here in our office and the description's so close that no one could mistake it. Welcome. Sit down, all of you. How did you get here?

HEDY. We rode at the bottom of a bricklayer's wagon out of Wilmington.

OLIVER *(laughs)*. Well, they'd never think to look there for you.

MOSES. Children, this is Oliver Johnson, head of the New York Anti-Slavery Office. And this is Hedy and Tom. *(They shake hands.)* And Linda. *(They shake hands.)*

OLIVER. I'm glad to see two such brave children. I'm glad to see all of you... here, and safe.

TOM *(admiring poster, tracing figure with his finger)*. What'd you do, Joe? How come they're willing to pay so much for you? Nobody seems even to miss me.

MOSES *(hugs TOM)*. You just thank the good Lord they ain't out lookin' for you, child.

JOE. Mr. Martin hired me out every day. I was an overseer of a plantation. And then I was sold to the same
man I'd been working for. $1,000 down and $1,000 to
come. My first lesson after I was sold was a beating.
Even though I'd worked from early morning to late at
night, sun and rain. It didn't matter to him. My first
lesson with my new master was a beating. And I went
to Moses's Uncle Ben and just said, 'Next time Moses
comes, let me know.' *(Suddenly angry, ripping poster
from wall and crumpling it.)* Well, they can't stop me
now. They can't! I'm going to farm that Canadian land,
just the way I planned. And I'm going to build us a
home there, just the way I planned. And I'm going to
help anyone of us coming North, because that's the way
I dreamed it. And that's the way I planned it. Mr.
Johnson, how far off is Canada now?

OLIVER. Three hundred miles to Niagara Falls on the
train. When you cross the rise in the tracks, you'll be
on the other side, and you'll be free.

JOE *(nervous)*. We're going on the train? An open train?
Shouldn't we keep right on going North the same way
we got here?

OLIVER. Not in the winter. You'd freeze in the cold inside of a week. Besides, the train's so obvious, they
won't even think of looking for you there. It's the road,
ditches and fields they'll be watching. And it's three
hundred more miles, remember.

HEDY. All that way to go, just to be free?

TOM *(to HEDY)*. Moses told us before, it's a long walk to
freedom.

OLIVER. And Moses has walked it nearly nine times. Do
you still remember the first time, Moses?

MOSES. That's the time I remember most.

TOM. Why?

MOSES. Well, I crossed the line into the free state of Pennsylvania just as the sun was coming up. I looked at my hands to see if I was the same person, now I was free. There was such a glory over everything. The sun came like gold through the trees and over the fields, and I felt like I was in heaven. (*Group sits transfixed. MOSES laughs gently.*) But there was no one to welcome me to the land of freedom. I was a stranger in a strange land. And I sat down and thought, 'My home is, after all, way down in the old cabin quarter right there with the old folks and my brothers and sisters.' I was free, and they should be free too. I decided to try and make a home for them up here in the North and, the Lord helping me, I would bring them all here. Oh, how I prayed then, lying all alone on the cold damp ground. I didn't have no friend then, and I needed help.

OLIVER. Harriet, Harriet, you've got to be careful now. There's a $40,000 reward out for your capture. I don't know how you've done it so far.

MOSES. I tell the Lord what I need, and He provides. (*Looks around at her group.*) We've made it this far. Canada's just further north.

OLIVER (*hands them tickets*). Here are your train tickets. And here are five bibles. There's a bible meeting up North in St. Catharines. That's past the border, and you're going to it—if anyone asks. (*He hands them the bibles.*)

HEDY. But I can't read!

OLIVER. Here's your first lesson. (*Demonstrates*) These white pages always belong on the right side when the gold letters are on the top. The gold letters spell bible. B-I-B-L-E.

HEDY. Tom...I'm learning to read, just like you said! *(She traces the letters with her fingers.)*

OLIVER *(distributes winter garments).* Watch out for the conductor. If he accepts your tickets, he's one of us and he'll let you cross the border. If he doesn't, be prepared to jump off that train, and don't talk to the passengers. They may sound friendly to fool you, but they may just want to get a better look at you before they try to collect the reward money. Keep your heads in these bibles. And you better leave now. Moses, you know the way to the station. *(They all start out except LINDA who sits there.)*

LINDA. Moses, I want to be free just like Joe said, you know I do. But I'm tired. I just don't think I can keep on going three hundred more miles. I don't want to go to no Canada.

MOSES. Mean to be free. Remember? If I can't trust Uncle Sam with my people no longer, I can bring 'em up clear to Canada, and that's what I plan to do. There's two things you got a right to: liberty or death. If you can't have one, you can have the other. But no one, hear me, no one is gonna take any one of us alive, ever. I never run my train off the track and I never lost a single passenger. We can fight for our liberty as long as our strength lasts, and when the time comes for me to go or for you to go, the Lord will take us in. No one else! I don't want to hear no more talk of givin' up. Three hundred miles! Why, that's nothing! Think how many miles we come so far!

Scene Four

SCENE: *Stage right, a railroad car. Stage left, the plat-*
form between cars. The train is bound for Niagara
Falls, Canada. MOSES, TOM, HEDY, JOE, and
LINDA are seated, pretending to study their bibles.

CONDUCTOR *(offstage).* Next stop, Niagara Falls, Ontario. Tickets, all tickets, please.

HEDY *(to TOM).* Does that mean Canada? Are we nearly
there?

TOM. Shhhh. Yes. Make believe you're asleep, so he
can't ask nothin'. And hold your book up, so he'll think
we're free and go to school. Remember what Mr.
Johnson told you. *(TOM studies bible cover, whispers.)*
Hedy, which way does it go?

HEDY *(looks at it carefully, turns it wrong side up).* This
way ... I think.

(The CONDUCTOR enters car. TOM nudges HEDY.)

TOM. Shhhh.

CONDUCTOR. You young folks have tickets? *(HEDY*
nods and gives him tickets. CONDUCTOR examines
tickets and looks at them carefully. He looks at MOSES,
JOE, and LINDA.) You all together? *(They look at one*
another apprehensively. There is a pause. Slowly,
MOSES answers.)

MOSES. We're together.

CONDUCTOR *(looks at them all closely again. Heartily).*
Well now, if you'll just give me your tickets, I won't
bother you any longer, and you can go right on with

your bible study group. Guess you're all heading up for that meeting in St. Catharines, up in Canada? *(MOSES nods gratefully. CONDUCTOR bends down, puts HEDY's bible right side up. He goes on down the aisle.)* I'll let you know when we get to the Falls.

(He goes towards platform as the two men come on the platform with the poster announcing reward for JOE. They study it carefully.)

FIRST MAN. We've searched nearly every car on this train. Haven't seen him yet.

SECOND MAN. But the man said he saw him get on.

FIRST MAN. You mean we paid a man fifty dollars to tell us that. You can't trust anyone these days. The whole country wants the reward money. Wait till I get my hands on him.

SECOND MAN. C'mon. Let's try the next car. We haven't got much time.

CONDUCTOR *(appearing as men try to conceal poster. They exchange long look)*. Tickets, gentlemen.

FIRST MAN. You have the tickets.

SECOND MAN. No, I don't! You do. *(He hunts through his own pockets to double-check.)*

FIRST MAN *(bullying him)*. All right, where'd you put 'em? You better remember...quick!

SECOND MAN *(scared, remembers)*. Coat pocket. That's where I put them. Five cars back. Conductor, you'll have to collect them later from us. We're in a hurry.

CONDUCTOR. Well, you'll just have to go five cars back and get them.

FIRST MAN. Conductor, we're looking for friends. We're supposed to meet them on the train. If you could just let us go into the next car to see if they're there...

CONDUCTOR. Sorry, gentlemen.

SECOND MAN. They'll be worried about us.

CONDUCTOR. As far as I know, you gentlemen are riding free on an international railroad. You can't go wandering around a train without your tickets. How am I supposed to do my job?

FIRST MAN. But conductor...

CONDUCTOR. Every passenger must show his ticket upon request as proof he has purchased one. That's the regulation.

FIRST MAN (*disgusted*). I told you to take those tickets!

SECOND MAN. Hurry up. We've still got time. (*They exit.*)

JOE. How much longer, Moses?

MOSES. Should be soon.

CONDUCTOR. Next stop, Niagara. Niagara Falls, Ontario. (*Walks to TOM and HEDY.*) If you keep watching out that window, you'll see the Falls.

TOM. When do we get to Canada?

CONDUCTOR. Soon as we hit that rise in the bridge. (*He exits, goes to platform.*)

HEDY. Tom! It's beginning now. Feel it?

LINDA. I can see the Falls!

JOE. Moses, are we here?

MOSES. Almost.

(*The men reappear attempting to show their tickets to the CONDUCTOR. At that moment, everyone is jolted by the center rise of the track.*)

That's it! That bump! That's the center. You're in Queen Victoria's free land. Look at the Falls!

FIRST MAN *(shakes SECOND MAN).* Canada! Now, what good are those tickets? All this way for nothing!

CONDUCTOR *(quietly).* Nice day to see the Falls, gentlemen. As long as you've come this far. *(They exit.)*

LINDA. Oh, Moses, I didn't believe it. I didn't think we'd make it.

JOE. On an open train.

LINDA. Oh Joe, after walking all that way ... we're here ... we're free! Ain't nothing can make you a slave again. *(They begin to put on wraps, standing up and gathering bundles.)*

TOM. Now we'll learn to read and write—just like Joe can. And no more stealin', I promise.

HEDY. Moses, when we get off the train you're staying here with us, aren't you?

JOE. Of course she will. We're all going to stay together and ...

MOSES *(interrupts).* No. Soon as you're settled I'm goin' back.

JOE. You can't. There's $40,000 reward out for you.

MOSES. Ain't nobody collected it yet.

LINDA. But it's dangerous.

MOSES. I know.

TOM. Do you have to go?

MOSES. Yes.

LINDA. Oh, Moses, you've done enough already. You've made the trip nine times crawlin' on your belly, goin' hungry. And now all that again? Is it worth it ... to risk your life?

MOSES *(calmly)*. So long as God wants to use me, He'll take care of me.

HEDY. Oh, Tom, I understand now. All this talk about freedom. It means I don't have to crawl on my belly no more, be silent no more, go hungry, no more creepin' in the dark. Every time Moses goes, some more of us stand straight. I can walk right off this train standin' tall as a pine tree, singin' as loud as I can. Singin'. The whole world's gonna hear us.

LINDA. Joe, we're safe. The freedom ride's over.

JOE *(slowly, thoughtfully)*. The way I look at it, it's just beginnin'.

THE END

Classroom Concepts

☙ The journey to freedom for an escaping slave was filled with peril. The danger and fear, however, were tempered with each successful step northward. The following exercise stimulates students to think about the hazards and the help that those aboard the Underground Railroad might have encountered. Best played with students seated in a circle, each person should contribute to the development of the plot. This activity can be repeated often with the same story starter, so long as an original plot develops each time.

Escape to Freedom

This is a continuous story and players may add as much or as little as they like in order to move the story forward. Plot reversals, however, are an important aspect of this activity in that a positive experience must be followed by a negative one. This good news/bad news pattern continues until the story has been completed. The story starter given by the teacher and an example of how it might begin to develop are below.

> *Teacher:* I am escaping to freedom with Moses on the Underground Railroad. Although I knew it was dangerous, I ran away from the plantation where I worked and hid in the woods until I found Harriet Tubman and the other passengers going on the journey north.

> *Student #1:* Just as it began to get dark, we could hear the dogs barking. They were coming near us. I was certain I'd be captured and returned to the plantation and

punished. I held my breath and waited for the worst to happen.

Student #2: Then I heard my master yell to the others that he had helping him search for me that they had to turn back. It would soon be too dark to see anything. They turned away.

Student #3: When we were certain that they were gone, we began to take our first precious steps toward freedom. I had joy in my heart as I thought about the new life I'd have in Canada.

☞ This play is about a black person but has been written by a white playwright. The following explores the potential issues that this may raise.

Black and White

Stage a debate which focuses upon this question: *Can a white person speak to the black experience portrayed in this play?* Follow this with a role-playing exercise wherein one person is Harriet Tubman and another is a contemporary playwright. What points does each raise in support of or against a white writer telling this story? Be certain to role-play the scenario twice, switching parts so that each student is cast both as Tubman and as the playwright. As a class, follow the debate and the role-playing exercises by discussing the points of view which surfaced through these activities.

☞ A concentration game is an enjoyable way for students to remember factual information about Harriet Tubman and her brave deeds. To play, students sit in a circle and should be encouraged to help one another if someone has difficulty remembering. If the class is large, the game can be played simultaneously in small groups.

Harriet Tubman Concentration Game

The first person begins with the phrase, 'I am Harriet Tubman' and states a fact about her life or her work. The next person repeats the phrase and the fact before adding another fact. The game continues in this way, with each person repeating previously stated facts before adding something new. An example follows.

> *Student #1:* I am Harriet Tubman. I was born on a cotton plantation.

> *Student #2:* I am Harriet Tubman. I was born on a cotton plantation. I have a scar on my head from an overseer throwing an iron weight at me.

> *Student #3:* I am Harriet Tubman. I was born on a cotton plantation. I have a scar on my head from an overseer throwing an iron weight at me. I first ran away to freedom in Pennsylvania.

As a class, students should research those who have helped secure freedom and civil rights for African-Americans. They may limit their investigation to Harriet Tubman, Thomas Garrett, and others who lived during the time in which *Mean to be Free* is set, or they may expand the scope of the assignment and include figures like Martin Luther King. It is important that all members of the class work from a shared list of those dedicated to achieving freedom and human rights for others. At the conclusion of the activity, biographical sketches and pictures may be displayed in the classroom.

Fighting for Freedom: Who am I?

After researching the lives and deeds of those individuals who helped African-Americans in their struggles for freedom and basic civil rights, each student should select one person who really interests him or her. Omitting the name, the student then writes a biographical sketch of this person. Then, in role, the young actor delivers that person's life story to classmates who see if they can guess the identity of the person being portrayed. If possible, after the freedom fighter has been named, his or her picture should be displayed.

This board game is unique in that students construct the course in the classroom and serve as players as well.

Living Board Game

As a class, design squares for a board game that takes the fleeing slaves in this play to freedom on the Underground Railroad. The first square should be labeled "Start" and the last square labeled "Freedom." Squares can be laid on the classroom floor in a south to north pattern. Episodes in the play should generate ideas for additional squares. Suggestions might include:

Escape from the plantation. Move ahead three squares.

Searchers are after you with dogs. Cover your trail. Go back two spaces.

Rest at Sarah and Thomas Garrett's home. Lose one turn.

As Hedy, Linda, Joe, and Tom are the runaway slaves, at least four pupils can play at a time. If Moses is added to the game, a fifth player is needed. The number of spaces a player may move can be determined by rolling dice.

ᐁ Analyzing a role for performance can be likened to detective work. Students become sleuths when they undertake the following task.

Role Analysis

Invite students to select a character from *Mean to be Free* and imagine that they have been cast in that role. As an actor preparing for the part, each should search for clues that will help in portraying that individual. Ask the class to look closely at the script for answers to the following questions. If students so desire, they may orally share their ideas.

How is this character like me and how are we different?

What does this character say about himself or herself in the play and are these statements true?

What do other characters say about this character and are their statements true?

What actions show what this character is like?

What does this character want most in the play and what is he or she willing to do to get it?

ᐁ Commemorative sculptures honor individuals and deeds that are significant. As artists in this activity, students will use each other, rather than materials such as clay or bronze, to create a statue.

A Tribute to Harriet Tubman

Students are invited to imagine that they have been commissioned to create a statue of Harriet Tubman. Their work may include Tubman and others from the past or present such as those who have helped African-Americans to attain freedom and civil rights, or it may portray only Tubman herself. The choice of content is the sculptor's, and he or she may pose as many or as few classmates as needed in order to create the desired image(s). Students should be told only that the title of the statue is to be *A Tribute to Harriet Tubman* and that their classmates are to be their medium. Stipulations can produce added interest. Having all figures connect, for example, by having a limb touching someone else in the composition adds excitement to this challenging project.

In Act Two, Scene Three (p. 101), Harriet Tubman (Moses) describes the first time she experienced freedom. That dialogue has been adapted here into a narrative pantomime paragraph. Insure that students have adequate space for movement and then read the narrative aloud, pacing delivery so that they have sufficient time to experience the feelings and show the actions reported. All students should portray Harriet Tubman and play in unison.

Moses' First Walk to Freedom

You are Harriet Tubman, also known as Moses. Although you've done it nearly nine times now, show that you remember clearly the first time you walked to freedom. Cross the line into the free state of Pennsylvania. Look at the sun just starting to rise in the sky. Now, lower your eyes to your hands and stare at them, wondering if they will look different now that you are free. Your hands look the same but your heart is light. Show your joy when you realize you are free at last! Look around. Everything appears glorious. How does this make you feel? What do you think? The sun is shining through the trees and over the fields and you raise your hand over your eyes to shield them from its bright golden rays. You use your arms to make wings and pretend that you are an angel. Then, you slowly let your body resume its shape as you realize you are all alone. No one greets you when you arrive in this free land. You sit down slowly on the ground and think to yourself about your home in the South. Show how much you miss your absent family. You make a decision and rise with determination. You will make a home for them in the North. You will return for them and bring them to live with you. You lie on the ground. The earth is damp and cold and you shudder. You begin to pray. You know that you will need help if your new mission is to succeed.

🙰 Several steps constitute the following activity in which students apply their knowledge of history through first-person narratives and visual interpretations.

Who Made It: Who Did Not

Students begin by researching aspects of slavery such as what plantation life was like for a slave, the risks associated with fleeing and the consequences of capture, as well as the struggles and opportunities that, for some, came with freedom. Next, students should work in pairs with each creating a first-person narrative for a slave who attempts escape. Student narratives may be as detailed as desired, but must include (1) the slaves' relationship to one another; (2) their individual reasons for running away; (3) a description of their flights to freedom; (4) whether or not each was successful in eluding capture; and, (5) what life was like after the attempted escape. These narratives are to be shared orally. Next, each is to use classmates to create a tableau depicting the most climatic moment in his or her flight to freedom. The student must include his or her partner in the frozen picture and then can add as many other classmates as desired.

ᗧᑫ As students read the plays in this anthology, they will recognize some common themes, character types, and ideas. In *Mean to be Free* and *Sunday Gold*, for example, there are slave characters. The two Holocaust plays call to mind the Nazi's belief that certain peoples were sub-human and fit only for slavery.

Enslaving Experiences

Working in groups of three, students should further explore these parallels. Using the format of a television news magazine, cast one student as the moderator, one as a former slave, and one as a Holocaust survivor. The moderator should ask questions of the other two which allow them to recount their experiences. Topics might include life in captivity, attempted escapes, and hiding. If possible, videotape these interviews. When each group has shared its program, as a class compare and contrast the experiences of slaves in America during the nineteenth century with those of perceived enemies of the Nazis during the twentieth century.

ᗧᑫ This activity helps students to understand character motivations and perceptions. They will need a working knowledge of cultural norms in the United States and Canada just prior to the Civil War as well as an understanding of the economics of slavery and the political positions of slave owners and abolitionists.

I Did It Because

Using "I did it because..." as the opening line, each student selects one of the *Mean to be Free* characters from the list below and creates a story which explains or attempts to justify his or her behavior. The story then is told orally from the character's point of view. Why, for example, might someone own slaves? Hunt slaves? Mistreat slaves? Help slaves? How could he or she defend this action?

Characters:
> Miss Nancy
> a slave hunter
> Oliver Johnson
> the railroad conductor
> a bricklayer

Next, students should review the script, noting clues which define that character such as whether he or she is greedy, altruistic, or an idealist. Then, with three classmates, each should improvise a scene in which this character is interviewed by journalists in 1857. The classmates should, respectively, play a Canadian, a southern, and a northern journalist. Their questions should reflect the prevalent points of view on slavery found in their geographic regions. This activity should be played four times so that each member of the quartet has an opportunity to experience each role.

☙ Students reading reports found in newspapers, magazines, and on websites will learn that slavery still exists in some parts of the world. This activity invites them to do investigative reporting.

Slavery Today

After identifying examples of slavery that exist in the world today, students should work in teams and imagine that they are creating a documentary on the subject. On-location reports should be a part of each team's program. They may wish to address historical aspects of slavery as well. The team members should write content for the documentary, be cast as journalists and figures key to their stories, and then stage their broadcasts. If video equipment is available, these shows actually should be taped.

Quick thinking is required as students work with the first images that come to mind here. These pantomimes reinforce their knowledge of Harriet Tubman and her accomplishments. Students will need to have adequate playing space and to imagine that they are Harriet Tubman. The teacher calls out a descriptive phrase or sentence and the students, playing in unison, pantomime the first thing that comes to mind to show *How Harriet Did It*.

How Harriet Did It

Possesses physical strength
Feels deeply religious
Escapes to freedom
Goes back nine times for other slaves
Guides 180 others to freedom
Serves as a brave scout
Spies for the Second South Carolina Volunteers

Tells Union officers where ammunition and cotton are
  stored and where slaves seeking freedom can be found
Works in a freedman's hospital
Raises money for freedman's schools
Helps the poor, sick, and disabled
Gives lectures after the war
Earns respect as a hero

 This activity provides students with an opportunity
to use a variety of historical documents in crafting a performance.

Slave Stories in Performance

Appropriate resources for this activity include the following: literary narratives, diaries, court records, handbills, autobiographical accounts, reward posters, excerpts from screenplays such as *Amistad* and *Gone with the Wind*, lyrics of spirituals and slave songs, folklore, excerpts from books and/or scripts such as *Uncle Tom's Cabin*, and political tracts. Students should craft a performance of dramatic readings and songs which chronicles the slave experience. Other classes may be invited to attend this presentation.

 Adapting and performing literature for the stage gives students experiences with both written and oral accounts of southern life in the nineteenth century.

From Page to Stage

Students begin this activity by reviewing slave and first person narratives which focus upon life in the southern United States from the antebellum period to the end of the nineteenth century. Websites such as that of the University of North Carolina-Chapel Hill Libraries are excellent places to find materials, i.e.,

http://sunsite.unc.edu/docsouth/specialneh.html *and* http://sunsite.unc.edu/docsouth/fpn.html.

First, each student should select a book and review it for classmates. Next, a scene or account from the book that the student finds stage worthy should be adapted in script form. Students then should work in groups, rehearsing each others' scenes. When they are at a polished level, a class period or evening can be devoted to performances for an invited audience.

＊￿￿ Contrasting family scenes makes evident how different life was for those who lived in a plantation's big house and those who lived in slave quarters.

Lifestyles

The character of Linda from *Mean to be Free* should appear in both of these scenes. First, working in groups, students cast themselves as a plantation owner's family. Improvisationally, they create a typical day at home in the big house. Who are the family members? What do they do during the day? How is Linda expected to serve them? Next, they create a second scene in which they portray Linda's family living in slave quarters on the plantation. Who are the members of this family? How do they spend their time at home? How is Linda's life different in each of these environments? When everyone has performed both scenes for classmates, invite each group to construct a chart which details differences in these lifestyles and display it in the classroom.

CHAPTER FOUR

Remember My Name

The Playwright Speaks

On my fourth birthday, I remember standing by our large Stromberg-Carlson radio phonograph. A few of my parents' friends were gathered in the living room. Suddenly the music of the New York Philharmonic Orchestra Sunday Concert was interrupted by an announcement. There was a hushed silence, which my father finally broke. "The party's over," he said. Pearl Harbor had been bombed. War had been declared.

It wasn't until four decades later that I began to investigate World War II Holocaust history. When I did I was horrified, not only by the events but by my own ignorance.

It was only when I found a simple sentence in a footnote about Le Chambon-sur-Lignon that I found what I wanted to say, that in the midst of evil there were those of conscience. (The term used today is Righteous People.)

I began to wonder about my friends and acquaintances. If I had knocked on a door, would the person have turned out the lights and pretended not to be home or would the friend have whispered, "Come in," and yanked me into a trembling safety. I could not even deal with the possibility that someone might have turned me in for a kilo of sugar. And I had to ask what I would have done if someone had come to my door. None of us knows what action we'd take in the midst of a crisis, whether we would be weak or strong, until we're tested. But I do know we can never take freedom, or for that matter, kindness, for granted. In the war-torn Europe of the early 1940s, most of the men were away at war. So I asked what kind of women opened their doors—and their hearts. Madame Barbière began to evolve in my mind.

A friend from my college days had been "hidden" during the war—not like Anne Frank but with a *faux nom* and a conspiracy of silence. What would a young, protected, bright, middle-class girl do, miss, want most of all? So Rachel/Madeleine Petit arrived.

I didn't want an army on stage. Yet, I needed a menacing Nazi presence but not a stock villain. I wanted someone who was educated, civilized in demeanor, intelligent, someone the school teacher might even be attracted to were it not for his prejudice and politics. So in strode Hans.

And what of the parents? I remember reading that so many families believed they should stay together. Yet it was those who separated who survived. What an agonizing decision for those parents! I tried to show the battle between them and within themselves.

A rescue story must have pressure, tension, danger. Enter the nosy Yvette Reynaud, who collaborates with the Nazis for sugar; Suzanne, the strong-minded, attractive teacher; and Julien, the resistance fighter whose ideals endanger them all.

So like the Potée de Madame Barbière, the ingredients began to simmer.

To augment my secondary research, I did primary research. I took the train from Paris to the Riviera to the Auvergne, I walked the cobblestone streets of Le Chambon-sur-Lignon, which I called St. Laurent des Pins, and I interviewed people who'd lost their jobs, homes, and families, whose greatest act of courage was somehow to go on living.

Courage isn't necessarily physical bravery and bravado. There are other kinds. What I call "kitchen courage" is a quieter kind. It's about a widow who wants no more trouble yet opens her kitchen door, risking her own life to save a child. It's about a small child without the comfort of family, friends, home, or real name, who is sent off to face the world alone—and thrives.

No, it's not a true story; but it was inspired by historical data. Facts that are unforgettable. Although these particular characters were invented, I hope Rachel's story will provoke audiences to ponder how to resist tyranny and oppression, how to protect those inalienable rights of human beings sharing one planet. As Madame Barbière comments, "We each say, 'No!' in our own way!"

Remember My Name (originally titled *The Devil's Orphan*) was the first-prize winner in the 1989 IUPUI National Playwriting Competition. It was produced at Indiana University-Purdue University at Indianapolis in 1989.

The Play

CHARACTERS

RACHEL SIMON (a.k.a. MADELEINE PETIT),
a student. Resourceful, idealistic, and curious, about 10.

PAULINE SIMON, her mother. Religious, family-
centered, cautious, 32.

LÉON SIMON, her father. A man of action, 37.

MARIE-THÉRÈSE BARBIÈRE, a war widow,
independent, proud, 60.

SUZANNE FLEURY, the village school teacher.
Knowledgeable, attractive. Assists the Maquis, 26.

JULIEN DELACOUR, a leader in the Underground
Resistance, the Maquis. By profession a journalist.
Intense, impulsive, 30.

GÉRARD LA SALLE, a gendarme. Enforces the laws
of France, no matter what they are. Sentimental, 55.

HANS SCHMIDT, a Nazi officer. Handsome,
well-educated man of the world, who follows party
policy assiduously, 35.

YVETTE REYNAUD, Madame Barbière's neighbor.
An opportunist, 45.

PÈRE ANTOINE, A Jesuit priest. Follows his conscience, 55.

VENDOR, non-speaking. Only hands and shadowy face
seen. Can be played by PAULINE or LÉON.

TIME

The play takes place during World War II, 1942-1945.

SETTING

The action takes place in Southern and South Central France, in the Unoccupied Zone.

Scenic design can be minimal, a unit set with levels, selected set pieces and possible projections to suggest atmosphere and locale. What is vital is that the story flows freely, the action moves quickly, and the production is taut.

ACT ONE
Scene One

SCENE: *A city street in Marseilles. The Unoccupied Zone of France. November 1942. The whistle of a French train. School boys beating someone up.*

RACHEL *(voice offstage).* No! Leave me alone. Let me go. No-o!

(Sound: A gunshot. The wailing of a French siren. RACHEL races on, fleeing a gang of school boys. She is resourceful, idealistic, and curious. But at present she is beaten up. Her uniform is torn and her face and knees are bleeding. She turns and realizes they're not pursuing her. RACHEL stops to collect herself, discovers injuries, wipes the blood from her face and puts a handkerchief around her bleeding knee. Stifling the tears, she continues running, halting only in the momentary safety of shadows. RACHEL exits. Sound: The whistle of a French train. Lighting comes up on a basement hotel room in Marseilles.)

AT RISE: *PAULINE is setting the table for supper. PAULINE SIMON is married to Léon and is the mother of Rachel. She is religious, family-centered and cautious. Thirty-two. LÉON peers out through a slit in the hotel curtain. LÉON SIMON is married to Pauline and the father of Rachel. He is a man of action. Thirty-seven. Sound: Gunfire, followed by the wailing of a French siren. PAULINE freezes. Suddenly past the basement window, there are running feet. Then the thudding sound of heavy boots and the blare of a military brass band. LÉON slumps in a chair.*

PAULINE. What's happened?

LÉON. They're here. In Marseilles.

PAULINE. This is the Free Zone. That's why we came here. The French and German governments made a pact.

LÉON. A devil's pact.

(LÉON crosses to the desk, searching for papers. PAULINE rushes to the window.)

LÉON. Stay away from the window!!! PAULINE!!!

PAULINE. Where's Rachel?

(RACHEL SIMON stands in the doorway.)

RACHEL. Maman.

PAULINE *(runs to her)*. RACHEL!

RACHEL. I don't have the bread, Maman. I don't have...

(Bursts into tears in her mother's arms.)

PAULINE. Léon, some clean rags and some hot water quickly.

(LÉON goes.)

PAULINE. Where were you?

RACHEL. Outside the cinema.

PAULINE. But that's nowhere near the bakery!

RACHEL *(between sobs)*. I wanted... to find out... what was playing. But I saw a big sign, "No Jews Allowed." Maman, it wasn't there yesterday.

(LÉON returns with rags. PAULINE begins to cleanse wounds.)

LÉON. Who was it? Who beat you up like this?

RACHEL. Some boys. A gang.

PAULINE. If you'd do what you're told and not be so headstrong! The cinema!

LÉON. Did you recognize any of them?

RACHEL. Some were from my school.

PAULINE. Your new school!

RACHEL. They had the same uniforms. But, Papa, they all had Nazi armbands. Except one. Brand new armbands. And one of them had a flag.

LÉON. The Nazis do a thorough job.

RACHEL. They started hitting me. One of them yelled, "Forget it. She's just a kid." But the one carrying the flag said, "This'll teach her a lesson she won't forget."

LÉON. Why didn't you run?

RACHEL. I did. They came after me. The one with the flag yelled, "We'll get rid of your kind."

PAULINE. Rachel, are you hurt? Is anything broken?

RACHEL. Oh, Maman, it wasn't the sticks. They were laughing at me!

PAULINE. Léon, she is not going back to that school!

LÉON (*thoughtfully*). No. No, she's not.

RACHEL. But I didn't cry, Papa. No matter how hard they hit me.

PAULINE. You can cry all you want now.

LÉON. How did you get home?

RACHEL. There was a gunshot. They turned to look. The boy without the armband whispered, "Run!" But, Maman, I forgot the bread.

LÉON. Never mind about the bread. (*Hugs her.*) Tonight we'll eat less.

RACHEL. Papa, why do they hate us so much? WHY?

LÉON. Because...we are a little different. *(Shrugs.)* Because it's easy.

RACHEL. Easy?

LÉON. Easier to blame us than try to solve the problem. *(To Pauline wearily.)* That's our history, isn't it?

RACHEL. Papa, I was scared. Awful scared. But I didn't let them know. And I bit one of them, too. He yelled!

LÉON *(laughs)*. Next thing you know you'll be a French spy!

PAULINE. How can you laugh at a time like this?

LÉON. There are times, Pauline, when you can either laugh or cry. Léon Simon chooses to laugh. My one and only daughter is saved by the gunfire of the Nazi invasion. But just before that happened, she bit the enemy, and he howled like a baby. It's a story for her grandchildren.

RACHEL *(giggles)*. Papa, you make things seem all right. You make me laugh. You always do.

LÉON. It comes with the job of being papa. And right now that's the only job I have. The only job I have—worth keeping. *(LÉON goes to the drawer and takes out an official identity card and an ink pad.)* Rachel, put your thumb in this, and then press it on the square right here.

(RACHEL does.)

LÉON. Now say, "My name is Madeleine Petit."

RACHEL *(repeats)*. My name is Madeleine Petit. But why, Papa? My name's Rachel Simon. Who's Madeleine Petit?

(Sound: Clock striking five.)

LÉON. As of five o'clock—you are!

RACHEL. But that's lying. You told me never to lie.

LÉON. The world's just turned upside down. When it's right side up, we can live again—and stop lying. For now you must forget you were ever Rachel Simon.

PAULINE. NO!

RACHEL. Why, Papa? I don't want to forget.

LÉON. You must forget you are a brave and beautiful Jewish girl.

RACHEL. PAPA!

LÉON. Not that Madeleine isn't brave and beautiful. She is. Definitely. But she is not Jewish. And she has never heard of Léon and Pauline Simon.

PAULINE. Léon, we discussed this, and I said, "No." Only if it were an emergency.

LÉON. What do you call this? They've invaded Marseilles.

PAULINE. She's not ready.

LÉON. Ready? Who is ready? Do you think I want to do this? But alone she has a chance to survive.

RACHEL. Alone? ALONE! Maman?

PAULINE. Léon, she's only ten years old.

LÉON. With a whole life ahead of her! And I won't let those barbarians take it away!

PAULINE (*frantic*). The family should stay together.

LÉON. The only way to survive is to separate.

RACHEL. Why can't we go together?

LÉON. Because, you're the only one who has the right papers. I am sending you to St. Laurent des Pins.

RACHEL. Where?

LÉON. A tiny village in the mountains. Snowed in all winter. A perfect place to hide.

RACHEL. But where is it?

LÉON. Auvergne.

RACHEL. I never heard of it.

LÉON. With a little luck the Nazis never heard of it either.

RACHEL. Do we have relatives there?

LÉON. No.

RACHEL. Friends?

LÉON. Madeleine Petit will make some.

RACHEL. Papa, Auvergne is so far away.

LÉON. Yes. Far from all this madness. That's why I'm sending you. Now here's your new papers: your identity card with photograph and thumb print, your birth certificate, a food ration card. You'll need these. Don't lose them. You're going to start a whole new life.

RACHEL. Papa, I can't.

LÉON *(his gesture interrupts her)*. You don't know what you can do until you try. Now, this is the most important of all. Don't ever tell anyone that you had another name. Not even someone you think you can trust. NEVER!

RACHEL. Why not?

LÉON *(stern)*. Promise me!

RACHEL. All right, I promise, but why not, Papa?

LÉON. Because one slip of the tongue, and you're dead.

RACHEL *(scared)*. Papa, can't you and Maman come too? Please!

LÉON. It's safer this way.

RACHEL. How will I get there?

LÉON. By train.

PAULINE. They'll arrest her. Jews can't travel.

LÉON. No. But Madeleine Petit can. And she will. Three hundred and fifty kilometers. All the way from Marseilles to St. Laurent des Pins. *(To Rachel.)* Don't look so frightened. Above all, don't give them any cause for suspicion.

RACHEL. But I am frightened.

LÉON. Of course, you are! It's dangerous. Some people think when you're brave, you have no fear. No. To be brave means you don't *show* your fear.

PAULINE. Léon, she's just a child.

LÉON. Not any longer! Go change. Your bag is under the bed. Packed. The train's at eight. Hurry.

(RACHEL exits.)

PAULINE. She won't know what to do.

LÉON. She'll learn.

PAULINE. It isn't right.

LÉON. The whole war isn't right.

PAULINE. I only have one child.

LÉON. And I will do anything to save her!

PAULINE. What if something happens to her?

LÉON. Did you forget what happened to our neighbors in Paris? The reason we ran?

PAULINE. Why St. Laurent des Pins?

LÉON. I told you before. They'll never let a child go hungry.

PAULINE *(desperate)*. Léon, can't we decide this tomorrow?

LÉON. Tonight there's confusion. Easier for her to escape. And wait for what? They took our business. They took our home. They're not going to take our daughter.

PAULINE. There must be some other way.

(Sound: Gunfire and the wail of a French siren.)

LÉON. Not now! *(Persuading her.)* In St. Laurent des Pins she'll lead an ordinary life.

PAULINE. Ordinary! Away from her own mother and father?

(Sound: Marching jackboots and orders shouted in German.)

LÉON. We are sending her away to live, Pauline. TO LIVE!

PAULINE *(looks at him shocked. Pause. Softly)*. All right.
  (Deliberately.) All right.
  (LÉON kisses PAULINE.)

PAULINE. Léon, I want her to remember the Sabbath.

LÉON. I'll get her. *(Exits.)*

(PAULINE gets out three Sabbath candles on a tray, one for each member of the family, and a wine goblet. As the reality hits her, she loses control and cries. But quickly she straightens herself up. She lights the three candles, covers her head with a white shawl, closes her eyes, and waves her hands toward her three times in the traditional welcoming of the Sabbath blessing. RACHEL and LÉON enter. PAULINE puts her hands before her face, closes her eyes and recites the Sabbath blessing.)

PAULINE *(recites in Hebrew)*. Ba-ruch a-ta, ha-shem E-lo-hei-nu, me-lech ha-o-lam, a-sher kid-sha-nu b'mitz-votav ve-tsi-va-nu-le-hud-lik-ner shel shab-bat.

[Translation: Blessed art Thou, the Eternal our God, King of the Universe, Who has sanctified us with His commandments and enjoined us to kindle the Sabbath lights.]

(LÉON raises the wine goblet and says the traditional blessing.)

LÉON *(recites in Hebrew)*. Ba-ruch a-ta, ha-shem E-lo-hei-nu, me-lech ha-o-lam, bo-rei pe-ri ha-go-fen.

[Translation: Blessed is the Lord our God, Ruler of the Universe, Creator of the fruit of the vine.]

(LÉON sips the wine. PAULINE and RACHEL each take a sip from the same goblet.)

PAULINE. We'll have to imagine the Sabbath loaf is in front of us.

LÉON, PAULINE, and RACHEL *(recite in Hebrew)*. Baruch a-ta, ha-shem E-lo-hei-nu, me-lech ha-o-lam, ha-mo-tzi le-chem min-ha-a-retz.

[Translation: Blessed art Thou, the Eternal our God, King of the Universe, who brings forth bread from the earth.]

(PAULINE mimes taking a piece of the Sabbath loaf and hands the tray to LÉON and RACHEL who each mime taking a chunk.)

PAULINE *(kisses Léon and Rachel)*. Good Shabbas.

LÉON. Good Shabbas.

RACHEL. Good Shabbas. Maman, where's the lace tablecloth?

PAULINE. Rented rooms cost money.

RACHEL *(horrified)*. You sold it!

(PAULINE nods upset.)

RACHEL. You said you'd never do that. No matter what happened.

(PAULINE looks at Léon unable to respond.)

LÉON. Things are replaceable. Lives are not! *(Gestures to soup tureen.)* She's got to hurry.

(They sit down to their meager supper. PAULINE ladles out soup. Lighting: The street is now dark. As they eat, RACHEL looks out the window nervously trying to gather courage. They eat a few spoonfuls in silence.)

RACHEL. I've never been out alone after dark.

PAULINE. I never let you!

RACHEL. When will—

LÉON *(interrupts)*. When the war's over. But stay in St. Laurent des Pins. *(A lighter tone.)* I don't want to have to hunt all over France for you!

RACHEL. What do I do first?

PAULINE. You see!

LÉON. A sensible question! Just what I'd expect from Madeleine Petit. The directions are easy. Finding a home will be harder. As soon as you arrive go to the village priest or the school teacher.

RACHEL. What do I tell them?

LÉON. Don't mention Paris. Just say that you've come from Marseilles.

RACHEL. I have.

LÉON. Tell them that when the Nazis invaded, you lost your home.

RACHEL. We did.

LÉON. And that your parents were deported for forced labor.

PAULINE. Léon!

LÉON *(to Pauline)*. She has to know! Marseilles was safe until today. Tomorrow it could be Paris all over again. *(To Rachel.)* Say you need a place to stay, and you'll work hard in exchange. A farm can always use extra hands.

RACHEL. It won't be long, will it, Papa? Will it?
(Sound: Roar of motorcycles, tramp of soldiers' jackboots. LÉON can't answer. PAULINE embraces her.)

PAULINE. My dearest, as soon as the first star appears, say goodnight; and I'll say goodnight too. For as long as we're apart.

RACHEL. Oh, Maman. Like letters. Our own special letters.

PAULINE. Be a good girl. Remember all I've taught you. But most of all, remember that I love you. *(Covering her emotions.)* You'll need your winter coat. I'll get it. *(Exits.)*

LÉON. You know the way to La Gare Saint Charles. You pass it every day.

RACHEL. Can't you go with me? Just that far?

LÉON. No. If they stopped us for an identity check, none of us would get through. Maman and I have to…arrange…for new papers… Remember how we used to make up stories?
(RACHEL nods.)

LÉON. This one you must always tell the same way. Ready?

RACHEL. Ready.

LÉON. Name?

RACHEL. Madeleine Petit.

LÉON. Occupation?

RACHEL. Uh…uh…student.

LÉON. Good. Which school?

RACHEL. Elementary School.

LÉON. Where are you going?

RACHEL. St. Laurent des Pins.

LÉON. Why?

RACHEL. Uh…uh…to see…uh…my relatives.

LÉON. Good. But don't hesitate. *(With a feigned kindly tone.)* Now what's your real name?

(PAULINE returns with coat and hat. The hat is a brimmed felt hat with ribbon in back.)

RACHEL *(slips)*. Rachel Simon.

LÉON *(slaps her face)*. NO!!!

RACHEL. PAPA!

PAULINE. LÉON! How could you?

LÉON. You don't think the Nazis will do worse? This is a
game of life and death. One mistake—and it's over. *(To
Rachel.)* Let's try again. Your name is?

RACHEL *(sniffling)*. Madeleine.

LÉON *(shakes her roughly)*. Madeleine what?

RACHEL. MADELEINE PETIT!

LÉON. Good! Say it again.

RACHEL. Madeleine Petit.

LÉON. Say it over and over. Until it's second nature.

RACHEL *(muttering)*. Madeleine Petit. Madeleine Petit.
Madeleine Petit.

LÉON. Good. Good. Now I'm going to give you some
money. I wish it were more. But it'll get you there. Are
you ready?

RACHEL *(scared)*. So soon? What time is it? *(Peeks in
his vest pocket, an old familiar gesture.)* Papa, where's
your watch?

LÉON *(picks up identity papers)*. Here! Genuine forged
false identity papers. The best in the black market. And
here. The money for your train ticket. It was a good
watch. It fetched a good price. *(Hands envelope to her.)*

RACHEL. Oh, Papa, you loved that pocket watch. It was
Grand-père's.

LÉON. Yes. *(Hugs Rachel tightly.)* But I love my daughter
more!

RACHEL *(crosses to Pauline and they hug goodbye)*.
Maman!

(PAULINE gives her her coat, which RACHEL puts on.)

LÉON *(shows directions on envelope)*. Here's the numbers
of the trains. From Marseilles you take one train direct
to St. George d'Aurac. You'll have to change trains
there for Le Puy. From Le Puy, it's only about twenty
kilometers to St. Laurent des Pins. *(Looks out the win-*

dow.) Better go out the back way. Wait until the street is empty. Make sure no one follows you. Go straight to the station. When you've bought your ticket get on the train immediately. Don't talk to anyone. I'm counting on you, Madeleine Petit!

RACHEL *(crosses to Pauline, scared)*. Adieu, Maman.

PAULINE *(quickly)*. No, no, not adieu. Adieu means goodbye forever. Au revoir means till we see you again. And we will see you again. I promise. *(Kisses Rachel tenderly.)* Au revoir, my darling.
(RACHEL picks up suitcase. LÉON and PAULINE cross with her to hotel door.)

LÉON. Au revoir, Madeleine.

RACHEL *(turns for one last look at her parents)*. Au revoir. *(Exits. PAULINE turns to LÉON crying. He holds her in his arms. Lighting fades.)*

Scene Two

SCENE: *A carriage in a French train bound for the Haute-Loire region in Auvergne in South Central France. Two days later. RACHEL sits stiffly in the carriage.*

AT RISE: *PÈRE ANTOINE, a Jesuit priest, a man who follows his conscience, fifty-five, sits reading a book. YVETTE REYNAUD, an opportunist, forty-five, is dozing. Sound: The train stops abruptly.*

YVETTE *(wakes up with a start)*. Where are we?

PÈRE ANTOINE *(peering out the window).* Just outside the station. Le Puy. *(Still peering.)* There's some sort of trouble.

YVETTE *(sighs).* That's all there is these days.

(Sound: Voices shouting.)

YVETTE. I can't make it out. It's all in German. What are all those soldiers doing?

PÈRE ANTOINE. Chasing someone.

YVETTE. Oh, I see him! I see him! *(Calls out window.)* Over there! *(Pause.)* The horse just knocked down the flower cart!

(Sound: A gunshot. RACHEL screams and buries her head. PÈRE ANTOINE immediately tries to calm her.)

YVETTE. Must they do such things in public! Scaring women half to death.

PÈRE ANTOINE. My God! They've just left the man. Beside the tracks!

YVETTE. Who was it?

PÈRE ANTOINE *(shakes his head).* A poor Jew trying to escape.

(PÈRE ANTOINE quietly recites a prayer in Latin from the liturgy of Good Friday under Yvette's next speech[1].)

Ego eduxi te de Aeypto	I led you out of the land of Egypt
Demerso Pharone in Mare	Destroyed Pharoah in the Red Sea,

---

1 The hymn from the liturgy of Good Friday describes the crucified Christ speaking to his "people." The suggestion to use this hymn was made by Father Frederick Tollini, Department of Theatre Arts and Dance, Santa Clara University, California. It was chosen to suit the emotions and situation of the scene. "The priest in the play could see the murdered Jew as a 'Christ figure' or conversely that Christ is made 'present today' in the figure of the Jew killed by the powers that are in control."

Rubrum, et tu
me tradidisti
Principibus
sacerdotum.
Ego ante te aperui
mare,
Et tu apereruisti
lancea
Latus meum.
Ego ante te praeivi
in columna
nubis,
Et tu me duxisti and
Praetorium
Pilatis.
Ego te pavi manna
per desertum,
Et tu me cecidisti
a lapis et fiagellis.

Ego dedi tibi
sceptrum
regale,
Et tu dedisti capiti
meo
spineam coronam.
Ego te exaltavi
magna virtute,
Et tu me
suspendisti,
In patibulo Crucis.

and you handed
me over
To the authorities of
the Church
I opened the sea
before you,
And you have
opened my side
with a lance
I went before you in
a pillar of
cloud,
And you led me to
the Tribunal of
Pilate.
I fed you with
manna in the
desert
And you have
struck me down
with slaps and
scourging.
I gave you a royal
sceptre,
And you gave my
head
A crown of thorns.

I raised you up in
great power,
And you have
suspended me
On the gibbet of the
cross.

YVETTE. He must have been a criminal! (*Grabs newspaper, searching.*) Why...did you know? There's a five-hundred franc reward for turning in a Jew! Right here. Look. On page two. And I saw him. Five hundred francs! I could have fed my whole family for a month! *(Sound: The train starts to move again.)*

YVETTE. All this stopping and starting. Next time my sister's sick, she can come and visit me.

(PÈRE ANTOINE finishes prayer.)

YVETTE. Père Antoine, you know I never pry; but why on earth did you say a prayer for him? Someone who doesn't even go to our church? And a criminal?

PÈRE ANTOINE. My dear Madame Reynaud, perhaps the differences down here don't seem as important up there!

GÉRARD *(calling offstage)*. Papers! All identification papers. Please, have your papers ready!

(GÉRARD LA SALLE enters. He is a gendarme, who enforces the laws of France, no matter what they are. Sentimental, fifty-five. GÉRARD checks Yvette's papers.)

GÉRARD. Yvette Reynaud. Ah, but you look younger than your photograph, madame.

YVETTE *(pleased)*. Oh, monsieur. Well, it's a wonder I do. Tending an ill sister all week.

GÉRARD. You'll soon be home, now. *(GÉRARD inspects Père Antoine's photograph closely.)*

PÈRE ANTOINE *(laughs)*. I can see you notice the difference. I'm thinner now. Before the war I ate better.

GÉRARD. We all did. These are hard times. Thank you, Père Antoine.

(PÈRE ANTOINE resumes reading. GÉRARD crosses to Rachel.)

GÉRARD. Hello there, young lady. And what is your name?

(RACHEL opens her mouth to speak and no sound comes out. Mutely she hands her papers over.)

GÉRARD. Madeleine Petit. *(Looks sharply at her.)* Don't you know your own name?

(RACHEL nods.)

GÉRARD *(shakes his head disapprovingly)*. Such times! I certainly wouldn't let my young daughter travel alone. Where are you going?

RACHEL. To ... to ... visit ... relatives.

GÉRARD. Let's see your train ticket.

(RACHEL hands it to him.)

GÉRARD. St. Laurent. That's the next stop. *(Scrutinizing papers.)* Ah, from Marseilles. I know it well. The best fish on the Mediterranean. *(Kisses his fingers.)* Ah, Père Antoine, what I wouldn't give for some bouillabaisse à la Marseillaise!

(PÈRE ANTOINE nods in agreement.)

GÉRARD *(to RACHEL)*. Is someone meeting you in St. Laurent des Pins?

(RACHEL hesitates.)

PÈRE ANTOINE *(takes him aside)*. Officer, can't you see the child is upset? She saw what happened.

YVETTE. It was practically under this carriage window. Almost like ... the movies!

GÉRARD. Ah! Ah, Père Antoine, something like that's happened every day this week. After awhile you get used to it. They try to run away. Our job is to stop them.

PÈRE ANTOINE. What kind of job is that for a decent Frenchman?

GÉRARD. We stop them... if we see them. Me? I never see them.

PÈRE ANTOINE. Officer, I was so absorbed in my book, I wasn't paying attention. The child is traveling with me.

YVETTE. She is!

GÉRARD. Well, well, why didn't you say so? Sorry, Father. *(Checks papers.)* Regulations. You understand.

PÈRE ANTOINE. Certainly. But she's very tired. It's a long way from Marseilles, Officer—and good bouillabaisse!

GÉRARD. Ah, Père Antoine, for a man who loves fish, as I do, to work in Auvergne... is purgatory! *(Catches himself.)* I hope I didn't offend you, Father.

PÈRE ANTOINE *(laughs)*. Not at all. Not at all. *(To Rachel.)* Rest now, Madeleine. I'll wake you, when we get there.

(RACHEL pretends to sleep.)

GÉRARD. Why is she going to St. Laurent des Pins?

PÈRE ANTOINE. If I had my way, Officer, I'd take all the children out of the city. War's no place for a child.

GÉRARD *(agreeing)*. No. *(Hands papers to Père Antoine.)* Here. Let her sleep. We have to check the papers on all the trains. Just following orders.

PÈRE ANTOINE. So am I.

GÉRARD *(exiting)*. Papers. All identification papers.

YVETTE. Such a quiet little thing. I had no idea that she was with you, Père Antoine. Why, she hasn't spoken the whole way to you.

PÈRE ANTOINE. Or to anyone else. She's well brought up. *(Pointedly.)* She knows better than to chatter, when I'm trying to prepare a Sunday sermon.

YVETTE. Oh! *(Pause.)* Then, is she a relative of yours?

PÈRE ANTOINE. In a way.

YVETTE. Oh, you people from Auvergne! You never ever talk. It's maddening. Where I come from in the south, we practice the art of conversation. But you Auvergnats, you hardly ever open your mouths. It must be the climate. Why my husband's family ...

(Sound: Train lurches to a stop.)

PÈRE ANTOINE. Ah, here we are! Permit me to help you with your baggage, Madame Reynaud.

YVETTE. Why, thank you. Thank you, Père Antoine.

(PÈRE ANTOINE opens carriage door and puts Yvette's luggage out.)

YVETTE. But why didn't you introduce us, when I got on at Nimes? Now, I know all about little girls. I raised six of them. So be sure to ...

PÈRE ANTOINE *(assisting Yvette out)*. Thank you, Madame Reynaud.

(YVETTE exits.)

PÈRE ANTOINE. Madeleine. Madeleine, we're here.

RACHEL. I'm awake. Why did you lie?

PÈRE ANTOINE. Lie? I didn't lie.

RACHEL. You said I was with you.

PÈRE ANTOINE. You are. I vowed to look after any child who's in need. But I didn't introduce myself. I'm Père Antoine from St. Laurent des Pins.

RACHEL. I'm Madeleine Petit.

PÈRE ANTOINE. Yes. But when the police officer asked you, you forgot.

RACHEL. No! No, I just lost my voice.

PÈRE ANTOINE. Madeleine, your name must be comfortable—like an old shoe. Particularly, if the name is new.

RACHEL *(stiffens)*. How do you know?

PÈRE ANTOINE. I don't! And what I don't know, I can't tell! Remember that.

RACHEL. You saved my life just now.

PÈRE ANTOINE (*lifts suitcase down and takes her hand. Casually*). Just following orders.

(*PÈRE ANTOINE and RACHEL exit through carriage door.*)

Scene Three

SCENE: *Immediately afterwards. The traditional kitchen-room of Mme. Barbière's stone farm house. There is a black cast iron stove with iron cooking pots and utensils hanging above it. There are fresh lace curtains at the windows and framed ornamental patterns of lace hanging on the wall.*

AT RISE: *MARIE-THÉRÈSE BARBIÈRE is making lace, peering through her glasses at the netlike fabric of thread. She is a war widow, independent, proud, sixty. She wears mourning black continually, and her white hair is pulled off her face in a bun. Over her somber attire is an apron that she rarely removes, as she is always hard at work. PÈRE ANTOINE watches.*

MARIE-THÉRÈSE. ...and they'd hung their Nazi flag in front of the Town Hall. The mayor stood there, tears in his eyes. But he could do nothing. Nothing. Then the regiment marched on to Le Puy. Ah, Père Antoine, what will happen to us now? Now, that they're here.

PÈRE ANTOINE. I don't know. In Paris meat's practically disappeared. The bread ration would barely keep a sparrow alive. Women are crying in the streets, because they can't feed their children.

MARIE-THÉRÈSE. Savages! What they can't kill, they starve! Well, they won't starve the Auvergnats! We can make a cabbage grow from a stone. *(Inviting him.)* I have some hot soup on the stove.

PÈRE ANTOINE. Thank you. Not now. I don't think they'll bother us. We're a poor mountain village. There's nothing to steal.

MARIE-THÉRÈSE. Except our five-month winter. And we'll give them that!

(They laugh. MARIE-THÉRÈSE holds her lace up to the light and deftly corrects a stitch.)

PÈRE ANTOINE. Madame Barbière, your lace is the finest in St. Laurent des Pins.

MARIE-THÉRÈSE. Thank you, Père Antoine. My lace is my company, since Henri died. *(Looks at him sharply.)* But whenever you compliment me there's a favor not far behind. Have I ever refused? What is it?

PÈRE ANTOINE. This is different.

MARIE-THÉRÈSE. What?

PÈRE ANTOINE. A child.

MARIE-THÉRÈSE. What kind of child?

PÈRE ANTOINE. Intelligent. Polite. They lost their home to the Nazis.

MARIE-THÉRÈSE. Her parents?

PÈRE ANTOINE. Deported.

MARIE-THÉRÈSE. Such times! French?

PÈRE ANTOINE. French!

MARIE-THÉRÈSE. An orphan?

PÈRE ANTOINE *(carefully)*. Alone.

MARIE-THÉRÈSE. Ah! Ah, no, Père Antoine. It is too dangerous!

PÈRE ANTOINE. She has papers. All in order.

MARIE-THÉRÈSE. Did you see them?

PÈRE ANTOINE. Yes. She boarded the train at Marseilles. She stared out the window for hours. In utter silence. I've never seen anyone look so forlorn. Then at Le Puy the Nazis killed a man, and she screamed.

MARIE-THÉRÈSE. Naturally!

PÈRE ANTOINE. When the gendarme came though, she couldn't speak. She needs a home.

MARIE-THÉRÈSE. Père Antoine, you can't hide her here. If she's caught, we'll both be shot. The way they killed my husband.

PÈRE ANTOINE. Henri was a brave soldier, Madame Barbière. Very brave.

MARIE-THÉRÈSE. I don't want any more trouble.

PÈRE ANTOINE. I understand. *(Picks up his hat casually.)* I thought she might be company.

MARIE-THÉRÈSE. My neighbor across the field, Madame Reynaud, looks in on me, even when the snow is knee deep. So how could I hide her with that one poking her nose into my cabbage soup every day?

PÈRE ANTOINE. Madame Reynaud! She was on the same train. I said Madeleine was with me.

MARIE-THÉRÈSE. Madeleine?

PÈRE ANTOINE. The child.

MARIE-THÉRÈSE. Where is she now?

PÈRE ANTOINE. Outside. *(Crosses to window.)*

MARIE-THÉRÈSE. Outside! Good Lord! Outside in the cold! Père Antoine, what were you thinking of? *(Crosses beside him.)*
(PÈRE ANTOINE points out the window.)
She looks half frozen. You didn't say she was so little! Poor child so young to be alone in the world. Bring her

in to sit by the stove, Père Antoine. At least she can get warm and have some hot soup. How could you leave a little child like that out in the cold? Bring her in here at once!

PÈRE ANTOINE *(suppressing a smile)*. Certainly, Madame Barbière.

(PÈRE ANTOINE exits. MARIE-THÉRÈSE rustles about the stove and stirs pot. PÈRE ANTOINE enters with RACHEL.)

PÈRE ANTOINE. Madame Barbière, this is Madeleine Petit. Madeleine, this is Madame Barbière.

RACHEL *(shyly)*. Hello, Madame Barbière.

MARIE-THÉRÈSE *(warmly)*. Come in, Madeleine. *(MARIE-THÉRÈSE takes Rachel's coat. RACHEL shivers. MARIE-THÉRÈSE looks at Père Antoine disapprovingly.)*

MARIE-THÉRÈSE. Sit by the stove and get warm. *(Puts coat near stove.)* This is ice cold! Where are you from, Madeleine?

RACHEL. Marseilles.

MARIE-THÉRÈSE. No wonder you're shivering. It's always summer there, isn't it?

RACHEL *(agreeably)*. Yes, madame. *(Shivers again.)*

MARIE-THÉRÈSE. Here, have some hot soup.

RACHEL. Thank you, Madame Barbière.
(RACHEL eats hungrily. Her manners disappear, and she gulps soup. MARIE-THÉRÈSE and PÈRE ANTOINE exchange glances. RACHEL stops, embarrassed by her appetite.)

RACHEL. This is wonderful soup.

MARIE-THÉRÈSE *(laughs)*. Hunger is the best seasoning, little one. But we are famous in St. Laurent des Pins for our cabbage soup.

PÈRE ANTOINE. And our lace.

(RACHEL looks up at framed lace. Puts bowl down and goes to look more closely.)

RACHEL. Oh-h-h-. Each one's different! Oh, Madame Barbière ...

(RACHEL stops in front of one particular piece.)

RACHEL. I like that one!

MARIE-THÉRÈSE *(softly)*. That's my favorite too. It's my own design. Do you think it would make a nice wedding dress?

RACHEL. Oh, yes!! Is it very difficult to make lace?

MARIE-THÉRÈSE. Come here. *(Shows Rachel how to do a stitch.)* Lace making requires sharp eyes, careful fingers, and patience. And while you work on each tiny piece you have to see the whole design in your head.

RACHEL. We had a lace tablecloth ... once. It was for Sh ... holidays. Maman said one day, when I got married, it would be mine. But ... but ... but now, it's gone.

MARIE-THÉRÈSE *(briskly)*. Well, then you must make your own. Just like the girls do here. They all have lace trousseaus. Madeleine, how old are you now?

RACHEL. Ten.

MARIE-THÉRÈSE. Well then, there's plenty of time before you get married! Plenty of time. *(Spontaneously takes Rachel's small hand.)* Oh, your hands are so cold! *(Rubs them.)* There! You need wool mittens when you go out in weather like this. *(Looks down.)* And wool socks. Madeleine, do you know how to knit!

RACHEL. No, Madame Barbière.

MARIE-THÉRÈSE. Good heavens! What do they teach at school these days?

RACHEL. I was learning French, history, geography, arithmetic, science, art, and music. Oh, and sewing, too.

MARIE-THÉRÈSE. Sewing. Now, that's something useful.

RACHEL. I was at the top of my class, too. I was even learning English.

MARIE-THÉRÈSE. English? Sometimes at night we can pick up the British broadcast on the radio. *(To Père Antoine.)* Now, the Nazis arrest you for listening. They don't want us to hear the *real* news! But I say no one is going to tell me what to do in my own house, in front of my own fire. No one.

PÈRE ANTOINE. It's getting dark, Madame Barbière. We'd better be on our way.

MARIE-THÉRÈSE. It gets dark so early these days. *(Looks out the window.)* It's starting to snow. *(Goes to get Rachel's coat.)* And her coat's not even warm yet. And she has no mittens.

PÈRE ANTOINE. But in an hour the roads will be too slippery.

MARIE-THÉRÈSE. Madeleine, someone must have sent you to St. Laurent des Pins. Who? Why?

PÈRE ANTOINE. Madame Barbière, the best kept secrets are the ones we don't know. *(Pause.)*

MARIE-THÉRÈSE. That's true. Madeleine, I'd like to help you, but I can't. If the Nazis pound on the door, and they find you curled in a closet, that will be the end of both of us.

RACHEL *(rises)*. Thank you for the hot soup, madame. *(Puts her coat on. Crosses to door.)*

MARIE-THÉRÈSE. Not so fast! Not so fast! Where will she go tonight, Père Antoine?

PÈRE ANTOINE. I'll think of something. The Lord provides. Come, Madeleine.

MARIE-THÉRÈSE. The Lord has more sense than to be out in a St. Laurent blizzard. Wait a minute. Let me think. When it snows here, Madeleine, it can be up to your waist in no time. But that can keep the soldiers away as well. *(Thinking of a plan.)* I can't hide her, Père Antoine, ... but ... you say she has papers?

PÈRE ANTOINE. Yes. The gendarme inspected them. A food ration card too.

MARIE-THÉRÈSE. Hmm. We'd need that if ...

(PÈRE ANTOINE and RACHEL look at one another.)

RACHEL. Oh, Madame Barbière, I wouldn't be any trouble, I promise! I'd be so quiet, you wouldn't even know I was here.

MARIE-THÉRÈSE. No, no, no, little one. A child should laugh. A child should sing. We were never blessed with a child. But there's a time in life, for everything. Père Antoine, I can't hide her but ... but ... my husband's cousin could come to visit, couldn't she? And she could go to school with the other girls, couldn't she? And in the evening she could learn to make lace.

RACHEL. Oh, yes, Madame, yes! And I could wash the dishes and run to the bakery for you and ... and ... *(Hides tears.)*

MARIE-THÉRÈSE *(gently puts an arm around Rachel)*. She can't leave without warm clothes, and that's that. Not with winter on its way. She needs warm wool mittens and socks ... and a scarf. And she's not leaving till she has them. But, Madeleine, you'll have to knit them yourself!

RACHEL *(crushed)*. But I don't know how to knit!

MARIE-THÉRÈSE. I will teach you, little one. I will teach you.

PÈRE ANTOINE. Madame Barbière, just how long do you think it will take to make all those clothes?

MARIE-THÉRÈSE. Oh, that's hard to say, Père Antoine. Hard to say. It could take...awhile. *(Removes Rachel's brimmed hat.)* It could take...till the end of the war.

Scene Four

SCENE: *The village school for girls, January 1943.*

AT RISE: *SUZANNE FLEURY is examining Rachel's schoolwork. SUZANNE FLEURY is the village school teacher, knowledgeable, attractive, twenty-six. RACHEL is in her seat, waiting nervously.*

SUZANNE. Excellent, Madeleine. You've done well in French grammar and in geography. Not as well in mathematics. So, I have assigned these extra pages. Bring them in tomorrow. However, we are happy to have you in the school. I hope you will continue to work hard and be an honor student.

RACHEL. Oh, yes! Oh, thank you. I will try, Mademoiselle Fleury.

SUZANNE. I'm sure you will. Madeleine...you said once that you studied English. Can you speak it?

RACHEL. Only a little. My last teacher liked Shakespeare. She used to read to us, and then we had to read aloud to her.

SUZANNE. Good practice. Now, you are excused, Madeleine. I must prepare tomorrow's lessons.

RACHEL. Goodbye, Mademoiselle Fleury.

SUZANNE. See you tomorrow, Madeleine.

(RACHEL exits with school bag. SUZANNE continues working. HANS SCHMIDT enters. He is a Nazi officer, a handsome, well-educated man of the world, who follows party policy assiduously. Thirty-five. He is not a caricature villain.)

HANS. I see you work late, fräulein.

SUZANNE *(startled)*. It is customary to knock before you enter!

HANS. I must examine a list of your students, your textbooks, your lessons, and your exams.

SUZANNE. There are several plants in the room. Would you like to examine those as well!

HANS. This is no joking matter, fräulein. I advise you not to be frivolous. In Belgium we found stacks of false identity and ration cards in the headmaster's desk. *(Opens hers and goes through contents.)*

SUZANNE. What happened?

HANS. Some desks, you know, have false bottoms, but I know how to discover them. *(Continues his inspection.)* Before I was promoted to be an officer in the Führer's army, I was a cabinet maker. I know desks. *(HANS crosses and knocks on wall.)* And I know walls, particularly hollow walls. Where someone may be hiding. *(Smiles at Suzanne.)* What happened? We shot him. Enemies, fräulein, can be anywhere.

SUZANNE. You are free to search the room. But I must get on with my work.

HANS *(places whip across her book)*. First you will answer my question, fräulein. It is a mistake to ignore me. You will give me the names of all Jewish students.

SUZANNE. What? What are you talking about?

HANS. Are there Jewish children in your school?

SUZANNE *(rises)*. We have only French children here! You must have something better to do than to storm into a village schoolhouse. Now, please leave.

HANS. Hand over the list.

SUZANNE. What list?

HANS. The list of names. Your student's names. The list. The list!

(SUZANNE hands it over. HANS checks it against his list.)

HANS. Um-hm. Um-hm. Hm-m. Why is this name not on my list?

SUZANNE *(looks)*. Oh, that's Madeleine. She came after the term started. She's a relative of the widow Barbière.

HANS *(checks his notes)*. Whose husband was a prisoner of war until...approximately a year ago, when unfortunately he refused to cooperate.

SUZANNE *(a growing apprehension)*. I don't know any of the details.

HANS. And you, you are Suzanne Fleury, a graduate of La Sorbonne, a teacher at the village school in St. Laurent des Pins, a former resident of Le Puy, but who on December 7th went to board with the widow Barbière. Why?

SUZANNE. How do you know all this?

HANS. The Kommondant is particular. Now, you will answer the question. Why did you move out after our soldiers took Le Puy? What are you hiding?

SUZANNE *(laughs)*. Hiding? You don't understand.

HANS. I warn you, fräulein, if you laugh at a German officer the results may not be so funny.

SUZANNE. Surely in your country, people laugh, monsieur—?

HANS. Herr Leutnant Schmidt. (*A broad smile crosses his face.*) We do laugh, fräulein. Personally, I like a good time. But you should never laugh at an officer.

SUZANNE. I'm not laughing at you, Herr Leutnant Schmidt.

HANS. No?

SUZANNE. Of course not. But it's clear you don't know the Haute Loire section of Auvergne. You ask what I'm hiding? Look out the window.

HANS. Snow! Again!

SUZANNE. Yes, Herr Leutnant Schmidt. Again and again and again. From November until May. And when the winds start, some of the mountain roads become impassable. That is why, when winter comes, I board in the village. From the look of that sky, I advise you to leave at once. The snow here falls fast.

HANS. I will return, fräulein. Have your books, your lessons, and your exams ready for inspection.

SUZANNE. When will that be?

HANS. Soon, fräulein. Very soon.

SUZANNE. I sincerely hope you will knock next time, Herr Leutnant Schmidt, and not surprise a lady!

HANS (*drawn to Suzanne*). You are young, spirited, I like that. If you cooperate, I will see to it you have a real school to teach in...in our New World.

SUZANNE. I already have a school to teach in...in this world!

HANS. This! This is nothing! A country schoolhouse filled with French peasants.

SUZANNE. Then why waste your time here?

HANS. We will see each other again, fräulein. But next time... (*A slight smile.*) I will knock first.

(SUZANNE gathers her belongings, puts on her boots. Sound: Knock at the door. SUZANNE hesitantly opens it. JULIEN DELACOUR enters quickly. He is a leader in the Underground Resistance Movement, the Maquis. By profession a journalist. Intense, impulsive, thirty.)

JULIEN. Mademoiselle Fleury?

SUZANNE. Yes. *(Glances out at snow.)* Can this wait until tomorrow?

JULIEN. No. No, it can't. *(Looks at her carefully.)* You don't recognize me, do you?

SUZANNE. No, monsieur...

JULIEN. I'm Julien Delacour. We were in the same philosophy class. La Sorbonne.

SUZANNE. Oh? Did we meet?

JULIEN. No, not officially. I sat three rows behind you. When I finally had the courage to say hello, it was too late.

SUZANNE. Too late?

JULIEN. It was the day the Nazis took over the university. The Gestapo came in and knocked the professor to the floor.

SUZANNE. I remember. But when he got up, he said—

JULIEN. "Do not forget what you just saw. A man can be knocked down—and stand up again. And so can a country!"

SUZANNE. The end of our education.

JULIEN. Or the beginning! Suzanne... may I call you Suzanne?

SUZANNE. Yes.

JULIEN. Suzanne, there are those of us who think the professor was right. We don't want to sit and wait for the Allies to rescue us.

SUZANNE. We can't wait! The Allies are still in North Africa.

JULIEN. We live here, and we must fight here. On our own soil. For our own country.

SUZANNE. A French underground?

JULIEN. Here in Auvergne, in St. Laurent des Pins, the Maquis will be born. We want this schoolhouse for a meeting.

SUZANNE. It's yours.

JULIEN. We need secrecy.

SUZANNE. We need success, Monsieur Delacour! The French are like puppets, obeying absurdities, ignoring atrocities. It has to stop!

JULIEN *(impulsively hugs her, then backs off embarrassed)*. Suzanne, you are the spirit the Maquis needs!

SUZANNE *(laughs lightly)*. Tell me, what can I do?

JULIEN. Leave the door open.

SUZANNE. That's all?

JULIEN. For now! The Maquis meets here tonight. Tomorrow we go into action. Oh, I'll meet you at the café. Five o'clock?

SUZANNE. Five o'clock!

Scene Five

SCENE: *The Town Hall. March 1944, fifteen months later.*

AT RISE: *HANS SCHMIDT is interrogating Rachel.*

HANS. Now, tell the truth.

RACHEL. I've told you.

HANS. I don't believe you. It's a crime to help a prisoner.

RACHEL. All I did was mail a letter.

HANS. What secret information was inside?

RACHEL. It was a birthday card for his little girl.

HANS. Idiot! Where would a prisoner get a birthday card?

RACHEL. He made it. From scraps.

HANS. Again. Where did you and the prisoner meet?

RACHEL. I've told you. I was on my way home from school, and he was sweeping the snow from the Town Hall steps. He just asked me if I'd mail this letter for him, because he wasn't allowed to leave.

HANS. Then you admit you spoke to him!

RACHEL. Yes.

HANS. That alone is a crime! *(Checks his watch.)* Now, Madeleine, you've been here for three hours. Aren't you getting tired?

RACHEL. Yes.

HANS. Then identify the prisoner, I'll give you your coat and let you go home! *(Bribing her.)* If you're a good girl, I'll even give you some real chocolate.

RACHEL. Chocolate? But there's no chocolate in France anymore. I know that.

HANS. Ah, you're wrong. *(Opens his desk and holds out a chocolate bar.)* Look!

(RACHEL looks longingly at it. HANS tempts her with chocolate.)

Just walk over to the window and point to the man. That's all. *(HANS crosses to the window with her.)* That one? Or that one?

RACHEL *(she struggles with decision, then lies)*. I don't know! I CAN'T TELL!!

HANS *(strikes her across the face)*. There are only five of them there. And you spoke directly to him. Now, which one was it?

RACHEL. I don't remember! They all ... look the same ... in prison clothes.

HANS. Why did you break the law?

RACHEL. I didn't know it was the law! And I won't do it again. Anyway, Herr Leutnant Schmidt, birthdays only come once a year!

HANS *(looks at her in astonishment)*. Madeleine, just how old are you?

RACHEL. Eleven.

HANS. Eleven! I wouldn't have believed you could be so naive. This is a waste of time! Now Madeleine Petit, never, NEVER, speak to strangers! A young girl of your age should know that. Why don't they teach you what's important at school? And if a prisoner ever tries to talk to you again, you are to come tell me at once. At once!

RACHEL. Yes, Herr Leutnant Schmidt.

HANS. Talking to a prisoner is treason. Punishable by death. Now, you don't want to be shot, do you?

RACHEL. No, Herr Leutnant Schmidt.

HANS. So, you must never break the law again.

RACHEL. Yes, Herr Leutnant Schmidt.

HANS. I'm talking to you just like a father.
(RACHEL avoids looking at him. HANS pulls her face towards him.)

HANS. AREN'T I!

RACHEL *(dully)*. Yes, Herr Leutnant Schmidt.

HANS *(gives Rachel her coat and helps her on with it)*. So, when you get home you can tell Frau Barbière and Fräulein Fleury that we had a nice little visit this afternoon and you learned an important lesson from Herr Leutnant Schmidt. *(HANS holds her by the shoulders until RACHEL nods.)* Now, run along. But remember, next time I won't be so lenient!

Scene Six

SCENE: *Madame Barbière's kitchen. June 1944.*

AT RISE: *MARIE-THÉRÈSE BARBIÈRE and YVETTE REYNAUD are having coffee.*

YVETTE. And as long as I was coming I thought I'd bring you some of my almond cake.

MARIE-THÉRÈSE. I haven't had a piece of cake in two years! It tasted like real sugar.

YVETTE *(giggles)*. It was.

MARIE-THÉRÈSE. Real sugar?

YVETTE. Madame Barbière, you never mentioned that dear little girl was coming. Why didn't you say something to me? I could have given you lots of help.

MARIE-THÉRÈSE. I didn't know.

YVETTE. You didn't know? All the way from Marseilles and you didn't know?

MARIE-THÉRÈSE. Well, that is... I found out... just before. Family's family. You don't refuse.

YVETTE. Henri's cousin, isn't she?

MARIE-THÉRÈSE. Yes!

YVETTE. She doesn't look a bit like Henry. Not a bit.

MARIE-THÉRÈSE. No. She resembles the other side of the family. The Marseilles side.

YVETTE. Was Madeleine born there?

MARIE-THÉRÈSE. Yes. Why?

YVETTE *(smug)*. She doesn't have a Marseilles accent.

MARIE-THÉRÈSE *(pause)*. No. No, her mother insisted on the best convent schools, so she would speak a pure French. Thank you for the cake, Madame Reynaud. It's the little things that make wartime so hard. Who'd have thought I would miss sugar in my coffee so much? Who'd have thought the war would last so long?

YVETTE. There's plenty of sugar if you know where to go.

MARIE-THÉRÈSE. Oh?

YVETTE. Down at the Town Hall, they have it every day.

MARIE-THÉRÈSE. The Town Hall?

YVETTE. My dear Madame Barbière, you don't think the Nazi officers pay attention to our rationing, do you? They have sugar and real chocolate and...I suppose you heard about the shooting in Le Puy?

MARIE-THÉRÈSE. No!

YVETTE. It's lucky I tell you the news. You don't go out.

MARIE-THÉRÈSE. My arthritis—

YVETTE. Anyway, they caught a Jew hiding in Monsieur Latour's barn.

MARIE-THÉRÈSE. Etienne?

YVETTE. Yes.

MARIE-THÉRÈSE *(fearfully)*. What happened?

YVETTE. Well, Monsieur Latour swore he didn't know anyone was hiding there. No one believed that. *(MARIE-THÉRÈSE is riveted. YVETTE sips coffee before continuing.)*
So they shot them. And the dog. As an example.

MARIE-THÉRÈSE. An example!

YVETTE. There was a reward, too—six hundred francs. But Herr Leutnant Schmidt said we should do our duty without a reward.

MARIE-THÉRÈSE *(pensive)*. Yes. If we can.

YVETTE. I spoke right up. Right from the crowd. Money always helps, I told him.

MARIE-THÉRÈSE *(still shocked)*. They shot Etienne!

YVETTE. Can you imagine the danger for his neighbors?

MARIE-THÉRÈSE. Yes.

YVETTE. But I don't know why they shot the dog. Someone would have taken it in.

MARIE-THÉRÈSE *(ushering her out as fast as she can)*. Be careful crossing the road, Madame Reynaud. It may be June, but there's still patches of ice.
(YVETTE exits. MARIE-THÉRÈSE closes the door, bolts it, and draws the lace curtains shut sharply. She opens the door to the armoire and turns on a radio. On the door is a map. Sound: Radio static.)

MARIE-THÉRÈSE. Suzanne! Madeleine!

SUZANNE. I'm coming.

(SUZANNE runs in followed by Rachel.)

MARIE-THÉRÈSE. I thought she wouldn't leave in time. Madeleine, stand here. Look out the window. Here. Through the crack in the curtains. If you see anyone, warn us.

RACHEL. All right.
(Sound: Radio static.)

BRITISH RADIO VOICE. Good evening. This is the British Broadcasting Corporation. Key points in the German defense line in Italy have fallen. American troops have captured Valletri and Valmontone. Allied forces continue to push forward toward Rome...

SUZANNE *(she has marked the map with pins)*. Madame Barbière, look. The Allies are here. The Nazis still hold Rome, but by tomorrow, maybe—

RACHEL. Someone's coming.

MARIE-THÉRÈSE. Turn off the radio! Hide everything!
(SUZANNE starts to close the armoire door.)

MARIE-THÉRÈSE. No. No. *(Looks about frantically.)* Put
it in the stove. Quickly.
(SUZANNE hides radio in stove compartment.)
MARIE-THÉRÈSE. Madeleine! Here!
*(MARIE-THÉRÈSE hands Rachel bowls, spoons, and a
pot of soup to put on the table. Sound: Footsteps on the
stone stairs. SUZANNE folds the map in her coat and
drops it on the floor of the armoire. She closes it.
Sound: Loud imperious knock at the door.)*
MARIE-THÉRÈSE. Who's there? *(Gestures to Rachel to
hurry.)*
HANS. Open up the door.
MARIE-THÉRÈSE *(sounding casual)*. Just a moment. Just
a moment.

*(MARIE-THÉRÈSE inspects to see if all signs are put
away. She motions Rachel and Suzanne to the table.
SUZANNE ladles soup so they can pretend to eat.
MARIE-THÉRÈSE opens door. HANS enters.)*

SUZANNE. Herr Leutnant Schmidt!
HANS. I told you I would always knock first, fräulein.
Am I not a man of my word?
(RACHEL starts to leave the table. HANS stops her.)
HANS. There is no need to run away, Madeleine Petit,
unless you have done something wrong.
MARIE-THÉRÈSE *(puts arm protectively around Rachel)*.
She's still ashamed she caused you all that trouble, Herr
Leutnant Schmidt. It won't happen again.
*(MARIE-THÉRÈSE guides Rachel away from Hans and
towards her lacework. She helps her begin.)*
SUZANNE. You must excuse the table. We were just hav-
ing supper. Are you hungry, Herr Leutnant Schmidt?

HANS. No. I have had my dinner. (*His eyes search the room.*)

SUZANNE (*distracting him*). But couldn't I tempt you with dessert—a piece of French cake and coffee?

HANS (*finds nothing amiss*). Yes, if you made the cake.

SUZANNE. Me? Ah, no, no, no. It was made by Madame Reynaud. Have you met her, Herr Leutnant Schmidt?

HANS. Madame Reynaud? Reynaud? I don't think so.

SUZANNE. She's famous for her almond cake. It's her speciality.

HANS. Then I'll have some.

SUZANNE (*cuts piece and gives it to him*). Here you are. Coffee?

HANS (*watching her move about*). Yes. With lots of sugar.

SUZANNE. We have no sugar, Herr Leutnant Schmidt. Rationing.

HANS. Ah. Perhaps...I could help you there. (*Takes a bite.*) Excellent. Excellent. (*Smacks his lips as he finishes the cake.*) Well, now, I must make it a point to meet this Madame Reynaud. (*HANS pulls out official paper.*) Someone reported that you were listening to a foreign radio station.

MARIE-THÉRÈSE. A radio? A foreign station? Why, you said yourself that was illegal.

HANS. I know what I said! Now, I won't sit at your table and then arrest you.

SUZANNE (*seizes the advantage*). Oh...you are not heartless, Herr Leutnant Schmidt. (*Sits beside him.*)

HANS (*doggedly*). But someone reported hearing English voices in this house.

MARIE-THÉRÈSE *(musing)*. I always wanted a radio. The music would be such a comfort on a long winter's night. But there were never enough francs.

HANS. Explain that!

SUZANNE. Of course! Shall we tell him about our English lessons?

(RACHEL looks uncertainly at Suzanne.)

HANS. Why does she look so frightened?

SUZANNE. This! *(Leans over touching Hans gently as she removes whip. He looks up at her eagerly.)* Don't you know young girls prefer...sweets. Next time you come to see us...

HANS. I'll bring some. *(Annoyed.)* I have to check this report.

MARIE-THÉRÈSE *(chopping carrots by the stove)*. Look for yourself.

(HANS crosses to the armoire.)

SUZANNE *(in pretty confusion)*. Oh dear! My coat fell down! My scarf, my gloves...all over the floor! Excuse me.

(SUZANNE scoops them up with the map and leaves the room. HANS investigates the armoire, knocks on the wall, overturns chairs. Sound: While HANS stalks the room in his jackboots, there is the counter-rhythm of Marie-Thérèse chopping carrots and Rachel clicking the bobbins, as she makes lace.)

HANS. There's nothing here!

SUZANNE *(returns and stands by the stove)*. Of course not.

HANS. Then explain.

SUZANNE. Won't you sit down again?

(HANS sits. SUZANNE signals Rachel with her eyes to listen closely.)

"The quality of mercy is not strained,
It droppeth as the gentle rain from heaven
Upon the place beneath... "

HANS. That's Shakespeare!

SUZANNE. A man who knows Shakespeare must be well educated.

HANS. I am!

SUZANNE. Then you must know it is always better to study poetry in the original. I try to teach some of the girls. Madeleine is learning. But the accent is ... very difficult. Particularly the sound of the "R." You see in French...

HANS. I didn't come here for a French lesson! Let me hear the little girl.

SUZANNE. Madeleine, recite for Herr Leutnant Schmidt. (*Crosses to Rachel and whispers.*)

HANS. What are you whispering?

SUZANNE (*with an angelic smile*). Not to be afraid of you.

RACHEL (*recites the same passage, mispronouncing a few words*).
"The quality of mercy is not strained,
It droppeth as the gentle rain from heaven
Upon the place beneath."

SUZANNE (*claps for her student*). Herr Leutnant Schmidt! No applause? No thanks? When she tried so hard and did so well.

HANS (*applauds briefly*). I see you are determined to teach me French manners.

SUZANNE. Good manners, Herr Leutnant Schmidt, are international.

HANS (*gets his coat. Holds Suzanne's hand lingeringly*). I wish you would call me Hans.

SUZANNE. Hans.

HANS. You are ... very ... clever ... and very ... pretty.

SUZANNE. Thank you!

HANS (*still holding her hand*). But I am not a fool! Auf Wiedersehen, fräulein, Frau Barbière, Madeleine. Another evening we will talk more. You will teach me the French "R." (*Exits.*)

RACHEL. Oh, Mademoiselle Fleury, I was so ...

(*SUZANNE rushes to Rachel, puts finger to her lips.*)

SUZANNE. Sh-h. You were brave, little one. That's all that counts. (*Hugs her.*)

RACHEL. How did you know ... what to do?

SUZANNE. It's a lesson we don't teach in school; but it's as old as the Trojan War. When a man meets the enemy, he fights. When a woman meets the enemy, she flirts.

(*Sound: Motor car.*)

MARIE-THÉRÈSE. Is he gone?

RACHEL (*looks out window*). Yes.

(*The tension breaks. MARIE-THÉRÈSE and SUZANNE laugh together.*)

SUZANNE. When you said stove—

MARIE-THÉRÈSE. He never looked.

(*Sound: The whistling of the beginning of a resistance song to the tune of "Auld Lang Syne." Their laughter halts. SUZANNE stands rigid. It is repeated. SUZANNE whistles the next phrase. SUZANNE checks the window and opens the door. JULIEN DELACOUR enters. He is frenzied and worn.*)

SUZANNE. Julien!

JULIEN *(enters nervously. Hugs Suzanne).* Thank God you're here. I was back this morning. But I had to wait until dark. Then I heard his car. I thought...thought... Thank God you're safe! What did he want?

MARIE-THÉRÈSE. A report. A radio. I told him I'd always wanted one.

JULIEN. Suzanne, I can't stay long. But I had to warn you. I—

(Exhaustion and hunger overtake him. SUZANNE and MARIE-THÉRÈSE help him to a chair.)

MARIE-THÉRÈSE. Madeleine, some soup, some bread. Quickly! *(To Suzanne.)* He probably hasn't eaten. *(RACHEL gets soup and bread.)*

SUZANNE *(holding him).* You're shaking.

JULIEN. I'll be all right. I just need to eat. *(Devours a hunk of bread.)*

SUZANNE. Where were you?

JULIEN. Marseilles. *(He eats more bread.)*

RACHEL. Marseilles! Please! Please tell me about Marseilles.

JULIEN. It's not for young ears.

RACHEL. Please! I must know. I must!

SUZANNE. Tell us, Julien.

JULIEN. You want the real news. Here! Read it in *our* paper, the *Maquisard.* *(Places resistance newspaper on table.)* They sent me down to write a story, conditions since the French surrender. *(Grips her arm.)* Suzanne, are you all right?

SUZANNE. I'm fine! What's wrong?

(JULIEN eats hungrily.)

MARIE-THÉRÈSE. He needs to eat, not talk.

JULIEN. No. No, I must talk. I must tell you.

RACHEL. Tell me about Marseilles. Please!

MARIE-THÉRÈSE. Her family was there. Henri's family.

JULIEN. There's no food in Marseilles. Except the black market. I saw a woman take off her wedding band to buy a slice of bacon. When I was in prison—

SUZANNE. Prison!

MARIE-THÉRÈSE *(looking at him closely)*. I thought so.

SUZANNE. Julien, what happened? What happened to you?

JULIEN. They're arresting all the Jews in Marseilles.

(RACHEL reacts.)

JULIEN. They're going house to house, alley to alley, hunting them down. And they're arresting anyone who hides them. Anyone who gives them food, anyone who helps.

MARIE-THÉRÈSE. They shot someone in Le Puy. An example to the rest of us.

SUZANNE. Julien, why were you in prison?

JULIEN. I was cutting through an alleyway in Marseilles, when I saw two soldiers beating up an old man. An old Jew with a beard. He was so weak, he hardly resisted. Then one of them set fire to his beard. I jumped the soldier from behind.

SUZANNE. Oh, Julien! Why?

JULIEN. I am who I am, Suzanne.

RACHEL. Did the old man get away?

JULIEN. That night he did. They beat me up instead, arrested me, dragged me off to prison. No food. No water. For four days. At the interrogation they accused me of being in the Maquis.

SUZANNE. What?

MARIE-THÉRÈSE. The Maquis?

JULIEN. A bluff to see if I'd break. They couldn't prove anything. But I found out about the ... the so-called labor camps ... in Poland, where they send—

MARIE-THÉRÈSE. Not in front of the child.

JULIEN *(points to paper)*. Then read it for yourselves later.

SUZANNE *(holds him, reassuring him)*. Julien, you're safe.

JULIEN. None of us is safe. Especially you.

SUZANNE. What do you mean?

JULIEN. Your last letter was in my wallet.

SUZANNE. My last letter? That was four months ago!

JULIEN. Yes.

SUZANNE. Why did you keep it?

JULIEN. Home! It reminded me of home. When they released me, they returned my belt, my watch, even all my money. But the letter was gone. I had to warn you, Suzanne. I had to warn you. *(Exhaustion takes over.)*

MARIE-THÉRÈSE. Let him sleep. Was *this* address on your letter?

SUZANNE. No.

MARIE-THÉRÈSE. Your last name?

SUZANNE. Just Suzanne.

MARIE-THÉRÈSE. Good! A man who's been in prison doesn't forget his fears so fast. Suzanne's a common name. Now, help me find a blanket for Julien. *(As she exits with Suzanne.)* Madeleine, cut some more bread and serve the soup. *(To Suzanne.)* Madeleine made the soup tonight all by herself.

(RACHEL steals over to the paper and reads the lead article. She is visibly shocked.)

RACHEL. No-o-o-o!!!

(RACHEL runs out of the room choking back sobs. MARIE-THÉRÈSE and SUZANNE return. SUZANNE

places blanket around Julien. MARIE-THÉRÈSE looks at table, irritated.)

MARIE-THÉRÈSE *(calls).* MADELEINE? MADELEINE?

(RACHEL emerges, newspaper behind her.)

MARIE-THÉRÈSE. I asked you to cut the bread and serve the soup! We're all hungry, and it's late.

RACHEL. I don't want any food.

MARIE-THÉRÈSE *(the stress of the day shows).* Other people live here besides you! There's no room for self-ishness in this house.

RACHEL *(overreacting).* Are you saying there's no room for me?

SUZANNE *(serving soup and slicing bread).* Madame Barbière, come sit down.

MARIE-THÉRÈSE. I'm too old for all this trouble!

RACHEL. I didn't know...you thought I was trouble! I thought— *(Runs out, dropping newspaper.)*

MARIE-THÉRÈSE *(tastes soup).* Needs more salt! *(Adds it.)* She doesn't listen to me anymore.

SUZANNE *(picks up newspaper and reads).* She was reading this.

MARIE-THÉRÈSE. When I was twelve, I did as I was told.

SUZANNE *(interrupts, reads aloud).* "Mass murder report confirmed. Jews told they would be sent to live in a resettlement area are selected for hard labor. Or death. Either way, few survive. For them the only new country is heaven, not Poland. Families torn—"

MARIE-THÉRÈSE *(reads newspaper with increasing agitation).* She shouldn't have seen this!

(MARIE-THÉRÈSE exits abruptly. SUZANNE crosses to Julien, adjusts blanket around him, sits beside him. MARIE-THÉRÈSE reenters with RACHEL, who is wiping away tears.)

MARIE-THÉRÈSE. We are all upset.

RACHEL. I'm sorry... I...I don't...want...to be trouble for you. I'll go somepl—

MARIE-THÉRÈSE. Now don't be foolish! Have some of your soup. It's very good. For a first time.

RACHEL *(refusing it)*. People in Marseilles are starving... and...

MARIE-THÉRÈSE *(sensibly)*. It doesn't help them if you go hungry.

RACHEL. This war will never stop!

MARIE-THÉRÈSE. Yes, it will.

RACHEL. When?

MARIE-THÉRÈSE. You will be taller, that's certain. And I'll be older, that's certain. But the end will come. It always does. Until then, you must have courage, little one. Courage!

(RACHEL rests her head against Marie-Thérèse and dozes. MARIE-THÉRÈSE, utterly exhausted, closes her eyes. SUZANNE crosses and reads the underground newspaper. She is visibly upset. JULIEN opens his eyes and watches her. SUZANNE sees he's awake, crosses to him. They speak softly, so as not to awaken the others.)

SUZANNE. How do you know this is true? Murder? Children murdered? It can't be. It can't.

JULIEN. In ancient Greece they killed the messenger who brought news they didn't like.

SUZANNE. But Julien, how do you know?

JULIEN. I can't tell you that. One of the Maquis was there ... and saw enough.

SUZANNE. It wasn't you, was it? Was it?

JULIEN *(places fingers on her lips)*. A friend. But you've got to be careful. They have ... your letter. Your signature.

SUZANNE. There are hundreds of Suzannes who write love letters in war time. They must have more to do than track each one of us down!

JULIEN. Listen to me, Suzanne! When Mussolini's men held Nice, they marched with mandolins. When the Nazis took over, the music stopped.

SUZANNE *(worried about him)*. You're not yourself. Stay here tonight.

JULIEN. I can't. War doesn't stop because the sun goes down.

SUZANNE. You need rest.

JULIEN. I'll sleep when it's over.

SUZANNE *(in a mock embrace. Loudly)*. Goodnight. *(Whispers.)* What are my orders?

JULIEN *(kisses her on both cheeks. Loudly)*. Goodnight. *(Whispers.)* Pick up the boots from the cobbler. *(Places note in her hand.)*

SUZANNE *(whispers)*. Where do I bring them?

JULIEN. To the café. At five o'clock. *(Another mock embrace, whispers.)* If there's danger, drop your gloves! *(Loudly.)* Goodnight, darling. Goodnight, Madame Barbière.

(SUZANNE looks at Marie-Thérèse with Rachel dozing by the fire.)

SUZANNE. Look at them. Oh, Julien, the world could be so beautiful—

(Impulsively, JULIEN kisses her.)

SUZANNE *(flustered)*. We don't need to pretend now. They're both fast asleep.

JULIEN. I wasn't pretending. *(Exits.)*

MARIE-THÉRÈSE *(opens her eyes)*. I like your young man.

SUZANNE. What? Oh, oh yes.

MARIE-THÉRÈSE. When you get married, I will make the lace for your wedding dress.

SUZANNE. Madame Barbière, no one said … anything about …

MARIE-THÉRÈSE. Suzanne, my eyes can't see the thread as clearly as they used to. But they see other things— very clearly. He's part of the Maquis isn't he?

SUZANNE *(startled)*. Madame Barbière!

MARIE-THÉRÈSE. He's among friends. But there are many different ways to fight.

RACHEL *(wakes, stirs, half-asleep)*. Papa? Papa!

(Automatically MARIE-THÉRÈSE comforts Rachel.)

MARIE-THÉRÈSE. We each fight the war in our own way. *(Strokes Rachel's head gently.)* Go back to sleep, little one. *(With strong conviction.)* We each say, "No!" in our own way!

ACT TWO
Scene One

SCENE: *Outdoor café. June 1944.*

AT RISE: *SUZANNE is at a table waiting to meet Julien. She looks around anxiously and sees HANS enter. Quickly she drops her gloves. Sound: The clock strikes five.*

HANS *(sees Suzanne, crosses to table)*. Good evening, fräulein.

SUZANNE. Oh, Herr Leutnant Schmidt.

HANS *(picking up her gloves)*. You dropped these.

SUZANNE. I guess I did.

HANS. Why are you so formal tonight? I told you to call me Hans.

SUZANNE. I forgot ... Hans.

HANS. Are you waiting for someone?

SUZANNE. No.

HANS. Then I may join you. *(Sits before she answers.)* Tea or coffee?

SUZANNE. Coffee.

HANS. I'll get it. *(Exits.)*

(SUZANNE quickly drops her gloves again. Looks about. Then powders her nose and looks in her mirror more carefully to see who is there. Sees JULIEN enter and she pointedly looks at her gloves. JULIEN exits.)

HANS *(returns)*. Two coffees! *(He sets coffees down. Sees gloves on floor.)* Is this a game? *(Picks up gloves and puts them in his pocket.)* They'll be safer here.

SUZANNE. No! I must have dropped them again. Please! *(Holds out her hand for her gloves.)*

HANS *(takes Suzanne's hand in his, smiling)*. I don't want to keep picking them up. After you and I have dinner, then I'll give them back to you.

SUZANNE. Dinner?

HANS. Your French rations are abominable. But I have sources. We'll eat at my hotel.

SUZANNE *(stalls)*. No, I really can't. Perhaps, some other time. But I have to correct papers this evening.

HANS. Then you certainly should eat dinner first.

SUZANNE. Oh, I couldn't. I'm not hungry yet.

HANS. I'm in no hurry. No hurry at all. Tell me about this village, St. Laurent des Pins.

SUZANNE. It began on the slope of that hill. Four hundred years ago. Some of the first stone houses are still standing. With the same families.

HANS. And the lace making? How old is that?

SUZANNE. Sixteenth century. I didn't know you were interested in all this, Hans.

HANS. Oh, I am. I am.

SUZANNE. Some of the women still pay homage to—

HANS *(interrupts. Takes her hand in his. Smiles).* To the patron saint of lacemakers, Saint Francois Régis. You see I did my homework.

SUZANNE. Hans, you pronounced the name perfectly!

HANS. The French "R" can be mastered with a beautiful woman to inspire me. Suzanne—

SUZANNE *(nervously).* They say the most beautiful lace is made right here, by hand, by women like Madame Barbière.

HANS. Interesting. *(Casually.)* And what do you know about Julien Delacour?

SUZANNE *(agitated).* NOTHING!!!

HANS. We know you are—or were—his girlfriend.

SUZANNE. A long time ago.

HANS. Good. I like the past tense. All we want to find out is where he is hiding.

SUZANNE *(rises angrily).* Find out yourself.

HANS *(detains her).* Suzanne, you are in no danger. Unless, you are lying.

SUZANNE. I don't know where he is. And I don't care. *(Takes out handkerchief and fakes crying.)*

HANS. A little bit of information now could protect you...
from further inquiries later. One word whispered, and
I'll never say where I heard it. Painless.

SUZANNE. How should I know where he is! We had a
fight. He left me. Months ago.

HANS. I see. Then next week you will do me the honor of
coming to dinner.

SUZANNE *(stalls)*. Next week? I have to prepare exams!

HANS. You are conscientious. I admire that. But you must
have some relaxation too. Why refuse an excellent dinner? Some women say I'm quite handsome.

SUZANNE. Oh, you are.

HANS. I'm glad you think so! Saturday, then. Whenever
you're finished.

SUZANNE. But it might be too late.

HANS. I'll wait. I have the car if you would like a ride
home now.

SUZANNE. No. No, thank you. I...I need the fresh air.

HANS. "Fleury." That means flower, doesn't it?

SUZANNE. Yes. Why?

HANS. It suits you. A flower looks fragile, but it can be
tough. We could use you in our New World. *(Exits.)*

*(SUZANNE's facade evaporates. She sits for a moment
nervously. Then begins to gather her things. JULIEN
comes from behind, puts a hand on her shoulder and
pulls her back to her chair. They use the device of an
embrace.)*

JULIEN. The boots?

SUZANNE. "The boots will be ready tomorrow." Julien,
they're looking for you! How could you endanger the
Maquis for one old man?

JULIEN. "The only thing necessary for the triumph of evil is for good men to do nothing." Edmund Burke.

SUZANNE. Go to Le Puy. But stay off the road.

JULIEN. Done.

SUZANNE. Now, go. The message must get there before noon.

JULIEN. It will. *(Exits.)*

(SUZANNE waits a moment to make sure he's gone then adjusts make-up, hair. Sound: Offstage scuffle. HANS appears a second later.)

HANS. Ah, good! You're still here! I was already back in my hotel when I discovered I had these. *(Tosses the gloves on the table.)*

SUZANNE. My gloves!

HANS. I thought you'd want them.

SUZANNE. That was kind of you.

HANS. Also profitable.

(SUZANNE looks puzzled.)

HANS. I found the man I was looking for, Delacour.

SUZANNE. Julien!!!

HANS. He was just outside the café when we arrested him.

Scene Two

SCENE: *Madame Barbière's kitchen. A half hour later.*

AT RISE: *RACHEL by the window, sees the first star.*

RACHEL. Goodnight, Maman. *(Blows her a kiss, hears Marie-Thérèse coming and darts back to her lacework.)*

MARIE-THÉRÈSE *(enters limping and counting the pieces of lace)*. Two meters ... let's see ... at fifteen francs per centimeter ... that's ... hm-m-m ... Lucky for us the arthritis is in my legs and not my fingers, Madeleine!

RACHEL. Maybe we can sell some of my lace.

MARIE-THÉRÈSE *(crosses to inspect)*. Um-m-m. *(Holds up a piece.)* Um-m-m. Ah! Twist the thread around the pins this way. Watch. *(Demonstrates.)* Now you do it. *(Observes Rachel.)* That's right. *(Ruffling her hair.)* You can't rush fine lace, little one.

SUZANNE *(bursts in)*. They arrested Julien!

MARIE-THÉRÈSE *(crosses to comfort Suzanne)*. Maybe it's routine.

SUZANNE. He was on his way to Le Puy with a message.

MARIE-THÉRÈSE. Can you go instead?

SUZANNE. Schmidt's watching every move. If I'm not at work, he'll get suspicious. Oh, why was Julien so ... stupid?

MARIE-THÉRÈSE. Not stupid, Suzanne. Kind. I don't want to live in a world where kindness is called stupid.

SUZANNE. The message must get to Le Puy. Before noon tomorrow.

MARIE-THÉRÈSE. If my legs were better ...

RACHEL. I'll go!

MARIE-THÉRÈSE. It's twenty kilometers from here, little one.

RACHEL. I went with you last summer.

MARIE-THÉRÈSE. It's much too dangerous for you, Madeleine. Le Puy is full of Nazis.

RACHEL *(stubbornly)*. I know the way ...

MARIE-THÉRÈSE. No! This is no business for a little girl.

SUZANNE. That's the point. Who would guess?

MARIE-THÉRÈSE. I promised to take care of her, and I will.

RACHEL. But I want to go! And I'm twelve years old now!

MARIE-THÉRÈSE. What else could I expect in this house?

SUZANNE. Tomorrow's market day. You could start out at dawn. Can you whistle?

RACHEL. Yes.

SUZANNE. Then listen. *(SUZANNE whistles beginning of partisan song to tune of "AULD LANG SYNE.")* Repeat it.

(RACHEL does.)

SUZANNE. Our contact will be at a flower stand. Go there and whistle that song. When you hear him whistle the second part of the song, you repeat the first. Then buy some flowers—yellow flowers—whisper the message. No other song. No other person. No other color. Can you do that?

RACHEL. OF COURSE! What's the message?

SUZANNE. "The boots are ready."

RACHEL. I don't understand.

SUZANNE. Just deliver it. You can borrow my bicycle. But we should have a reason. A village girl wouldn't ride twenty kilometers to buy spring flowers.

RACHEL *(excited)*. I could sell some of Madame Barbière's lace. I've helped her before.

MARIE-THÉRÈSE. But not all by yourself.

SUZANNE *(excited)*. Yes, you could sell some lace. Let's fill the basket. Good thinking, Madeleine.

MARIE-THÉRÈSE. And what if someone asks her why I'm not there? Have you thought of that?

RACHEL. I'll say you're ill. Your leg is bad. It is!

MARIE-THÉRÈSE. She'll miss school. Her history test.

SUZANNE. Tomorrow, Madeleine will make history!

MARIE-THÉRÈSE *(holds Rachel)*. It is very dangerous. You don't know. You can't know.

RACHEL. Madame Barbière, you said we each must fight the war in our own way.

MARIE-THÉRÈSE *(relents)*. I did. But remember this.

RACHEL. What?

MARIE-THÉRÈSE. Many people have died for France. You, Madeleine, must live for France.

Scene Three

SCENE: *Early morning, the next day, Le Puy. Around the cobblestone square are outdoor stands and large café umbrellas to protect the fruits, vegetables and plants displayed. A lace store is at the edge. Just off the square is a narrow alley with a "No Parking" sign at the entrance. The sign is the traditional French red circular sign with white lettering. Sound: Carts over cobblestones, vendor's cries.*

AT RISE: *RACHEL rides bicycle to the edge of the square, parks her bike hastily at the entrance to the alley and whistles the first few bars of the Resistance song. There is no response. MADAME REYNAUD enters with a large straw market day basket.*

YVETTE. MADELEINE! Why aren't you in school? Is Madame Barbière here with you?

RACHEL. She's ill.

YVETTE. Ill! I just saw her yesterday, and she was well enough.

RACHEL. It's her leg, her arthritis.

YVETTE. Well, no wonder, keeping up with the likes of you! I warned her, young girls have to be watched every minute.

RACHEL. She sent me here.

YVETTE. You can't fool me!

RACHEL. She did. To deliver the lace.

YVETTE. Then where is it?

RACHEL. On... on my bicycle.

YVETTE. On your bicycle? When did you get a bicycle? You're just enjoying yourself. I wouldn't keep the likes of you in my house, young lady.

RACHEL *(blurts out).* I wouldn't stay in your old house. *(Quickly covers.)* Excuse me, Madame Reynaud. I—

YVETTE. Well!!! It's no concern of mine what happens to a girl like you. I don't go around interfering... like some people. *(Exits.)*

(RACHEL pretends to look at various stands, whistling the first few bars of the Resistance song over and over. Periodically, she looks back at her bike. At the furthest point from it, she sees Gérard, the gendarme, approach her bike to examine it. This time there is a response to her whistle. RACHEL is torn. She hears the refrain repeated. RACHEL whistles the first few bars. The refrain is repeated, and she locates the sound. RACHEL carefully selects a bouquet of flowers. She counts out the money to pay for them as the VENDOR gives her the flowers in newspaper.)

RACHEL *(recites)*. "The boots are ready." *(She takes the bouquet and races to her bike, where GÉRARD is writing a ticket.)* No! No! Please.

GÉRARD. You're in a no parking zone, mademoiselle.

RACHEL. I'm sorry, officer.

GÉRARD. Is this your bicycle?

RACHEL. Yes.

GÉRARD. It's nice. Don't leave it like that. Someone could come and steal it.

RACHEL. Officer, do you have to write a ticket? I didn't know.

GÉRARD. You can read, can't you?

RACHEL. Of course.

GÉRARD *(points to the No Parking sign, and hands Rachel the ticket)*. It should be fifteen francs. I made it five. First offense.

RACHEL *(digs in her pocket and pays him)*. Thank you.

GÉRARD *(walks a few steps up the alley)*. Park it here.

RACHEL. But that's nearly the same place.

GÉRARD. But there's no sign.

(YVETTE enters with HANS, who carries her basket.)

HANS. Officer!

GÉRARD *(tips his hat)*. Good morning, Herr Leutnant Schmidt.

HANS *(curtly)*. Good morning. *(Stares at bike.)* Whose bicycle is that?

(GÉRARD gestures to Rachel.)

HANS. Arrest her!

GÉRARD. It was parked in the wrong place, that's all. I gave her a ticket.

HANS. And pocketed the fine? Arrest her!

GÉRARD *(stalls)*. Why?

HANS. The bicycle isn't hers. It's stolen.

YVETTE. I knew it! I knew it! Herr Leutnant Schmidt, it's just lucky I saw you.

GÉRARD *(disbelieving)*. Stolen? Are you sure? No. She doesn't look like a thief.

YVETTE *(smugly)*. Looks can deceive.

GÉRARD *(reluctantly, gently)*. Is it true? You can tell me. A pretty bicycle...a pretty day...you wanted to ride it around the square once. If you tell me now, it'll go easier for you.

RACHEL. No. It's not true.

GÉRARD. Ah, see. A mistake. All around. Bicycles look alike.

HANS. You call yourself a policeman? Afraid to arrest a little girl? No wonder France has lost the war!

(HANS shoves him out the way disgusted. GÉRARD and the bicycle both topple.)

GÉRARD *(rising slowly)*. Some land, monsieur. Some battles. But not the war!

HANS. I'll deal with you later.

(HANS turns to interrogate Rachel. As GÉRARD exits, he glances back at Rachel.)

HANS. Now, Madeleine, you will tell me why you have Fräulein Fleury's bicycle.

YVETTE. Mademoiselle Fleury!

RACHEL. I...I borrowed it.

YVETTE. And she told me she had to deliver lace for Madame Barbière.

RACHEL. The lace is right there!

HANS *(gives Yvette her basket)*. Don't let me detain you. Frau Reynaud.

YVETTE. Oh, Herr Leutnant Schmidt, I can wait. You said—

HANS. If she's who you think she is, Frau Reynaud, you'll get your reward. Now, leave us.

YVETTE. But—

HANS. LEAVE US!

YVETTE. I'm just going. *(Exits.)*

HANS. Now, Madeleine, we are going to talk. *(HANS leads her into alley. A shadowy face peers out from the plant and flower stand, sees that bicycle and flowers are strewn about, and puts up a sign that reads, "Closed.")* You see, Madeleine, I have a puzzle. A nice, neat puzzle, except there's a piece missing. And now you're going to help me find it.

RACHEL. Yes, Herr Leutnant Schmidt.

HANS. You're not her cousin, are you?

RACHEL. Whose?

HANS. Madame Barbière's.

RACHEL. Yes, Yes, I am!

HANS. You said before you were her husband's cousin. Which is it?

RACHEL. That's what I meant. Her husband's cousin!

HANS *(casually removes revolver)*. We will do whatever's necessary—to get the truth. Do you understand?

RACHEL *(concealing her fright)*. Yes.

HANS. Now, then, why did you steal the bicycle?

RACHEL. I didn't steal it. I...I borrowed it. To deliver the lace.

HANS. Lace? *(Rips open package.)* LACE!

RACHEL. I told you.

HANS. Then why didn't you deliver it? Or sell it?

RACHEL. I just got here!

HANS. You had time to buy flowers. Who are the flowers for?

RACHEL. For Madame Barbière. She's sick. That's why I came.

HANS. What's your real name?

RACHEL. Madeleine Petit.

HANS (*consults notes again*). Before you came to Auvergne, where were you?

RACHEL. Marseilles.

HANS. Did you always live there?

RACHEL. Yes.

HANS. And you were born there?

RACHEL. Just outside.

HANS. Frau Reynaud says you don't sound like someone from Marseilles.

RACHEL. Because my mother wanted me to speak French properly, without an accent.

HANS. Hand over your papers.

RACHEL. You already saw them.

HANS (*slaps her face*). Don't play the fool. You see, we ferret you all out. No matter where you hide. We find you. (*Holds out his hand.*)

RACHEL (*hands papers over*). I'm Madeleine Petit!!

(*HANS takes time to examine papers thoroughly. Sound: The whistle of the Resistance song. RACHEL turns her head slightly to listen. Sound: The phrase is repeated. HANS studies Rachel thoughtfully. She does not flinch.*)

HANS (*slowly*). Your papers...are in order. So it should be no trouble for us to get more proof.

RACHEL (*startled*). More!

HANS (*watches her*). Someone who knew you in Marseilles, who can swear you are Madeleine Petit.

(PÈRE ANTOINE and GÉRARD enter. GÉRARD points to bike. PÈRE ANTOINE crosses, looking for Rachel.)

PÈRE ANTOINE *(puts bike upright).* Madeleine! *(Crosses to them. GÉRARD exits.)* This child should be in school, Herr Leutnant Schmidt. Spring in this part of France. They won't stay inside. But I'll take her back.

HANS. That's not the issue!

PÈRE ANTOINE *(innocently).* No?

HANS. No! *(Points to her.)* She's been accused. Is she a Jew?

RACHEL *(insists).* I'm Madeleine Petit!

PÈRE ANTOINE *(laughs).* Herr Leutnant Schmidt, we'd be insulted if this accusation weren't so absurd! Naturally, she's Madeleine Petit! Ever since I've known her, she's been Madeleine Petit.

HANS. Did you know her in Marseilles?

PÈRE ANTOINE. I brought her to St. Laurent myself.

(Puts arms protectively around Rachel.)

HANS. This is no trifling matter.

PÈRE ANTOINE. I know.

HANS. You are telling the truth?

PÈRE ANTOINE *(indignant).* It is my duty to do so.

HANS. Then you will vouch for her identity?

PÈRE ANTOINE. Certainly.

HANS. Perjury, Père Antoine, is punishable by death. Even for a priest.

PÈRE ANTOINE. Especially for a priest! We're taught not to lie in the eyes of God. As a priest I may think about heaven, but I'm in no rush to get there.

HANS. Do you swear that she is Madeleine Petit?

PÈRE ANTOINE. I know her by no other name.

HANS. You swear?

PÈRE ANTOINE. I swear.

HANS. A priest's word is sacred.

PÈRE ANTOINE. So they say. *(Pause.)*

HANS. I will accept it. *(Shakes hands with Père Antoine.)* Yvette Reynaud is a fool.

PÈRE ANTOINE. Ah! *(Gesture indicates he agrees.)* There's one in every village.

HANS *(a slight bow)*. My apologies, fräulein ... for the little ... inconvenience. *(Exits.)*

PÈRE ANTOINE. Madeleine, you must forgive stupidity.

RACHEL. No!

PÈRE ANTOINE. For your soul.

RACHEL. You can forgive stupidity for your soul. But I have to fight it, for my life!

Scene Four

SCENE: *Madame Barbière's kitchen. August 25, 1944.*

AT RISE: *MARIE-THÉRÈSE, PÈRE ANTOINE, and SUZANNE study the map of France, which SUZANNE has marked to indicate the progress of the Allies and Axis forces. RACHEL is a lookout at the curtain.*

PÈRE ANTOINE. We're just outside of Paris.

SUZANNE. So close. So close. We need Julien.

MARIE-THÉRÈSE. It'll get worse before it gets better.

RACHEL. Why?

MARIE-THÉRÈSE. They're desperate. Madame Reynaud said the Nazis shot three hostages and left them dead in the street.

SUZANNE. We must get Julien out.

PÈRE ANTOINE. They've arrested the Bishop of Montauban.

MARIE-THÉRÈSE. The Bishop!

SUZANNE. Why?

PÈRE ANTOINE. For saying "all men are brothers, created by the same God." For saying that "the Anti-Semitic measure violated human dignity." It was a fine speech. There are many brave men in prison, Suzanne.

SUZANNE. Too many.

RACHEL. Is it time now?

MARIE-THÉRÈSE. Madeleine, you must learn some patience.

RACHEL. I can't stand waiting. I want to do something!

MARIE-THÉRÈSE. You did. Delivering that message to Le Puy was dangerous enough. Now, you stay home.

RACHEL. But I did more than that. I saved them too!

MARIE-THÉRÈSE. WHAT!

(SUZANNE signals Rachel to be quiet.)

What did you say?

RACHEL. Well, who'd suspect a girl just jumping rope. That was my idea.

MARIE-THÉRÈSE. SUZANNE! How could you let her?

RACHEL. Oh, I was only a lookout, Madame Barbière. They wouldn't let me pull out the train tracks.

MARIE-THÉRÈSE. I should think not!

RACHEL. We had to!

SUZANNE. A deportation train. Headed East.

RACHEL. We had to let them escape.

MARIE-THÉRÈSE. What if you'd been caught?

RACHEL. What if I did nothing!

MARIE-THÉRÈSE. To survive is enough! Suzanne, I want a live child at the end of the war, not a dead hero.

SUZANNE. Look at her carefully, Madame Barbière. *(Crosses to radio.)* She's a young woman now. *(Turns radio on.)*

(RACHEL goes to lookout post. Sound: Cheers, yelling, clapping, voices sing "La Marseillaise.")

MARIE-THÉRÈSE. La Marseillaise!!

(Sound: Church bells ringing, horns honking.)

PÈRE ANTOINE. It must be!

SUZANNE. Sh-h-h.

BRITISH RADIO VOICE. An incredible sight, ladies and gentlemen. This morning French tanks entered Paris. Crowds line the street, waiting for the procession to pass. And when it does, Parisian women climb upon the tanks to kiss the soldiers and toss them flowers. On every balcony in Paris the tricolor has reappeared. Some are flags that have been hidden for years, some are rags tied together. But everywhere blue, white, and red fly in the summer breeze. Never has the sun seemed brighter than today, August 25, 1944. All over the city there are signs, "Paris est libéré. Vive la France." Ladies and gentlemen, Paris is free!!

(They hug each other excitedly.)

RACHEL. Is the war over?

SUZANNE. Not quite.

RACHEL. But you said Paris is the heart of France.

SUZANNE. It is! Now we must free the rest of her!

MARIE-THÉRÈSE. And Julien. Before they kill him.

PÈRE ANTOINE. There's only one person who can walk in and out of prison at any hour without suspicion.

RACHEL. A guard?

PÈRE ANTOINE. A priest! I have an idea...

Scene Five

SCENE: *A dark, tiny room in the detention prison at Le Puy. There are no furnishings. Only a tattered blanket on the floor. Late at night, August 1944.*

AT RISE: *JULIEN is pacing the room. Sound: Boots walking; keys in a lock.*

PÈRE ANTOINE *(to Guard outside)*. Five minutes, Guard. No longer. *(Enters and says loudly.)* I've come to hear your confession, my son.

JULIEN. Père Antoine! What's happening? Why are you here?

PÈRE ANTOINE *(loudly)*. Kneel, my son, and pray for God's forgiveness. KNEEL!
(JULIEN kneels and automatically recites a prayer.)
Is he gone?
(JULIEN nods.)

PÈRE ANTOINE. I gave him a cigarette. Paris is liberated. *(Removes a hidden cassock.)*

JULIEN. We've been waiting two years to hear that! And I'm locked in here.

PÈRE ANTOINE. The door is never locked to a priest. Put this on. *(Helps him dress.)*

JULIEN. Why?

PÈRE ANTOINE. They need you out there. They need you more than they need me.

JULIEN. You can't take my place!

PÈRE ANTOINE. Don't argue. There's no time. I'm going to call for the guard. When I do, throw the blanket over me. They won't check till morning. By then you'll be far away from here. Take my hat.

JULIEN. You can't do this. They want to kill me.

PÈRE ANTOINE. They won't kill a priest! Go, Julien. Go! *(Calls loudly.)* Guard! I'm finished. *(PÈRE ANTOINE lies down and puts blanket over himself.)* Cover me. *(JULIEN covers him, then pulls blanket off his face for a split second.)*

JULIEN. Bless you, Père Antoine.

(JULIEN again covers Père Antoine's face with the blanket. JULIEN exits. Sound: Boots walking; keys in lock. Lighting: Fades. Sound: In the dark, there is a gunshot. Silence. Then the rising sound of church bells pealing. They signal peace. Gradually they are mixed with "La Marseillaise." The war is over.)

Scene Six

SCENE: *Madame Barbière's kitchen, mid-May 1945. It is decorated with miniature French flags and tri-colored ribbon.*

AT RISE: *MARIE-THÉRÈSE and SUZANNE are singing "La Marseillaise" as they work. They are preparing platters of cheese, French bread, and fruit. JULIEN is slicing sausage. RACHEL stares out the window, immobile.*

MARIE-THÉRÈSE. She's been like that ever since the war ended. Standing by the window, hour after hour. For ten days. I don't know what to do.

(SUZANNE crosses to Rachel, puts an arm around her.)

RACHEL. They said they'd come! As soon as the war was over! They promised.

(*SUZANNE and JULIEN look at each other.*)

JULIEN (*crosses to Rachel*). Some promises can't be kept.

RACHEL. I won't listen to you!

MARIE-THÉRÈSE. Madeleine, there are some things in life we must accept. Like Père Antoine's death last summer.

JULIEN. He said the plan was perfect. A change of clothes, and they'll never kill a priest.

MARIE-THÉRÈSE. He was always ... very persuasive.

JULIEN. He saved my life.

RACHEL. Mine, too. When Maman and Papa come, we have to tell them all about Père Antoine.

JULIEN. Madeleine, not everyone comes back.

RACHEL (*refuses to listen*). They'll come! I know they will.

(*OTHERS look at one another helplessly.*)

MARIE-THÉRÈSE (*practical*). Well, until then you'll stay right here. And there's a lot to do before the festival tonight!

(*RACHEL crosses to Marie-Thérèse. Sound: Cabrettes. [A French instrument similar to the bagpipe.]*)

SUZANNE. The band! The first time since the war. Julien, did you ever see a more beautiful day?

JULIEN (*gazing at her*). No. We'll dance the Boureé all night long.

SUZANNE. You too, Madeleine.

RACHEL. I don't know how.

JULIEN. Let's show her! (*He grabs SUZANNE and they show Rachel a few steps during the next few speeches.*) Every Auvergnat dances the Bourée!

SUZANNE. It's a traditional dance.

JULIEN. And at the end the man kisses his partner on the cheek three times.

MARIE-THÉRÈSE. In my day, if the lady gave him a flower, then the gentleman knew she liked him.

RACHEL. Are you going to give Julien a flower?

SUZANNE *(embarrassed)*. Oh, Madeleine, I just pretended to be Julien's girlfriend during the war to pass messages.

(JULIEN is looking at her.)

SUZANNE. We fooled everyone! *(To Marie-Thérèse.)* Even you.

MARIE-THÉRÈSE. Madeleine, go try on your party dress.

RACHEL. I already did.

MARIE-THÉRÈSE *(pushing Rachel out of the room)*. I need to check the length of the sleeves.

(RACHEL and MARIE-THÉRÈSE exit.)

JULIEN. Is that true?

SUZANNE. What?

JULIEN. What you just said.

SUZANNE. It was their idea. The Maquis. Not yours.

JULIEN. That's how it started. That's not how it ended. Suzanne, I came back to marry you.

SUZANNE. That sounds like another order from the Maquis.

JULIEN. I thought about you, about us, the whole time. It's what kept me alive.

(SUZANNE waits for him to continue. JULIEN misinterprets her silence.)

But if your answer is no, I'll leave.

SUZANNE. Julien Delacour, how can I answer yes or no, when you didn't even ask me a question?

(Sound: Bourée music continues. SUZANNE dances a step of the Bourée. JULIEN joins her. He kisses her on the cheeks three times. SUZANNE smiles, hands Julien a flower.)

JULIEN. Suzanne Fleury ... will you ... please ... marry ...
me?
SUZANNE. Oh, yes, Julien! Yes! *(In his arms.)* Oh,
Julien, YES.

*(They embrace. Sound: A knock at the door. JULIEN
ignores it. Sound: Another knock at the door. Reluctantly JULIEN goes to answer it. LÉON stands there,
gaunt, grey haired. His clothes are army hospital sur-
plus. He is a shattered man, a shadow of himself.)*

LÉON. I'm looking for Madeleine Petit. They said Ma-
dame Barbière's house.
(JULIEN hesitates, looking at Léon's appearance.)
I'm her father.
SUZANNE. Come in!
(LÉON enters.)
SUZANNE *(to Julien).* Go get Madeleine.
(JULIEN exits.)
SUZANNE. I'm Suzanne Fleury, her teacher. *(They shake
hands.)* Please sit down.
(LÉON sits.)
SUZANNE. She has been waiting by the window, hoping
her maman and papa would come.
LÉON. I've come alone.

*(MARIE-THÉRÈSE enters nervously with her hands
firmly on Rachel's shoulders. As RACHEL enters, she
stops, stares, stunned by Léon's altered appearance.
SUZANNE exits.)*

RACHEL. Papa? *(Pulls away from MARIE-THÉRÈSE and
crosses slowly to him. There is a long look.)* Papa!

(They embrace.) I knew you'd come. They said—but I knew you'd come. *(Runs to the door.)* Maman.

LÉON. She's not there.

RACHEL. Where is she?

(LÉON doesn't answer.)

RACHEL. Papa, where is she?

(LÉON shakes his head.)

Papa! Tell me!

LÉON. Typhus. She died of typhus in the camp.

RACHEL. No! Not Maman! NOT MAMAN. Maybe she escaped. Maybe—

LÉON. You can't understand. You weren't there. There was only one escape.

RACHEL. I made a lace tablecloth just for her. And every evening as soon as the first star appeared, I said good-night. Just the way we said we would. *(Turns on him violently. All the pent-up rage and fear pour out.)* She can't be dead. She can't be. Why didn't you stop them? *(MARIE-THÉRÈSE pulls her away.)*

I hate them. I HATE THEM! I HATE THEM!

LÉON *(drained)*. Hating won't bring her back.

MARIE-THÉRÈSE. But it helps. *(Gathers Rachel in her arms.)* I'm Madame Barbière. *(RACHEL sobs. To Léon.)* When a river is swollen, it floods. Let her cry, monsieur, let her cry. Nature knows more than we do about healing.

LÉON *(far away)*. I...can't...cry.

(SUZANNE and JULIEN have reentered.)

SUZANNE *(to Léon)*. This is Julien Delacour, my fiancé. *(They shake hands.)*

MARIE-THÉRÈSE. Ah! Fiancé! Did you hear that, Madeleine?

(There's a little nod amidst the sobs.)

RACHEL *(raising her head)*. Papa, where were you?

LÉON. Many places.

SUZANNE. Tell her the truth.

LÉON. I...I can't.

RACHEL. You were in one of those camps, weren't you?

(LÉON nods.)

RACHEL. In Poland?

LÉON. Poland, Germany. After awhile it doesn't matter. They can only kill you once. *(To Rachel.)* But you still have one of us left.

RACHEL *(crosses to him slowly)*. So do you, Papa. So do you. *(Looking at him.)* You look so...so...so different.

LÉON. The Americans sent me to a hospital to fatten me up!

MARIE-THÉRÈSE *(dryly, bringing him some food)*. They didn't finish.

RACHEL. What about Maman?

LÉON. Too late. *(Touches her face.)* You're so healthy! Madame Barbière, you've given me my daughter! A reason to hope.

MARIE-THÉRÈSE. War is strange, monsieur. I could say the same.

LÉON. How can I thank you?

MARIE-THÉRÈSE. Don't take her away so soon. Stay with us...a few days.

LÉON. I owe you too much already.

MARIE-THÉRÈSE. We'll talk about that later. Later. Right now you need mountain air and rest. And more than a day of it. Even with our famous cabbage soup, I can't work miracles.

LÉON *(gazing at Rachel)*. I think you already have.

RACHEL. Papa, stay. Until you're stronger.

SUZANNE *(softly to Léon)*. It would give her some time, too.

RACHEL. Please, Papa, stay.

LÉON. All right, Rachel. All right.

MARIE-THÉRÈSE, SUZANNE, and JULIEN *(together)*. RACHEL?

LÉON *(to Rachel)*. I haven't said it aloud since the night you left.

RACHEL. Neither have I, Papa.

LÉON. Two and a half years.

RACHEL *(a slow realization)*. Madame Barbière, they wouldn't really have shot you, would they?
(She doesn't answer.)

RACHEL. WOULD THEY?

MARIE-THÉRÈSE. I couldn't leave you out in the snow.

LÉON *(seated. Far away)*. Others did.

RACHEL. Papa? *(Touches his face gently.)* You sound so ...so far away.

LÉON *(a trace of tears beginning in his voice)*. Rachel. My dearest Rachel. I'm coming home...slowly.
(LÉON is seated, his head down. RACHEL stands behind him, her arms on his.)

RACHEL. It's over, Papa. The war's over. We can stop hiding! I can have my name back. My own name. RACHEL SIMON!

THE END

Classroom Concepts

❧ A number of hints will help students to play this activity. Encourage students to explore the following as preparation.

> The location of the town in Auvergne in South Central France
>
> André Trocmé, Huguenot minister
>
> The climate

Town Meeting

Work with your students in planning a town meeting in which they must make decisions about rescue issues. Will they, as villagers of the fictional town of St. Laurent des Pins, assist Jews who are fleeing? Make certain that students prepare both pro and con arguments and can support their positions.

❧ This activity asks students to put themselves in a situation similar to Rachel's and to create a new identity for themselves. Give the following directions to class members.

Who Am I Now?

Imagine that, like Rachel, you had to leave your home and family. What new identity would you create for yourself? What political or personal situation would cause you to go into hiding or exile with a new identity? What possessions would you take with you and why? Are you fleeing during World War II or during another time period? After making these decisions, create a new autobiography for yourself. Write and deliver a monologue in which you reveal your new identity and the reasons for it. If desired, look through books, magazines, and photo albums for a picture that represents what you would look like under your new identity. If possible, assume this characterization using costume and make-up in order to realistically create this new look for yourself.

꿀 This activity and the variation which follows afford students an opportunity to analyze and design settings for this play.

Scenically Speaking

Ask students to imagine that each is the scenic designer for a school production of *Remember My Name*. They are responsible for creating color sketches or a three-dimensional model of (1) the Simon apartment in Marseilles; (2) Mme. Barbière's traditional farmhouse kitchen room; or, (3) the village school for girls. These should be shared with classmates. Student designers must next explain the rationale for their choices and describe how they took historical accuracy into account. When all have shared their work, as a class compare and contrast these settings in terms of scenic interpretations and requirements.

As a variation, students may elect to use projected scenery for a school production of the play. Slides could be taken of geographic locations that might serve as projected scenery and then presented to classmates.

꿀 Like the previous scenic design exercise, this activity invites students to function as costume designer for this play.

Figures and Forms

Invite each student to imagine that he or she is the costume designer for a school production of *Remember My Name* and to create color renderings of costumes for the characters in the play. These are to be shared with classmates. Student designers are expected to explain the rationale for design choices and to take historical accuracy into account. When all have shared their work, as a class compare and contrast these costume designs.

The punishments for hiding Jews from the Nazis could be severe. In this activity, students have an opportunity to weigh courage of convictions against serious consequences.

Would You Risk It?

Working in small groups, students should investigate the punishments faced by those caught hiding Jews. What might have happened to those who helped Rachel had they been discovered? What risks might Mme. Barbière have faced by hiding Rachel in her home? Next, ask group members to imagine themselves in Mme. Barbière's place. When Père Antoine sought shelter and safety for the little girl, what would each of them have done? Next, group members should imagine living in St. Laurent des Pins during the Second World War and improvise a scene in which they are asked to care for Rachel. The outcome of this scene need not replicate the one in the play. Decisions, however, be they to accept or to refuse the child, must be legitimately based upon investigation of the possible consequences and students' willingness to take the necessary risks.

Rachel says that there is no more chocolate in France (p. 157). What other commodities were in short supply? How might these goods be used by the Nazis to further their cause? In addition, Yvette says that there is a five hundred franc reward for turning in Jews (p. 139-140). What other rewards were offered for this? Challenge students to consider what goods or rewards they would find tempting if they were residents of St. Laurent des Pins during the Nazi occupation of France. Next, play the concentration game, *Hans Schmidt Offered Me*, which follows.

Hans Schmidt Offered Me

Students should sit in a circle for this concentration game. The first person begins by saying the phrase, Hans Schmidt Offered Me and stating something the Nazis used to reward or bribe French citizens in order to get information from them. The student then concludes with the phrase, "...but I said no." Each person following says the opening phrase and repeats the item or items already given. The student then adds his or her own and concludes with "...but I said no." An example follows.

Student #1: Hans Schmidt offered me sugar, but I said no.

Student #2: Hans Schmidt offered me sugar and money, but I said no.

Student #3: Hans Schmidt offered me sugar, money, and a chocolate bar, but I said no.

As a variation, replay the game. This time, allow each student to say "yes" or "no" at the conclusion of his or her recitation. At the end of the activity, as a class, discuss these personal responses. Why might someone agree or refuse to take these offers?

❧ In the following activity, students have an opportunity to imagine that they, like Julien, are members of the Maquis. The exercise has both writing and dramatic improvisation components.

Member of the Maquis

Ask students to imagine themselves as members of the Maquis and to investigate conditions in Nazi-occupied France, as Julien did when he went to Marseilles. They then should describe what they have learned in articles to be published in an underground newsletter. Next, they should compile columns that they and their classmates have written and actually publish a newsletter for distribution to other classes or school groups.

Either before or after publishing the class newsletter, each student should take on the role of a member of the Maquis and report observations resulting from investigations. In character, they should tell their comrades what they have seen and experienced. The setting for this report should be a secret meeting of the group.

❧ Acts of resistance took a number of different forms during World War II. Students can demonstrate some of these in *Saying "No."*

Saying "No"

In the play, Mme. Barbière says, "We each say, 'No!' in our own way" (p. 173). Invite students to analyze the script and determine how each of the characters who resists the Nazis does so. Next, encourage students to investigate other acts of resistance in France from 1942-1945 and then to cast themselves as survivors who engaged in acts of resistance. Each student should develop a clear characterization of the survivor as well as a detailed understanding of the act of resistance. After casting several class members as reporters, these personal stories of resistance can be shared using a television or radio interview show format.

๛ In conjunction with their reading of the play and study of events and conditions in wartime France, do the following exercise with students. If desired, they can create and perform *The Time Between* for more than one of the characters in the exercise. Students also might identify other places in the script which lend themselves to this treatment.

The Time Between

After selecting one of the characters below and investigating applicable circumstances in France from 1942 through 1945, students should write a monologue describing what happened to the character. These monologues should be memorized, staged, and performed for classmates. Costumes might be worn to enhance performances.

> I am Léon. After the war ended but before I found Rachel, I...

> I am Pauline. After Rachel left home but before the war ended, I...

> I am Julien. After the Maquis held its first meeting at the schoolhouse but before I came to Mme. Barbière's to tell Suzanne about the letter, I...

> I am Hans. After my first visit to Suzanne at the school but before investigating the report of English being spoken at Mme. Barbière's, I...

I am Suzanne. After agreeing to allow the Maquis to use the schoolhouse for meetings but before Julien came to tell me my letter had been confiscated, I...

&ed; There are several places in the play wherein a character says something but really means something else. An example of this can be found in Act One, Scene Six (p. 160) in the following exchange.

> *Yvette:* There was a reward, too—six hundred francs. But Herr Leutnant Schmidt said we should do our duty without a reward.
>
> *Marie-Thérèse:* Yes. If we can.

In the above, Yvette thinks Mme. Barbière is referring to doing her duty for the Nazis when, in fact, she means obeying the dictates of her conscience. In order to communicate the true meaning of her lines, students must understand "subtext," the real meaning underneath the words that influences how the dialogue is delivered. The *Subtext* exercise provides students with an opportunity to analyze and interpret lines of dialogue.

Subtext

Students begin by searching the script for lines which have subtextual content. Next, as the character to whom the lines are assigned, volunteers deliver the dialogue at least twice, giving a different interpretation and meaning each time. All students should discuss how meaning changed in these varying interpretations.

◌ Prior to engaging students in this exercise, prompt them to study what happened to concentration camp prisoners at war's end. Encourage them to have a working knowledge of displaced persons and their experiences, including the psychological adaptations incumbent upon reuniting families. Then, divide students into groups and have each group create and dramatize *The Next Scene*.

The Next Scene

Remember My Name ends with Rachel and her father staying with Mme. Barbière for a while. With classmates, students should create a scene showing what happens to them during this period and immediately afterward.

◌ Mme. Barbière teaches Rachel many things, including how to make lace and how to prepare soup. Pair the students and cast one as Mme. Barbière and one as Madeleine (Rachel) for this mirroring activity. Remind them that when mirroring, the goal is to be as synchronized as possible so that onlookers cannot tell who is initiating action and who is reflecting it.

Mirroring

The student playing Mme. Barbière should pantomime actions which demonstrate what she teaches her young charge. The student playing Rachel should precisely and at the same time copy these actions. Players then can switch roles and repeat the exercise.

◌ In this narrative pantomime, students play in pairs with one taking on the role of Rachel (Madeleine) as she arrives for the first time at Mme. Barbière's home. The second player assumes the role of Marie-Thérèse. Before playing, remind partners that when pantomiming they are expected to use the body rather than the voice to communicate. The teacher serves as narrator here.

Narrative Pantomime: Arriving at Mme. Barbière's

You are Rachel arriving at Mme. Barbière's home for the first time. You step into her kitchen and she asks you for your coat. You remove it and shiver because you are so cold from walking and waiting in the snow. She directs you to sit by the fire. You walk to the stove, sit, and warm yourself. Mme. Barbière brings you a bowl of soup. You gulp it eagerly. You put the bowl down and stand. You walk over to look at Mme. Barbière's lace work. You admire the pretty lace and Mme. Barbière shows you how to do a stitch. You try to do exactly what she shows you. Mme. Barbière takes your cold hands in hers. She rubs your hands and they feel warmer.

It is time to leave. Mme. Barbière pauses at the window to look at the snow before she gets your coat. You take the coat from her, put it on, and thank her for the soup. As you start to go, Mme. Barbière tells you that she has an idea. She tells you her plan. You can stay with her. What do you think of this? How does this make you feel? As Madeleine Petit, you have found a home!

CHAPTER FIVE

Angel in the Night

The Playwright Speaks

Playwrights usually create their own characters, plot, time, and place. But how do you handle a commission when most of the main characters are alive and well? The idea of a play about Marysia Szul, an eighteen-year old Polish Catholic girl who rescued four Jewish fugitives during World War II, was the brainchild of the Honor of Humanity project and the Avenue of the Righteous. The latter seeks innovative ways to promote greater understanding amongst different races, creeds, and cultures. René Roy, Director of the Theatre Arts Program at National-Louis University, eagerly took on the stewardship of the project, which was monumental: to engage a playwright, develop a script, and mount a premiere production to be followed by a tour.

But my initial reaction when he first telephoned requesting me to write a play on the Holocaust was that I already had one. Wouldn't they like to use that?

I was flown out to Chicago where, apparently, I met the approval of those assembled to interview me and so work began.

"The play will write itself," someone said to calm my jangled nerves.

Wrong! Wrong! Wrong!

The material was inherently dramatic but gathering the facts proved to be more difficult than anticipated. Some facts were easy to validate—when a ghetto was established or liquidated. Other facts were more elusive.

A story must have a beginning, a point of attack. "When did this happen?" I asked Frieda, a survivor.

"It was autumn. Harvest time. I remember we were running through the fields. The stalks of grain were over my head," Frieda told me.

"It was spring. Planting time. I remember we were planting potatoes," Marysia said.

Finally, I managed to get the two of them together and asked the question again. They answered the same way simultaneously.

Marysia smiled at Frieda benignly. "What do you know?" she asked. "You were eight years old!" Later, that became the last line of the Prologue to segue into Act One.

When I first met Mania to interview her, she told the story of her comfortable upbringing as an assimilated Polish-Jew, a distinct rarity at that time, of going to a Polish school, of the horror of losing her entire family and of her escape from the ghetto. She told it with eloquence and emotion, and after two hours I felt as if I'd known her for years. Then I asked, "What did you do, hiding in the bunker?"

"Nothing."

"Well, what did you talk about?"

"We didn't talk."

"Was there tension?"

"No, no tension."

Great, I thought. No conversation. No tension. No play!

But I couldn't accept that. There had to be tension. Cramped together. Cooped up in the dark. Unable to have privacy. Terrified. Two years. When the play opened, whether Mania was being polite or whether my intuition was on target, she said, "Joanna, it was just like that!"

Although by then I'd read reams on the Holocaust, I knew little of Poland. National-Louis University arranged a research trip with a video crew and both Marysia and Frieda, with her daughter, went with the director, public relations director, a board member, a Polish faculty member, and me. No one except René quite understood my need to walk the ground, to smell the air, to visit the ethnographic museum, and to see the faces of the people who wished to erase the uncomfortable past. As a group we visited castles, churches, cemeteries, monuments, and concentration camps.

Frieda, a stunning woman, aged before my eyes as she stared at the dusty tattered collection of labeled suitcases at Auschwitz. "I could have been one of those children," she whispered. It wasn't hyperbole.

One afternoon, at a cathedral in Warsaw, I asked Marysia, "How was it you never said anything? When they hurt you, you were silent."

She looked at me the way you might look at a dense child. "If I die, why should others die, too?"

I began to think about my protagonist, Marysia. She made no lengthy philosophical statements, no impassioned protest for a cause, had no intellectual position. But she possessed an innocence and goodness that nothing shook. When the Nazis interrogated her, starved her, beat her, she thought it was better to die than to betray those she'd promised to protect. For Marysia, it was simply a matter of doing what was right. That's all.

I came across a line from the Hebrew writer, Hazaz. "All the darkness can't extinguish a single candle yet one candle can illuminate all its darkness."

For the four people she saved, Marysia was that candle.

Why is she called Pawlina in the play? When we had the first reading, the audience had trouble distinguishing amongst similar-sounding Polish names, Mania (the teen), Mundek (the baby), and Marysia. So for clarification, I wound up using the main character's middle name, Pawlina.

One of the great pleasures of the project was working with the staff, students, and drama director at NLU and the members of the committees who hosted and helped me in every conceivable way. Under René Roy's careful coaching, students who had minimal theatre training were creating powerful improvisations that brought tears to my eyes. The material was strong, but so was their commitment.

Whenever I came to Chicago, Mania would insist on tea and her fabulous homemade cookies. "Eat!" She would look at me skeptically, as if she worried whether I could even finish the script if I didn't have another delectable bite. "You're too thin!" she would say in motherly concern. Although it was far from the truth, there's no doubt that some of those Polish cookies inspired me and they are now part of the Prologue. It was on one of those occasions Mania confided, "First there is God. Then there is Marysia!" But Marysia, like so many of those who helped, always waived such praise aside.

There was so much material that a lot of my research and early drafts got tossed and became "take-out scenes." The play in its published version is a tight, one-hour script. But I still miss some of the moments we had to give up, some of the compromises that had to be made.

But edit and cut I did, as I wanted this story to be part of the American students' learning experience.

Despite all the evidence, there are still those who say the Holocaust was invented. I remember the chilling trio of short, square Pinteresque men who, on the eve of the premiere, marched up to say I'd made a mistake. "No Anti-Semitism," they insisted. "We were good to those Jews!"

Marysia was an ordinary young girl growing up on a Polish farm when, reluctantly, she became the protector of four fugitives for nearly two years. Feeding them, carrying out their slops, washing their clothes, calming their terror—is that the work of a hero? Some would say it's the work of an angel. And so the title.

The Play

SETTING / TIME

The Epilogue and Prologue occur in a Chicago suburb, the present. The play takes place in Southeast Poland near the city of Zoborow, during World War II, 1942-1944.

CHARACTERS

(4 men, 4 women, 1 girl, minimum with doubling. May be expanded to 9 men, 7 women, and 1 girl)

MANIA (in the present), mid-60s

MARYSIA PAWLINA (in the present), late 60s

FREIDZA (in the present), late 50s

MARYSIA PAWLINA (in the past), a young Polish woman, 18

DOMICELA, her mother, 48

GOLDA, a Jewish fugitive, 27

FREIDZA (in the past), her daughter, 8

MUNDEK, her baby son

HANKA, her former Polish neighbor

HENRYK, her husband

TADEUSZ, a Polish neighbor, 22

MANIA (in the past), a Jewish fugitive, 14

BRUNO, a German soldier, 37

ERNST, a German captain, 23

OTTO, a German officer

LUTHER, a German soldier

KURT, a German prison guard

WALDO, a German prison guard

STANISLAUS, a Polish guard in a German prison, 50s

Author's Note

At the edge of the city of Jerusalem in Israel there is a center for research on the Nazi Holocaust and a memorial to the lives lost. Yad Vashem was established in 1953.

Beyond its somber walls is a tree-lined avenue commemorating the bravery of those who helped to save others. They were called Righteous Gentiles. Among them were leaders of nations and menial laborers. Each Righteous person had to be recommended by survivors and proof presented. A tree was then planted to honor the individual and a medal presented with the following inscription, "Whoever saves a single soul, it is as if he had saved the whole world."

Outside of Chicago there is a similar Avenue of the Righteous Park located in Evanston, Illinois. It was dedicated in 1987.

In both parks a tree was planted in Marysia Pawlina Szul's honor.

Prologue

SCENE: *Mania's living room. An affluent Chicago sub-urb. The present. The tea table is set with a fresh linen cloth, silver tea service, tall glasses in metal holders and a banquet of Polish pastries.*

AT RISE: *MANIA is adjusting her centerpiece of fresh flowers. PAWLINA appears in the interior doorway.*

PAWLINA *(from the doorway).* Stop fussing!

MANIA *(without turning).* But I haven't seen her in years. She's ... so ... successful.

PAWLINA *(enters room and parades in her new outfit).* How do you like it?

MANIA *(turns, inspects and impulsively hugs her).* Perfect! Pawlina, the blouse is perfect on you. It goes with your suit. It goes with your eyes—

PAWLINA *(breaks in laughing).* You picked it out. But, Mania, are you sure this is what they wear to plant a tree?

MANIA. You don't have to plant it. You just have to stand there. Someone else will do the digging. You're our celebrity, remember?

PAWLINA. I'd rather do the digging. *(They look at each other. Sound: Doorbell. MANIA crosses, glances in the mirror and stops to fix her hair.)* Answer the door!

MANIA. She's here. Oh, I wish I hadn't gained so much weight. *(Sound: Doorbell again.)*

PAWLINA. Go! *(MANIA exits to open the front door. PAWLINA crosses to the table. In Polish:)* Ummmmm. *Herbatniki!*[1] *(PAWLINA takes a tiny pastry from the pyramid.) Bezy!*[2] *(She swallows it appreciatively and selects another.) Piernik Wyborny!*[3] *(She savors the taste of the teacake.)*

MANIA'S VOICE *(offstage)*. Freidza!

FREIDZA'S VOICE *(offstage)*. Mania!

BOTH VOICES *(offstage)*. You look WONDERFUL!

(FREIDZA and MANIA enter. PAWLINA and FREIDZA look at one another, then embrace.)

FREIDZA. Panna Pawlina.

PAWLINA. Little Freidza. *(They sit.)*

MANIA. Did you have trouble finding the house?

FREIDZA. No. I had a long-distance conference call. A buyer from Tokyo. It's hard with the time difference.

MANIA. Sure.

FREIDZA *(looks at tea table, astonished)*. Mania, who's coming?

MANIA. I want there should be enough. In my house there should be enough.

FREIDZA. If the whole city of Chicago comes, you've got enough. What'd you do, buy out the Polish bakery?

MANIA. I made them! *(Rising.)* Come. It's a long drive.

FREIDZA. Relax. They can't dedicate the park without the star.

---

1 Tea cakes.
2 Similar to a meringue.
3 Similar to a fruitcake.

PAWLINA. Star! I'm not a star. Mania, why such fancy cakes? We only had those at Christmas—or christenings.

MANIA. We wouldn't be here without you. There's no name for what you did.

FREIDZA. There's a name *(Takes newspaper from briefcase.)* Right here on the front page. "Righteous person."

PAWLINA. Freidza, Mania. What does that mean? I only did what was right.

FREIDZA. It means most people didn't.

PAWLINA. You know the proverb. It was my mother's favorite. *(In Polish.)* *Przyjaciel w domu yest bóg w domu.* A guest in the home is God in the home.

FREIDZA *(slowly)*. We weren't exactly guests. And your mother didn't want us. *(Rises.)* No one wanted us. No one in the whole country wanted us.

MANIA. Freidza, it's late. We really should go.

FREIDZA. I remember running through the hayfields trying to hide. It was autumn.

PAWLINA. It was spring, Freidza.

FREIDZA. No. Fall. Harvest time. The hayfields were taller than I was.

PAWLINA. What do you know? You were eight years old.

(Lighting: fades on women as they exit. Sound: Polish folk music. OTHER ACTORS set up haystack and a suggestion of Domicela's house and barn. When the stage is set, a young FREIDZA dashes on anxiously looking around. It is May, 1942. FREIDZA tears off her white armband with the blue Star of David, flings it aside and darts into the haystack. Sound: Rifle shots in the distance, bloodhounds howling.)

ACT ONE
Scene One

SCENE: *A field in rural southeast Poland. It is late after-noon, towards the end of May 1942. At the edge of the field is a high mound of hay. Sound: Distant church bells.*

AT RISE: *PAWLINA sings to herself, filling her apron with wildflowers (poppies, daisies). She crosses to put them in the water pail. Suddenly the haystack moves. PAWLINA stops in her tracks. She crosses herself. A pair of frightened eyes are now visible. Then a hand grabs PAWLINA's skirt. A desperate face follows.*

GOLDA has lost her husband, her home and all that they owned. She has fled from the ghetto with two small children. Her Polish has a Yiddish accent.

GOLDA *(softly)*. Don't be frightened, Panna Pawlina.

PAWLINA *(looks closer)*. Paniusia Schachterova!!!

GOLDA. Sh-h. We escaped.

PAWLINA. From the ghetto?

GOLDA *(nods)*. Freidza's with me too. *(FREIDZA's scared face appears.)*

PAWLINA. Hello, Freidza. Is your husband with...

GOLDA. No. Murdered.

PAWLINA. Oh, my God!

GOLDA. We've been hiding for three days.

PAWLINA. You have to get away from here. It's not safe. *(FREIDZA's face disappears.)*

GOLDA. Nowhere is safe, Panna Pawlina. I have to talk to you.

PAWLINA. It's too dangerous. Someone might see us.

GOLDA. Just keep picking flowers. *(PAWLINA bends down near the haystack and picks wildflowers.)* My baby's going to die if we don't get some water. He's only a few weeks old. Please, just some water.

PAWLINA *(demeanor changes)*. A baby. I didn't know. I didn't see him. *(She reaches down and touches the baby's head in the haystack.)* He's burning up!

GOLDA. Mundek's been like that all day.

PAWLINA *(sings softly)*. Hello, Mundek.

GOLDA. Just some water, Panna Pawlina. Water. Please.

PAWLINA. As soon as it's dark, slip around to the barn. I'll bring you water. And bread. And then, Paniusia Schachterova, go where they don't know you.

GOLDA. Bless you, Panna Pawlina. Bless you. *(Her face disappears. PAWLINA starts to run off forgetting her flowers. She runs back to scoop them up and drops one by the haystack.)*

PAWLINA *(whispers)*. For you, Mundek. *(Haystack is silent.)*

Scene Two

SCENE: *Outside DOMICELA's thatched-roof farmhouse. Twilight.*

AT RISE: *A soldier attaches a notice to the side of the barn. PAWLINA is pumping water. On the ground is a yoke with buckets. Under her apron is a round loaf of dark bread.*

DOMICELA. Why so much water?

PAWLINA. For the animals.

DOMICELA *(looks at her suspiciously)*. One horse! One cow! And there's a bread missing.

PAWLINA *(innocently)*. Maybe a neighbor came in.

DOMICELA. Tadeusz would have told me.

PAWLINA. Was Tadeusz here?

DOMICELA. Repairing the roof. He hung around waiting to see you all afternoon.

PAWLINA. When did he leave?

DOMICELA. When I had to get dinner for your brother and sister. Why were you so late? *(DOMICELA crosses to PAWLINA, pulls the bread from her apron and waits for an explanation.)*

PAWLINA. It's for Paniusia Schachterova...from the next village.

DOMICELA. Are you crazy? What good do you think one loaf of bread will do?

PAWLINA. It's terrible what they're doing...behind that barbed wire fence.

DOMICELA. Who told you to look? When you take the cart to market, go a different way!

PAWLINA. Mamusia! I could hear the women screaming. And then...I saw a baby...at the end...of a bayonet. You wouldn't kill a sick animal like that.

DOMICELA. There's a war going on, Pawlina. Stay away from there. It's not safe. Not with all those soldiers around. For a pretty girl like you, there's worse things than being killed. You can't save Paniusia Schacterova.

PAWLINA *(quietly)*. She's in our barn.

DOMICELA. Mother of God! Do you know what they'll do if they catch you helping a Jew? *(Crosses to poster and reads.)* "Anyone caught helping or hiding Jews will be punished by death." *(PAWLINA doesn't answer.)* They'll shoot you, Pawlina. And then they'll shoot me. And then your brother and sister. And then maybe they'll throw in Krasula the cow for luck!

PAWLINA. What if we were in trouble, Mamusia?

DOMICELA. We're not Jews. We're Poles. Pawlina, I have nothing against Paniusia Schachterova. But it's her neck or mine. Her family or mine.

PAWLINA. Mamusia, you always said we're all the same. In the eyes of God we're all the same.

DOMICELA. It's not his eyes I'm worried about! It's the eyes of those Nazi soldiers. They took most of our food.

PAWLINA. Mundek's so tiny he doesn't eat solid food.

DOMICELA. Who's Mundek?

PAWLINA. Her brand new baby. He's ill.

DOMICELA. Ill! Mother of God, what if he cries? Tiny, sick babies have strong lungs. There's no sure way to keep a baby quiet.

PAWLINA. The Nazis found a way.

DOMICELA. Marry Tadeusz and have your own baby. Forget about this one. *(Sighs.)* To be born into a world like this.

PAWLINA. Mamusia, just let them hide in the barn until he's better.

DOMICELA. No!

PAWLINA. Then at least until they're rested. They're worn out.

DOMICELA. I know you! When you were little you brought in birds with broken wings and fussed over them until they flew. Who else is out there?

PAWLINA. Her little girl, Freidza. Mamusia, she hasn't eaten in three days!

DOMICELA *(pause. Sighs and gives her bread).* Here!
When you milk Krasula, give them half. *(PAWLINA
looks at her still waiting.)* All right, all right. Let them
rest in the barn. Oh my God, I wouldn't want to be in
her shoes with one in her arms and one at her skirt.
(Firmly.) But before sunrise, Pawlina, they go! *(PAWL-
INA kisses her mother. She places the yoke across her
shoulders. Sound: In the distance, soldiers shouting excitedly—in unintelligible German. Howl of bloodhounds.)*

Scene Three

SCENE: *The storage barn that night by the dim light of a
kerosene lamp.*

AT RISE: *GOLDA, the baby MUNDEK and FREIDZA are
visible. PAWLINA ladles milk from the pail into earth-
enware cups. FREIDZA gulps hers down.*

PAWLINA. I told Krasula the milk was for you. *(Gives
her more.)*
FREIDZA *(impressed).* Can you talk to Krasula?
PAWLINA. I sing to her. She understands.
FREIDZA. Could you teach me how to milk her?
PAWLINA *(uncomfortably to GOLDA).* My mother says
you have to leave.
GOLDA *(startled).* When?
PAWLINA. Before dawn. So the neighbors don't see.
GOLDA. But the baby's still sick.
PAWLINA. I'll give you some food to take with you.

GOLDA *(distraught)*. Where can we go? How many hay-stacks can we hide in?

PAWLINA. There are so many people around at planting time. She's afraid they'll hear the baby cry. And the German police are everywhere.

GOLDA. Hunting for Jews! Panna Pawlina, I want to save my children! Help me! Please help me! *(Sound: MUN-DEK wakes up and starts to cry.)* Sh-h! Sh-h! *(Instantly GOLDA sings a Yiddish song softly, MUNDEK quiets down.)* If he starts to cry, I'll sing to him. He won't make a sound.

PAWLINA *(quoting)*. We're a poor family, Paniusia Schachterova. There's no food.

GOLDA *(interrupts)*. But we'll pay for our food and pay you to stay! My husband—*(Starts to cry.)* they beat him up. With clubs. The men who used to work for him in the wheat fields. They beat him up and left him in a ditch to die. And when I found him, I couldn't recognize his face. The police just laughed. But once upon a time, Panna Pawlina, we were respected people in the village.

PAWLINA. I know.

GOLDA. Just before the Nazis took our home, my husband buried my jewelry in the garden. He hid our silver tea service up in the attic. Panna Pawlina, it's all yours if you'll let us stay. *(PAWLINA doesn't answer.)* Freidza, you remember where Tateh hid everything, don't you? *(FREIDZA nods.)* I don't dare leave Mundek alone. But Freidza, you could show Panna Pawlina where we hid our valuables.

PAWLINA *(tries to explain)*. My mother's frightened.

GOLDA. Who isn't? Night and day I'm frightened. But one day this war will end and God will bless you. What good are all my things? It's the children that matter! *(PAWLINA thinks. GOLDA removes MUNDEK's diaper and from the seam removes a gold bracelet. Puts it on PAWLINA's wrist.)* Here. My husband gave me this gold bracelet when Mundek was born. Now, maybe it can keep him alive.

PAWLINA *(hesitates)*. It's beautiful!

GOLDA. Wear it, Panna Pawlina. Or sell it. But let us stay here.

PAWLINA. For how long?

GOLDA. How long can this war last? Three weeks? Two months at the most. Just keep us here until it's over, and you can have all that I own.

PAWLINA. I'd like to help you, but...

GOLDA *(distraught)*. My husband murdered, my house taken, my baby ill. What's next?

FREIDZA. I'm here, Mameh.

GOLDA *(hugs her)*. Yes! Yes! *(Sound: MUNDEK starts to fret.)*

PAWLINA *(picking up baby)*. Sh-h, Mundek. Sh-h. *(PAWLINA softly sings a Polish lullaby. Instantly the baby is quiet, transfixed.)* Oh, so you like Polish singing too! *(GOLDA watches.)*

GOLDA. Go. Go now. Take everything you can. We gave some neighbors our best winter clothes. They promised to keep them safe. Panna Pawlina, you can give your mother my fur coat.

PAWLINA. No! Wherever you are, you'll need it.

GOLDA. Ask her again. Please. We could hide in your barn. There's room.

PAWLINA. I want to help you, Paniusia Schachterova; but my mother said you had to leave. It's a terrible risk.

GOLDA. Maybe if you tell her we can pay, she'll change her mind. Try.

PAWLINA *(looks down at MUNDEK sleeping in her arms)*. Look, Paniusia Schachterova! He's sleeping quietly now. And there's a little tiny smile. He's getting better.

GOLDA. Panna Pawlina, our lives are in your hands!

PAWLINA *(struggling)*. I don't want to hurt anyone. Not you. Or me. Or my family.

GOLDA. We could dig a hole.

FREIDZA. And cover it up with straw.

PAWLINA *(crosses thoughtfully with MUNDEK still in her arms to place where bunker will be)*. Maybe...a bunker...

FREIDZA. No one will ever know we're here.

GOLDA. Hide us. Please. Don't send us out there to die! *(Sound: MUNDEK whimpers.)*

PAWLINA *(kisses him)*. Sh-h-h. *(Hums refrain. LIGHTS: fade.)*

Scene Four

SCENE: *A wooded area near HANKA's thatched-roof farm. A moonless night.*

AT RISE: *PAWLINA and FREIDZA are cutting through the woods.*

FREIDZA. Why are we going this way?

PAWLINA. Better to stay off the road.

FREIDZA. I never saw my house like that, all empty. They took everything. Everything except the staircase.

PAWLINA. We were too late, Freidza.

FREIDZA. But Tateh said no one would ever find Mameh's jewelry. I helped him cover the hole with grass and leaves. When we were done, you couldn't tell it was there.

PAWLINA. Somebody dug up the whole garden.

FREIDZA. Even my rose bush. I planted it all by myself. In the ghetto—(*PAWLINA covers FREIDZA's mouth. FREIDZA whispers.*) We couldn't have flowers. Mameh's going to blame me. She'll say that I didn't hunt hard enough.

PAWLINA. I'll tell her we both hunted. Now let's get the clothes. You can't spend a Polish winter in a summer dress!

FREIDZA. Will you go to the door with me?

PAWLINA. No. You have to go alone.

FREIDZA. You're not supposed to help us, are you?

PAWLINA. That's what the Nazis say. (*Sound: Owl hooting. Night wind in the trees.*)

FREIDZA. Can you hold my hand until we get there?

PAWLINA (*holds her hand*). Just tell them that your mother sent you to collect the clothes she left, that she needs them. That's all. Don't tell them anything else.

FREIDZA. Some kids smuggled food in, sugar and flour, and one boy, littler than me, he brought in two eggs. He climbed the wall with two eggs, and the guards never caught him. (*They approach the door to the thatched-roof farm.*)

PAWLINA. I'll wait for you in the woods over there. Go on.

(*PAWLINA pushes her gently. FREIDZA knocks timidly at the door. Then boldly, she knocks louder. HANKA, a stern-faced farm woman answers the door peering out into the night. She looks down and sees FREIDZA.)*

HANKA. Jesus, Maria! Will you look who's here. I thought you were ... Well, what is it?

FREIDZA. I came for my mother's things.

HANKA. What things?

FREIDZA. Our clothes. The two wool dresses, her black fur coat and my rabbit muff.

HANKA. What are you talking about?

FREIDZA *(insisting and taking a step in)*. We need our clothes. She sent me.

HANKA *(slaps her face)*. It's against the law to keep Jewish property. *(Calls.)* Henryk.

(A huge man stands in the doorway.)

HANKA. The little Jew wants her rabbit muff! She says her mother left a fur coat with us.

FREIDZA. She did! She did! I know she did.

HENRYK *(removing his leather belt)*. When children lie, there's only one way to cure them. *(Whacks her.)*

FREIDZA. I'm not lying! She sent me! *(Sound: Offstage, German soldiers marching and chanting.)*

HENRYK *(calls)*. Hey, over here! Here's a Jewish brat! *(Sound: Soldiers continue singing. HANKA has a firm hand on FREIDZA.)*

HANKA. Get them, I'll hold her.

HENRYK *(hollering)*. Hey, over here. Come over here. *(Exits.)*

(FREIDZA kicks HANKA hard. In surprise, HANKA lets go. FREIDZA flees to the woods. HENRYK reenters with the SOLDIERS.)

HANKA *(points)*. That way. Hurry!

LUTHER. Halte! *(Sound: A shot rings out in the air.)*

OTTO. Halte! *(Sound: Another shot. FREIDZA hides, crouching under a tree trunk in the woods. In the dark, the SOLDIERS run right over the tree trunk.)*

LUTHER. Halte! *(Sound: Another shot. FREIDZA is terrified.)*

HENRYK. Why didn't you hold her?

HANKA. Why didn't you come faster?

HENRYK. They need a higher fence around that ghetto!

HANKA. We lost the money, Henryk. Fifty zlotys. Even if they do catch her, we won't get it now.

PAWLINA *(whispers)*. Freidza. Quick. We'll cut through the birch trees. *(FREIDZA crawls to meet PAWLINA.)*

FREIDZA. Panna Pawlina, are you going to kick us out now? *(Lighting: There is moonlight on them both. PAWLINA wipes away a tear on FREIDZA's face. Pause. PAWLINA takes FREIDZA's hand and they dart through the trees, alert to any sound.)*

Scene Five

SCENE: *Domicela's kitchen. The next day.*

AT RISE: *DOMICELA is sweeping. PAWLINA is at the table kneading bread dough.*

DOMICELA. No! I said one night, and now it's the next day. We can't have her here. I have two little ones.

PAWLINA. So does she! What if you were being hunted and killed?

DOMICELA. If they stay here, we will be! The only way a Pole survives is to stay out of the enemy's way, plant your potatoes and keep your mouth shut.

PAWLINA. No one will know. We can dig a bunker. Tonight.

DOMICELA. No.

PAWLINA. Tadeusz will help.

DOMICELA. Tell them to go somewhere else. Let someone else hide them. They can do it better than we can.

PAWLINA. Who, Mamusia? Her old neighbors told the soldiers to shoot. To shoot a child!

DOMICELA. If the moon had been out, the soldiers would have shot you too!

PAWLINA. Please, Mamusia.

DOMICELA. Take them some food, and send them away. Tell them that's all we can do. (*PAWLINA doesn't move.*) Fast! Go!

PAWLINA. I can't. Mamusia, they didn't do anything wrong. They're not criminals.

DOMICELA. They're Jews. That's enough. For the Nazis that's more than enough.

PAWLINA. Mamusia, they're people!!

DOMICELA. So are we!

PAWLINA. She has such a sweet baby. He smiles when I sing Polish to him. Just let them stay until he's better. (*Slowly brings out bracelet.*) Paniusia Schachterova gave me this bracelet, Mamusia, to pay us.

DOMICELA (*astonished, bites it*). Gold! Pawlina, this is real gold. Do you know what I could buy with this?

(*Pause.*) Give it back. If I try to use that, fifteen soldiers will be firing questions at me and then their rifles.

PAWLINA. Then I'll give it to Tadeusz. He'll know what to do. One week, Mamusia. Maybe then the war will be over.

DOMICELA. Maybe then Krasula the cow will talk! Why is it so important?

PAWLINA. Because I keep thinking what if it were you and me? And Jurek and Bronia? (*Pause.*)

DOMICELA (*decides*). Leave your brother and sister out of this. They're too young. They'll talk.

PAWLINA. Mamusia!!

DOMICELA. Just until the baby's strong enough to travel.

PAWLINA (*hugs her*). Oh, Mamusia, thank you. Thank you.

DOMICELA. Pawlina, I don't want to see them. I don't want to hear them. I don't want anything to do with them. If the German soldiers come knocking at the door, I don't want to know anything about it.

PAWLINA (*hugs her*). You won't even know they're here! I promise!

DOMICELA. Yesterday I saw the captain wipe his boots on the Polish flag. (*Spits in disgust.*) When the mushroom season starts, we'll send him a basket—some of those large, shiny ones that look so good. (*Winks at PAWLINA.*)

PAWLINA. The poisonous ones?

DOMICELA (*presenting an imaginary basket*). A little present from the Polish people! (*They laugh.*) As for that family out there, you're on your own! (*DOMICELA exits and returns a few seconds later with precious flour, which she plunks down on the table.*)

Here's the last of the flour. You better bake another bread!

Scene Six

SCENE: *The storage barn, just before dawn. The next day. There are mounds of fresh earth. In the background are piles of hay.*

AT RISE: *TADEUSZ and PAWLINA finish digging out a narrow bunker. They have been working all night. Sound: The shovels hitting the dirt. TADEUSZ smooths the sides with his shovel, checks their work and then gestures to PAWLINA to bring the fugitives out. PAWLINA leads the frightened FUGITIVES from the haystacks to the bunker, where there is only enough room to sit in a row. TADEUSZ and PAWLINA help them climb in. They stare out terrified, as TADEUSZ and PAWLINA cover the opening with straw.*

FREIDZA. Mameh!!

GOLDA. Sh-h. (*PAWLINA and TADEUSZ complete the camouflage. Exhausted PAWLINA sinks to the ground. TADEUSZ lifts her up. Wearily they start loading the earth into baskets.*)

TADEUSZ (*low voice*). We've got to get rid of it now, before the sun comes up.

PAWLINA (*low voice*). I didn't think it would take all night. I'm so tired, Tadeusz, I could fall asleep standing up.

TADEUSZ. Me too. Remember not too much dirt in any one place. Hurry, Pawlina.

PAWLINA. Can we go together?

TADEUSZ. No. Better not. *(Kisses her cheek.)* The Underground could take lessons from you.

(TADEUSZ exits with a basket of earth. PAWLINA struggles with a heavy basket of earth and lumbers out with her load. Sound: Music to indicate passage of time. PAWLINA brings in MANIA. MANIA has just escaped from the ghetto. Her blonde hair is in two braids worn down the front, fastened with two small ribbons at the bottom. PAWLINA helps others out of bunker to stretch.)

PAWLINA *(introducing her)*. Mania, this is Paniusia Schacterova and her daughter, Freidza.

GOLDA *(Yiddish)*. A gezunt af dir. [Translation. Health be unto you that you're with us.] *(GOLDA hugs her. MANIA doesn't answer.)* You don't speak Yiddish?

MANIA *(proudly)*. We only spoke Polish at home, and I went to a Polish school.

GOLDA *(suspicious)*. What kind of Jewish girl doesn't speak any Yiddish?

MANIA *(admits)*. I understand it.

GOLDA. You look like a little Polish girl. Such pretty hair.

MANIA. My sister Regina's hair was beautiful. It was so long, she could sit on it. She looked just like a painting before... *(Cries.)* They "liquidated" her section yesterday.

FREIDZA *(wanting attention)*. Do you have a brother? *(Pause.)*

MANIA. I used to, Freidza. A little brother. Then they said, "We can't feed little children who can't do anything." They took their rifles... they made us watch.

GOLDA (*a deep sigh. Yiddish*). *Oy vay.* When does it stop? (*Shakes her head. FREIDZA, jealous, brings MUNDEK over.*)

FREIDZA. I have a little brother. His name is Mundek. (*MANIA reaches out to touch him and FREIDZA pulls him away.*) You can't touch him. He's *my* brother.

GOLDA. Freidza!

FREIDZA. It's our hiding place. We were here first. Panna Pawlina, how long have we been here?

PAWLINA. A month.

FREIDZA (*whispers subversively to MANIA*). Panna Pawlina can kick you out too.

PAWLINA. Shake hands, right now, and say you're sorry. (*They shake hands and FREIDZA mumbles that she is sorry.*) That's better. (*Brings bucket over.*) I've brought you dinner—potatoes and milk. (*Gives bowl to MANIA first, who devours it. GOLDA and FREIDZA take food.*) I'll bring you food whenever I can. But if the Nazis ever catch you, swear you never saw me. You don't even know what I look like. Say you found this empty storage barn and hid here. Promise?

MANIA (*nods*). I promise.

GOLDA. I promise.

FREIDZA. I'll never tell them anything.

PAWLINA. And if I see them coming anywhere near you, I'll yell my brother's name twice.

MANIA. What's his name?

PAWLINA. Jurek.

FREIDZA (*to MANIA*). How'd you escape?

MANIA. Yesterday, I woke up early. I don't know why. When I peeked out the window, it was still dark; but I saw hundreds of soldiers. They were very quiet like they were waiting for something. I knew something aw-

ful was going to happen. *(Shows amber ring.)* My
mother gave me this. A year ago. She said, "Amber
protects you." So, I crawled through a secret hole in the
attic, and then I lay down and inched along the roof
gutters, until I reached the other side. I was so scared
I'd fall, so scared they'd shoot me. But it was dark, and
the soldiers never saw me.

FREIDZA *(mesmerized)*. It was the amber ring. Can I try
it on?

MANIA. Just for a minute.

FREIDZA *(puts ring on)*. It looks like firelight. Is it really
magic?

MANIA *(shakes her head)*. Some people say so. On the
first day of school Regina would always say, "Every
bead of my amber necklace is a different story." When
the children were good, she'd tell them one. She
was ... such ... a ... good ... teacher. *(Cries inconsolably.
PAWLINA puts an arm around her.)*

FREIDZA *(solemnly returns the ring)*. If I'm good, will
you tell me one of her stories? *(MANIA nods.)* What
happened to the necklace?

MANIA. Our maid took it. She said, "Now I'll be something; and you'll be nothing." She had Regina's necklace on and a meat cleaver in her hand. When my
mother couldn't get her wedding band off, she lifted the
cleaver up in the air and screamed, "Get it off or I'll
use this."

FREIDZA. How come she didn't take the amber ring?

MANIA. It was lost. But it was in my pocket the whole
time.

FREIDZA. See, it did save you. *(PAWLINA has helped
them all back into the bunker.)*

GOLDA (*crosses to MANIA*). Mania, from now on, you'll be with us. Whatever happens...will happen to all of us. (*They stare into the dark.*)

Scene Seven

SCENE: *The kitchen, Domicela's farmhouse. Mid-June 1943, the day of the Corpus Christi celebration. There is a hallway and a ladder that leads to the attic.*

AT RISE: *PAWLINA is singing as she arranges spring leaves on the mantle of the stove, decorating for Corpus Christi Day. On the table are bottles of vodka, mineral water, tumblers, and a plate of Polish sausage. She removes a freshly-baked bread from the baking compartment of their old wood-burning stove and sets it and a sharp knife on the table. DOMICELA rushes in.*

DOMICELA. I see them. They're coming here. I told you this would happen. Leave that and get out of here.

PAWLINA. Here! You're sure?

DOMICELA. I sent your brother and sister on ahead. Hurry, Pawlina. It's that baby!

PAWLINA. Mamusia, they've been here over a year. No one knows. Let me think.

DOMICELA. There's no time.

PAWLINA. We have to warn them!

DOMICELA. Soldiers, Pawlina!

PAWLINA (*points to attic*). Oh, God, the baby's diapers are up there drying.

DOMICELA. I'm going!

PAWLINA. Mamusia, when you run past the barn, yell Jurek's name—twice. They'll understand.

(DOMICELA exits. PAWLINA grabs her broom and rushes to the ladder and scrambles up. Sound: Soldiers knocking at the door. They knock again, insistently. PAWLINA scrambles down, as the door opens and two German SOLDIERS enter. BRUNO and ERNST, the captain. Both speak with a slight German accent.)

ERNST. When you deal with these Polish pigs, use your rifle. Either end, Bruno. Either end.

BRUNO *(spies PAWLINA's comely legs coming down the ladder)*. Do I have your permission, Captain.

ERNST *(claps him on the shoulder)*. We didn't teach you Polish to play with the ladies.

BRUNO *(slyly)*. But the Führer wants children too. *(They laugh.)*

ERNST. Either women or drink will be your downfall, Bruno.

BRUNO *(too familiar)*. But a pleasant way to go, Herr Captain. A pleasant way to go.

ERNST *(sternly)*. Do your job first. For the Führer and the fatherland. I'll look outside. Heil Hitler. *(Gives Nazi salute.)*

BRUNO. Heil Hitler. *(Returns salute. ERNST exits. Sound: In the distance DOMICELA yells, "Jurek! Jurek!")*

PAWLINA *(all smiles and charm)*. Your friend is leaving?

BRUNO. He'll be back. What were you doing up there?

PAWLINA *(holding broom)*. What do you think? Sweeping. My mother told me to.

BRUNO *(alert)*. Where is she now?

PAWLINA. At church. It's Corpus Christi Day. Didn't you know?

BRUNO. Why aren't you there?

PAWLINA. I've got one more loaf of bread in the oven. *(With an ingratiating smile.)* And now there's a handsome soldier in my kitchen.

BRUNO *(poking her with his rifle but not very hard).* You're hiding Jews, aren't you?

PAWLINA. Jews! Are you kidding? There aren't any left! They took them all to the city and killed them. *(BRUNO is appraising her. PAWLINA points to his rifle.)* That could go off and ruin my bread. Sit down and have some vodka. It's a holiday. *(BRUNO is torn.)*

BRUNO. I'm going up that ladder.

PAWLINA. There's nothing up there but spiders.

BRUNO. I'll look for myself... *(Looking at PAWLINA.)* in a minute.

PAWLINA *(flirts).* You're a good-looking soldier. *(Tosses her long blond hair.)* Or maybe it's just the uniform.

BRUNO *(grabs her).* Or maybe it isn't. We could find out.

PAWLINA. What would your girlfriend back home say?

BRUNO *(a wave of homesickness).* You look almost like a German fräulein... with that long blond hair.

PAWLINA. Why don't you put your rifle down. Have some vodka.

BRUNO. I'm on duty. If you're hiding anyone, they'll hang you.

PAWLINA *(lightly).* It's too hot a day to talk about hanging.

BRUNO. In Germany we drink beer on a day like this. *(Sits down, nostalgic.)* A tall stein of beer.

PAWLINA. You're in Poland now. *(Pours two glasses.)* Here! Polish men drink it in one gulp. But Polish men are pretty strong.

BRUNO. So am I. *(They clink glasses and toast each other. The drink hits him.)* What kind of vodka is this?

PAWLINA. The best. Homemade. Invite your friend. *(PAWLINA pours him more and gives it to him. They toast each other again. BRUNO is getting warmer, puts his rifle down and opens his collar.)*

BRUNO. On a day like this, we'd sit in the beer garden and eat sausages and dance the polka. *(BRUNO bangs the table and hums a polka tune. PAWLINA passes him the small plate of sausage.)*

PAWLINA. This is kielbasa, Polish sausage. Try it.

BRUNO *(tasting it)*. Not as good. But it'll do. It'll do. *(He eats all that's there, while PAWLINA refills his glass with vodka. BRUNO downs it. She takes mineral water.)*

PAWLINA. There'll be plenty of dancing tonight. A handsome man like you won't have any problem finding girls to dance the polka with. *(PAWLINA pours more vodka. BRUNO notices her empty glass.)*

BRUNO *(thickly)*. You have some more too. I'll teach you how we do the German polka and maybe a few other things. *(Laughs and puts an arm around her.)* What's your name?

PAWLINA. Pawlina.

BRUNO. I'm Bruno. *(Pours himself more vodka and refills her glass.)* To my Polish Pawlina!

PAWLINA. Careful, that's strong stuff, if you're not used to it.

BRUNO *(drunk)*. I'm a strong man. Pawlina, Pawlina, pretty soon you'll find out just how strong I am.

(ERNST enters.)

ERNST. Heil Hitler! *(Gives Nazi salute.)*

BRUNO *(struggles to his feet)*. Heil Hitler! *(Returns salute. The cordial, drunken host.)* We're having a party. This is Pawlina. My Polish Pawlina. Give him some vodka, *liebchen.*

ERNST *(smashes BRUNO's glass to the ground)*. You're a disgrace. Get drunk on your own time. And with a German girl, not a Pole.

BRUNO. She's very nice. Pawlina's very nice, Herr Captain.

ERNST. I've done the outside. All the haystacks. They crawl in there sometimes. Did you check the house— before you started drinking?

BRUNO. Sure I did. There's no one here. It's...What's the name of that holiday again?

PAWLINA. Corpus Christi Day.

BRUNO. It's one of their holidays. Her mother's out. C'mon, Captain. I'm going to teach her the German polka.

ERNST *(walks into hallway)*. Where's that ladder go?

BRUNO. Upstairs! *(Laughing at his own joke.)*

ERNST. Bruno! Get over here.

BRUNO. I'll be back, Pawlina. Don't go away. *(BRUNO, with difficulty, starts up the ladder. PAWLINA crosses, ready to crash it.)*

ERNST. Stand back. That's an order.

PAWLINA. I was just going to hold it steady. It's rickety.

ERNST *(with disgust)*. You Poles don't know how to do anything right. Not even how to build a ladder. *(PAWLINA starts to hold it. ERNST strikes her arm off.)* Leave it alone. *(Pause, while BRUNO drunkenly searches.)*

BRUNO. Nothing up here, Captain. Ow! Nothing but spiders. *(BRUNO comes down nursing a finger.)* One bit me. What do you feed those spiders.

PAWLINA. Polish vodka!

BRUNO. Polish vodka! *(Laughing at her joke.)* Polish vodka! You and I are going to get along just fine!

ERNST. You're going back to the barracks. *(ERNST roughly pushes BRUNO out the door.)*

BRUNO. See you later, Pawlina.

(BRUNO and ERNST leave. PAWLINA sinks into a chair overwhelmed by the narrow escape. Sound: TADEUSZ whistling the same song PAWLINA was singing earlier. TADEUSZ knocks and enters.)

TADEUSZ. Pawlina? *(PAWLINA rushes towards him.)*

PAWLINA. They were here!

TADEUSZ. Is everyone all right?

PAWLINA. I don't know yet. *(PAWLINA is trembling. TADEUSZ holds her.)* I'm frightened. Tadeusz, I'm frightened. What if they come again? What if next time we're not so lucky? I thought I could protect them. But now ... I'm not so sure. What if I can't go through with it? What if in the end ... Tadeusz, I'm frightened!!

TADEUSZ *(calming her)*. I'll stay with you.

PAWLINA. No. No! I have to check the barn.

TADEUSZ *(crosses to the door)*. I left some tools in the barn anyway. You wait here.

(TADEUSZ exits. Momentary silence, then ... Sound: A shot. PAWLINA screams. ERNST and BRUNO reenter with TADEUSZ, who is holding his arm in pain.)

ERNST. I thought we'd picked up all the young Polish pigs. Looks like we missed one.

PAWLINA. No! He didn't do anything!

ERNST. Ah, the boyfriend! *(BRUNO rises and gets his rifle. Looks at table.)* You see, Bruno, you never learn. You're not very observant. And you thought the party was for you. *(To TADEUSZ.)* Put your hands up! *(TADEUSZ hesitates.)* Bruno! *(BRUNO kicks him. When TADEUSZ rises, he puts his hands over his head.)* That's better. When you get to Germany you'll learn how to do what you're told without even thinking.

TADEUSZ. But it takes two Germans to stop one Pole!

ERNST. Bruno! *(BRUNO kicks him again. TADEUSZ groans. He staggers, and they force him up. He is dazed. BRUNO and ERNST push TADEUSZ to the door, a gun at his ear and a gun at his back.)*

PAWLINA *(frantic)*. Where are you taking him?

ERNST *(turns and gives a mock bow)*. Don't worry, fräulein. We take good care of our Polish workers.

BRUNO *(a drunken grin)*. Because they're all volunteers. *(They exit. PAWLINA stands by the kitchen table for a second, stunned, then collapses.)*

Scene Eight

SCENE: *The bunker at night, March 1944.*

AT RISE: *GOLDA, FREIDZA, and MANIA sit in a row, all facing the same way. There is no room to stand. It is dark. MUNDEK is asleep beside GOLDA.*

FREIDZA. Move over. I can't breathe.

MANIA. Freidza, there's no place to move. You're grow-ing, that's all.

FREIDZA. Mameh, look at all the room Mania has.

MANIA. Baby! Do you have to complain to your mother about every little thing?

FREIDZA. My mother's still alive! *(MANIA grieves for her family.)* Made you cry! Made you cry!

GOLDA *(in Yiddish)*. Shah! Quiet! The two of you.

MANIA. A year and a half in a dirt hole. Like we've been buried. Buried alive.

GOLDA. It's the same for all of us.

MANIA. But you have each other! You have each other! *(Cries.)*

FREIDZA. And she called me a baby.

GOLDA. Freidza, Mania is like a sister now. You must be nice to her.

FREIDZA. No, she's not. I don't want a sister. And tell her to be nice to me.

GOLDA *(to MANIA)*. Try to set a good example.

MANIA. It's spring and I want to see the sunlight. I want to walk along the river. I want to smell fresh air. The air in here is putrid.

FREIDZA. What's "putrid."

MANIA. Go look it up.

FREIDZA *(wistfully)*. I wish I had a book. Any book. *(Forgets argument and snuggles up.)* Tell me a story, Mania.

MANIA. About what?

FREIDZA. Something happy.

MANIA *(quietly)*. I don't know about anything happy.

FREIDZA. Make it up then.

MANIA. Once there was a place where you could eat all you wanted. The table was piled with...chicken...and wild strawberries...

GOLDA *(joining in)*. And loaves of fresh-baked *challah*.

FREIDZA. And black currant jam. *(Pause.)* Mameh, I'm so hungry!

GOLDA. Every day we wait is another day we're alive. Praise God.

MANIA. I don't believe in God any longer.

GOLDA. You don't mean that.

MANIA. Where was God when they shot my brother? Where was God when they shot my sister? Where was God when they shot my mother and father? Where was He then? Where was He?

GOLDA. I'm not going to listen to this anymore. *(GOLDA rearranges them, and it is very difficult in the cramped quarters.)* Mania, sit there. Freidza, sit there. Now, not another word until after dinner.

FREIDZA. Dinner! How can you call a half a slice of bread dinner?

GOLDA *(slaps her hand)*. Be grateful for what you get.

MANIA. Mundek can have mine. I'm not hungry.

FREIDZA. Can I have part?

GOLDA. No. Mania, you can't stop eating. You need your strength.

MANIA. For what? To die? *(Sound: MUNDEK starts to scream. GOLDA tries to soothe him but can't. MANIA sobs.)* Shut him up! Shut him up! *(Strikes MUNDEK.)* Shut up!

(Sound: MUNDEK wails at being hit. PAWLINA, entering with bucket and small kerosene lamp, has raised the straw on the above.)

PAWLINA. Give him to me. *(PAWLINA takes MUNDEK and rubs his mouth with a rag, tickles him, plays with him. MUNDEK is quiet.)*

GOLDA. What did you do?

PAWLINA. A little homemade vodka.

GOLDA. To a baby. You want to kill him?

PAWLINA. Just the pain. *(Examines MUNDEK's mouth.)* That's what I did when Jurek got his back molars. *(To MANIA.)* He's only crying because it hurts. *(She gives the baby back to GOLDA and helps them out of bunker.)* I've got some clean clothes here. I washed them last night.

GOLDA. Thank you, Pawlina. Thank you. *(They take clothes.)*

PAWLINA *(teasing)*. Freidza, you have to stop growing or your skirt will be way above your knees.

FREIDZA *(looks at food bucket)*. What did you bring?

PAWLINA. Some boiled potatoes with milk. And a chunk of bread. It's all we had.

GOLDA. We'll divide. *(GOLDA and FREIDZA eat.)* Bless you, Panna Pawlina.

MANIA. What's it like outside?

PAWLINA *(to MANIA)*. The snow's melting. And I saw a crocus in the meadow. *(To GOLDA.)* They say the Russians are beating the Germans. They'll be here by summer.

GOLDA. Did you hear that, Mania?

MANIA. I can't wait that long. I've got to get some fresh air, Panna Pawlina. Let me go to the meadow with you tomorrow.

PAWLINA. You know you can't.

MANIA. Just ten minutes. Before everyone's up. I just want to stand up straight and walk outside like a human being. I want to know I'm still a human being.

PAWLINA. Have some potatoes.

MANIA. I don't want any. I want to get out of here. I dream about the sun, sunlight on the mountain peaks, sunlight in our garden. *(Crying.)* Mama had roses.

FREIDZA. They killed our garden.

MANIA. I want to see the sun again before I die.

GOLDA *(in a low voice to PAWLINA)*. I never thought we'd be here this long.

PAWLINA. Neither did I. It's too crowded, Golda. Freidza's growing. Mundek needs to walk. Mania's a young lady.

GOLDA. Children grow in spite of everything.

PAWLINA *(crosses to MANIA. Tries to feed her)*. Eat, Mania.

MANIA. Do you know what it's like to be in the dark all the time? So dark you can't even see your fingers? And when you bring the kerosene lamp for ten minutes and leave, it's worse; because then it goes all dark again. It's always night. A night that never ends. I don't want to hide any longer. *(Sobs.)* Let them shoot me too.

PAWLINA. No! You've survived this long. Just a little longer. You have to be brave, Mania. Brave!

MANIA *(softly)*. Just to see the sun.

PAWLINA. I couldn't take you out, Mania, not even for a minute, unless you knew all the prayers.

MANIA *(eagerly)*. Which prayers?

PAWLINA. The Our Father, the Hail Mary, the Rosary of the Blessed Virgin and the Apostles's Creed. Every Catholic girl knows those by heart. And any soldier could ask.

MANIA. I could learn them! I won a prize once at school for reciting poetry.

PAWLINA. These are much harder.

MANIA. Why?

PAWLINA. They're all in Latin. But I have an idea, Mania. A way to give you all more room, Golda. It'll take some time. Some planning. But by spring, Mania, if you can learn those prayers, you'll see the sun!

ACT TWO
Scene One

SCENE: *The storage barn and bunker. May 1944. Two months later.*

AT RISE: *PAWLINA is outfitting MANIA to look like a Polish country girl (blouse, long skirt, apron, bare feet, hair in long braids wound around her head. PAWLINA places large cross around MANIA's neck. MANIA recites Pater Nostra in Latin.*

MANIA.	(Translation)
Panem nostrum quotidianum da nobis hodie et	Give us this day our daily bread.
dimette nobis debita nostra, sicut et nos dimittimus debitoribus nostris	And forgive us our trespasses, As we forgive those who trespass against us
Et ne non inducas in tentationem.	And lead us not into temptation.
Amen.	

PAWLINA *(corrects her)*. You forgot the last line. *"Sed libera nos a malo."* Then, Amen.

MANIA *(repeats correctly)*. *Sed libera nos a malo.* What does that mean?

PAWLINA. Deliver us from evil. Remember to cross yourself a lot too. Like this. *(Demonstrates touching with the three fingers of right hand, the forehead, heart, left shoulder, right shoulder. MANIA repeats.)* It's little things like that that could give you away. Now here are your papers, put them in your pocket.

MANIA *(reads)*. Cecylia Kozlowski.

PAWLINA. She died three months ago.

MANIA *(frightened)*. What if they know that?

PAWLINA. The church records burned in a fire. They can't check. It wasn't easy to get.

MANIA *(whirls around)*. OUTSIDE! I'm going outside. Thank you, Panna Pawlina. Thank you.

PAWLINA. You can thank me by not doing anything foolish.

MANIA. What do you mean?

PAWLINA. Don't look frightened. Walk with your head up, straight back, walk as if you worked in the fields. A country girl walks like this. *(There is a slight sway to her walk.)* Her feet are tough. Let's see you. *(MANIA walks.)* Too much of the city in that. Swing your arms. And talk back to them.

MANIA. Talk back to them! Are you sure?

PAWLINA. Sure I'm sure. A farm girl would.

MANIA. You'll be with me, won't you?

PAWLINA. Yes. But you have to know what to do in case. I wish you weren't so pale.

MANIA. In case of what?

PAWLINA. Trouble. Any kind of trouble.

MANIA. Why do you have to work for the Germans?

PAWLINA. There's no choice. They took all the young Polish men to Germany. The women they've kept here. But it's still the same. Forced labor.

MANIA. Where are we going?

PAWLINA. Zoborow. A kommandant's home.

MANIA. You mean a home they took over?

PAWLINA. Probably.

MANIA. A Jewish home?

PAWLINA. I don't know. I haven't seen it. We'll go through the woods, so you can drink in the fresh air. Remember you're a cousin on my mother's side. They haven't seen you before, because you just came. What's your new name?

MANIA. Panna Pawlina, couldn't I just go outside without all this fuss?

PAWLINA. Mania, if you want to go out, the safest place in the world is right under the enemy's nose. A Jewish girl would never be working for Nazis! But if the soldiers see a pretty face they haven't seen before, a girl who says she's just out for a walk, they'll be suspicious. Now do you want to go out or not?

MANIA. Yes! What are we going to do there? Cook?

PAWLINA. Clean. His wife is coming, and he wants it spotless by tonight, so I said I needed help and I'd bring my cousin.

MANIA. Did you say clean?

PAWLINA. Yes. Clean. Sweep, mop, dust, scrub the floors, wash the windows, beat the rugs. Whatever has to be done, we'll do.

MANIA (*as they exit*). But Pawlina, I've never cleaned before!

PAWLINA. It's easy. I can't show you here; but when we get there, I'll explain everything. *(Reassuring her.)* Don't worry. If my little sister Bronia can clean, so can you. That part's simple!

Scene Two

SCENE: *The storage barn and bunker, late June 1944.*

AT RISE: *GOLDA is talking to MANIA in the bunker. FREIDZA is listening.*

GOLDA *(in Yiddish). Meshugenah!* Crazy! That's what you are. You had to have fresh air and sunshine! Now the whole German army is hunting for Cecylia Kozlowski.

FREIDZA. I wouldn't try to go clean a house, if I didn't know how.

GOLDA. We're all in trouble because of you. You couldn't leave well enough alone.

MANIA. It was Panna Pawlina's idea too. She got the papers.

GOLDA. You can't stay here any longer. You're crazy. *(In Yiddish.) Meshugenah.* Get out!

MANIA. You can't throw me out. It's not your home.

FREIDZA. We were here first. Me and Mameh and Mundek.

MANIA. And what about Mundek. All this time I was terrified someone would hear him scream. And I never complained, did I?

FREIDZA. Not much. I don't want to die because of you. I'd like to see sunshine too. I'd like to run in the park and swim in the river. I'd like to go to school. I'd like to do a lot of things, if we ever get out. And now you've ruined it.

GOLDA. Go.

MANIA. Where? I don't know anyone. My family's gone. Where am I supposed to go?

GOLDA. Go wherever your eyes take you.

MANIA. I'll do what Panna Pawlina tells me to do.

(PAWLINA enters with food, clothes, lifts bunker cover and brings MANIA out.)

PAWLINA. Bruno was just here. They're suspicious. It's over, Mania. They're looking for *you*. But, if you can get to the Russians, you'll be safe.

GOLDA. How close are they?

PAWLINA. A few weeks, and this whole war will be over.

GOLDA. A few weeks. Praise God.

MANIA. Please let me stay! I won't go out again. I won't complain, I promise.

PAWLINA. It's for your own safety, Mania. If they find you here, you're dead. *(She helps her change clothes.)* They're hunting for you.

FREIDZA. How could you scrub a chair with soap and water? Even Mundek wouldn't be so stupid.

MANIA. This is the only home I have. Please let me stay.

GOLDA. Do you want to kill all of us?

PAWLINA. You must go.

MANIA. Where? Where?

PAWLINA. Head for the Russian front. Head for Tarnopol. And stay off the road. *(Kisses MANIA on both cheeks.)* May the saints go with you. Here's bread.

Hurry. Before they come back here. *(MANIA, now dressed in long skirt, shawl, flowered babushka and barefoot, exits. PAWLINA gives GOLDA and FREIDZA food.)* There's no time for you to come out and stretch. I have to look for another hiding place for you. If I don't come back by tomorrow, run.

FREIDZA. Why?

PAWLINA. Because it means we're all in danger. *(PAWL-INA kisses each goodbye on both cheeks.)* Goodbye. Remember if anyone is caught, no one talks. *(PAWL-INA covers bunker and exits.)*

Scene Three

SCENE: *The kitchen, Domicela's farmhouse and nearby countryside. Dawn. The next day.*

AT RISE: *PAWLINA hurriedly gathers a few belongings and some food. She stops briefly in front of the icon on the wall and prays. Sound: A loud insistent knock at the door. PAWLINA crosses herself and opens door. ERNST enters.*

ERNST. You're up early, fräulein.

PAWLINA. The cow has to be milked.

ERNST *(examines the room)*. Is the cow far away?

PAWLINA. In the barn.

ERNST *(lifts package with PAWLINA's belongings)*. Are you going somewhere?

PAWLINA. What do you want?

ERNST. You know what I want. Where's the girl? The one you brought with you? Cecylia Kozlowski.

PAWLINA. She left.

ERNST. Then we'll have to find her.

PAWLINA. She's gone.

ERNST *(insists)*. Where?

PAWLINA. I don't know!

ERNST. You and I are going to take a ride, fräulein. If you don't point her out, we have a very nice German prison about seventy kilometers from here. It helps people remember. Once you get there you Polish people never want to leave. *(ERNST throws her package on the floor and the contents spill out.)* You're under arrest.

PAWLINA. For what? I haven't done anything.

ERNST. You're a spy.

PAWLINA. No!

ERNST. Or she's a spy. Or a Jew. Either way, I'll find out, fräulein. I'll find out.

PAWLINA. I have nothing to tell you.

ERNST *(smiling)*. Ah, that's what they all say the first day. But by the third or fourth... *(PAWLINA tries to make a run for it. ERNST catches her at the doorway and throws her to the ground. He ties her wrists.)* Very foolish, fräulein. My soldiers are right outside. *(Opens door and calls.)* Tie her to the motorcycle. And search this house. *(Yanks her up.)*

PAWLINA. There's no one here. *(ERNST slaps her across the mouth.)*

ERNST. And gag her. *(Pushes her out the door, PAWLINA struggling.)*

PAWLINA *(offstage)*. JUREK!! JUR—

Scene Four

SCENE: *A German prison, eight days later. There is a table in the room with food.*

AT RISE: *PAWLINA is being interrogated by ERNST. It is evident that she has been beaten by the bruises and swellings on her body. Her face is black and blue. ERNST goes to the table, puts food on a plate, crosses to PAWLINA whose hands are tied behind the chair.*

ERNST. Who did you spy for?

PAWLINA. I'm not a spy. I don't know anything.

ERNST. She was a Jew, wasn't she? You hid an enemy of the Third Reich!

PAWLINA. No.

ERNST. How many at your house?

PAWLINA. Four. (*ERNST slaps her battered face. PAWLINA winces.*)

ERNST. How many at your house?

PAWLINA (*breaking*). Stop it! Stop it!

ERNST. Ah, we're getting somewhere. Finally. Look, Pawlina, there's a whole plate of food here. For every question you answer correctly, there's some food. For every question you don't answer, there's this. (*Fondles his whip. Unties her hands.*) I'll even let you hold the plate. Take some. After eight days, you must be hungry. (*The smell of the food is overwhelming. She is starving. She pushes food into her mouth. It is just enough to make her more hungry.*) That's enough. (*ERNST takes the plate away and puts it back on the table.*) You had your choice of jobs. Why did you choose the Kommandant's house?

PAWLINA. It was indoors. *(ERNST gets the plate of food but holds it just out of reach.)*

ERNST. What information did you hear?

PAWLINA. That his wife was coming at seven. *(ERNST strikes her shoulders with whip. PAWLINA winces.)*

ERNST. I'll break you yet. How many people at your house?

PAWLINA. Four! Four! I've told you four!

ERNST. And the girl who came to clean? Where did she live?

PAWLINA *(pauses).* With us. *(ERNST strikes her legs hard with whip. PAWLINA cries out.)*

ERNST. Ah, then it was five! Say it.

PAWLINA. Five.

ERNST. That's right, Pawlina. You must try harder to remember things correctly. If you want to eat, you must try much harder. How many at your house last month?

PAWLINA. Five.

ERNST. That's right. And who was the extra person? *(ERNST gives her a small piece of potato on a fork.)*

PAWLINA. My cousin. *(The whip comes down across her face.)*

ERNST. That's not right! *(Calls.)* Guards!

PAWLINA. No! Not that again. No.

ERNST. Are you ready to talk? *(PAWLINA with the strength of fury, leaps up, grabs fork from plate.)*

PAWLINA. Kill me. Go ahead. But first—*(Takes fork and jabs his eyes. A trace of blood comes.)*

ERNST *(bellows).* GUARDS!!!

(Two guards come running in, KURT and WALDO.)

ERNST *(wiping his face).* Take her to Cell D. *(KURT and WALDO surround a struggling PAWLINA.)*
KURT. Cell D!
WALDO *(to KURT).* Even the rats die in Cell D!
ERNST. Do as you're told!

Scene Five

SCENE: *A German prison cell in Brzezany, Poland and corridor outside.*

AT RISE: *KURT carries PAWLINA in and tosses her on the floor of the cell. She falls like a sack of potatoes. He looks at her, pokes her. She is motionless. KURT shakes his head, leaves cell and locks it.*

STANISLAUS enters. He is a temporary guard dressed in the clothes he was picked up in, another Polish "volunteer" for the German labor force (baggy trousers, old sweater, work boots, cap). They nod to each other. In the dim light, KURT opens the window grill of the cell and with a flashlight looks in. He hands STANISLAUS the flashlight to do the same.

STANISLAUS. She looks half dead. Who is she? *(KURT gives STANISLAUS the key and lights a cigarette.)*
KURT. Just another Pole. Like you, Stanislaus. Like you. Only she wasn't a volunteer. *(Exits laughing.)*

(STANISLAUS walks down the corridor. Lighting: Comes up slowly. PAWLINA is now huddled on the floor against a wall, motionless. STANISLAUS enters

*with a container of soup under an old blanket. He un-
locks the cell and enters.)*

STANISLAUS. Hello. You sat up. *(PAWLINA doesn't
move.)* I brought you some soup. *(There is no response.)* Tomato soup. I heard what you did. They said
you were like a wild animal. *(STANISLAUS looks her
over. She is shivering. Gently he puts a blanket around
her.)* You don't look like a wild animal. You look more
like my sister's child. May she rest in peace. *(Pause.)*
Why are you here anyway?

PAWLINA. I don't know anything. Nothing. *(STANIS-
LAUS lifts her face and looks at it.)*

STANISLAUS. Pigs! Treating our Polish women like that.

PAWLINA. Are you Polish?

STANISLAUS. From the Tatra mountains. *(PAWLINA
gives a little smile.)* That's better. *(Looks at her puffy
eyes.)* Can you see all right?

PAWLINA. Yes.

STANISLAUS. Here. Try a little soup.

PAWLINA. I don't know if I can. They beat me ... so
hard ... everywhere.

STANISLAUS. I'll feed you. *(He feeds her a few spoonfuls, which she manages to swallow.)* Can you walk?
(PAWLINA shrugs.) I was watching you. They threw
you in here earlier. You've been asleep for hours. I was
afraid you were dead.

PAWLINA. I will be soon.

STANISLAUS. Are you a spy?

PAWLINA. What's a spy? What do they mean? I live on
a farm in Halczyna near Zoborow.

STANISLAUS. Zoborow! You're only seventy kilometers
away. *(PAWLINA shrugs indifferently. STANISLAUS*

whispers.) The Russians will be here any day. They're only a few kilometers away. Are you Jewish?

PAWLINA. No.

STANISLAUS. Then why are you still in jail?

PAWLINA. They came and arrested me. They beat me for nothing. And they left me to die.

STANISLAUS *(thoughtfully)*. I like pigs. We have some on the farm. I keep them inside in the winter. They're friendly. It isn't really fair to call those soldiers "pigs," is it? *(PAWLINA stares at him.)* Bastards! That's what they are. *(Looks at her.)* Say it, and you'll feel better.

PAWLINA. What does it matter?

STANISLAUS. It matters to my pigs! *(Feeds her. PAWLINA tries to smile.)* Here. A little more soup. You've got a sweet smile. Well, it will be, when the swelling goes down. How do you feel?

PAWLINA. I wish I were dead.

STANISLAUS. You're young. You'll get better. *(Pats her shoulder gently.)*

PAWLINA *(groans)*. OW!

STANISLAUS *(surprised)*. Did I hurt you?

PAWLINA. Look what those bastards did. Look. *(Shows him her shoulder. The wounds are raw.)* I'll never leave here alive.

STANISLAUS. Oh my God, they beat you that way!

PAWLINA. Tell me what they're going to do to me. Tell me.

STANISLAUS. I'm supposed to guard the prisoners at this end, that's all I know.

PAWLINA *(shrugs)*. I don't care anymore. Just make them do it quickly. Please.

STANISLAUS. Can you stand up? *(He helps PAWLINA up.)*

PAWLINA. Yes.

STANISLAUS. Walk around the cell.

PAWLINA. Why?

STANISLAUS. Do it! *(He walks with her.)*

PAWLINA. What are you going to do? *(Louder.)* What are you going to do to me now?

STANISLAUS. Sh-h. Help you get out of here. But we've got to be quiet. There's a big steel door. You saw it when you came in.

PAWLINA. I don't remember.

STANISLAUS. At the end of the hall. I'll get you there.

PAWLINA. Then what?

STANISLAUS. There's a dozen empty houses near here. Jewish homes once. Stay in one of them until morning. As soon as you hear people going to the fields, go home. Just start walking. Don't look back. *(PAWLINA sinks to the floor wearily.)*

PAWLINA. I can't. I can't even walk across this cell.

STANISLAUS. Yes, you can! You can! Go home, child.

Epilogue

Sound: *Polish folk music. OTHER ACTORS replace suggestion of Prologue set.*

SCENE: *Mania's living room. The present. The dedication reception is over. The guests have gone. The pastries have been demolished.*

AT RISE: *MANIA, FREIDZA and PAWLINA sit with their shoes off and their feet up.*

MANIA. Do you remember that first Christmas, when we were down in the bunker?

PAWLINA. How could I forget?

MANIA. There was a storm outside, and the wind was howling.

FREIDZA. My mother said you couldn't possibly come out.

MANIA. And suddenly you were there with a kerosene lamp. When the light fell on your hair, you looked like an angel, an angel in the night. You pulled out a napkin full of Christmas cookies from your shawl. And for a minute I forgot the cold. I forgot the dark. I forgot to be frightened.

FREIDZA. Pawlina, weren't you ever scared?

PAWLINA. Are you crazy? Of course I was scared, Freidza. But there was no point in telling you that. My God, when I saw what they'd done to our home...all that way...barefoot...my feet were covered with blisters...and all that was left of our farm was a chicken coop. You could still smell the smoke.

FREIDZA. When we heard the Russian soldiers singing, Mameh crept out. They were giving all the children chunks of rye bread.

PAWLINA. But when I tried to find Mania, I nearly gave up. I almost walked right past you, Mania, huddled in that doorway.

MANIA. I thought you would never talk to me again. None of you. Pawlina, I didn't mean to get you in trouble. Freidza, I never meant that.

PAWLINA. Sh-h. Sh-h. Mania, tell me the name of my tree again.

MANIA. A flowering crab apple.

PAWLINA. We didn't have those in Zoborow.

FREIDZA. There's a lot we didn't have in Zoborow.

PAWLINA. But when I was little, it was nice. I remember standing on a stool and helping my mother bake bread. We were so happy then, and we didn't even know it!

FREIDZA. What would your mother say now if she knew that this afternoon you had a tree planted in your honor for saving Jews?

PAWLINA. She wouldn't believe it. But then she'd probably say "A guest in the home—" *(MANIA and FREIDZA join in.)*

ALL. "—is God in the home." *(They laugh, arms around each other and all together say it in Polish.)* Przyjaciel w domu yest bóg w domu.

THE END

Pronunciation Guide for Portion of Pater Nostra in Latin:

Panem nostrum quotidianum
da nobis hodie et
dimette nobis debita
nostra, sicut et nos
dimittimus debitoribus nostris
Et ne non inducas in
tentationem
Sed libera nos a malo.
                    Amen.

PAHN-em NOHS-troom quo-ti-dee-AH-num
dah NOH-bis HO-dee-ey eht
dee-MET-tay NOH-bees DEB-ee-ta
NOHS-tra, SEE-koot eht nohs
dee-met-TEE-moos deb-ee-TOHR-ee-boos NOHS-trees
eht nay nohn een-DOOK-as een
ten-tats-ee-OHN-em
said LEE-behr-a nohs ah MAHL-oh.
                    ah-MEN.

Pronunciation Guide continued

POLISH – Characters

Marysia Pawlina	mah-REESH-a paav-LEEH-na
Paniusia Schachterova	pan-USH-a shack-ter-OV-a
Domicela	dom-eh-TSEL-ah
Krasula	krah-SU-la
Jurek	YUR-ek
Bronia	BROHN-ya
Hanka	HAHN-ka
Henryk	HEN-rick
Tadeusz	tah-DE-oosh
Mania	MAHN-ya

Regina	ray-GHEE-nah
Cecylia Kozlowski	sa-SEEL-ya koz-LOUSE-ki
Stanislaus	stahn-EE-swawf

Terms

Mamusia	ma-MOO-sha
Panna	PAHNN-na
Zlotys	ZLOT-eez
Herbatniki	hehr-BAHT-nik-ee
Bezy	BEH-zay
Piernik wyborny	PYER-nik-vee-BOR-nee

Places

Zoborow	zuh-BORE-ov
Halczyna	hahl-ZEEN-ah
Brzezany	brehj-JA-nee
Tatra	TAT-ra
Tarnopol	tar-NOPE-uhl

Expressions

Przyjaciel w domu	puh-shay-YA-shill ve DO-moo
Yest bóg w domu	yest BOOHG ve DO-moo

YIDDISH – Characters

Golda	GOL-dah
Freidza	FRIDJ-ah
Mundek	MOON-dek

Terms

Mameh	MA-meh
Tateh	TA-teh

Challah   KCHAHL-ah

Expressions

A gezunt af dir   ah-guh-ZUNT-af-deer
Oy vay   oee vaay
Meshugenah   muh-SHUG-uh-nah

GERMAN – Characters

Bruno   BRUN-oh
Ernst   EHRNST
Otto   OTT-toe
Luther   LUTH-er
Kurt   COURT
Waldo   VALL-do

Expressions

fräulein   FROY-line
heil   HY-l
liebchen   LEEP-shin

Classroom Concepts

꧁ Learning about people who rescued others during the Holocaust makes an interesting and informative project. Students can begin this study with the exercise below.

Rescue

Remember My Name and *Angel in the Night* take the Holocaust as their subject and, in both, Jews are rescued. Direct students to compare and contrast these scripts, giving particular attention to the methods of rescue in each.

꧁ The Germans thought both Jews and Poles to be inferior peoples. Assign students to research developments in Poland during World War II. How did the country change once it fell to the Germans? What would life have been like for non-Jewish children? for Jewish children? Students should then play *Before and After*, utilizing the information gained from their investigation.

Before and After

Each student may contribute as much or as little as desired during this exercise. It is imperative, however, that episodes alternate. The first student, therefore, should begin with something that describes the life of a Polish child before the Nazi invasion and the next player should contribute a descriptive statement about life after the invasion. This alternating pattern should remain in effect until all students have had an opportunity to participate. Students should speak in the first person. The example shows how the activity is played.

Student #1: Before the Germans occupied Poland,
   I always had enough to eat.

Student #2: After the Germans occupied Poland,
   I always was hungry.

᳁᳁ Script analysis is involved in playing *Angel in the Night* as a sequence game. In this type of activity, the dramatic action is identified and important events are placed on index cards, generally one per card. Each card contains not only the action but the cue which the student is to look for in order to recognize when it is his or her turn to perform. Cues are written in one color or font and actions in another so that they are clearly distinguished. It is also helpful if the action, when written as a cue, retains as much similarity in wording as possible. Cards should be distributed randomly but should not be numbered. The teacher, however, should keep a master list showing the correct sequence of the cards, in case students err or need assistance.

   On one card appears only an action which begins, "You start the game. Come to the center of the room and..." The action is then given. The person with this card is the first player. When his or her action is recognized by another student as that person's cue, the second student then performs. When his or action is recognized by someone as their cue, that individual plays next. The game continues in this manner.

   Several cards are provided below to suggest how the story might be depicted using this format. As a class, determine what other actions are necessary and place these on cards.

   This rendition is played in pantomime.

Angel in the Night: A Sequence Game

> You start the game. As Pawlina, come to the center of the room and pantomime picking flowers when you discover Golda, Freidza, and Mundek hiding in a haystack.

> **The person before you has pantomimed Pawlina picking flowers and discovering Golda, Freidza, and Mundek hiding in a haystack.**
>
> You come to the center of the room and pantomime Pawlina begging her mother to allow her to hide Golda and the children in the barn until they are rested, hugging her mother for saying, "Yes," and then putting the yoke across her shoulders and going off to do farm work.

> **The person before you pantomimed Pawlina begging her mother to allow her to hide Golda and the children in the barn until they are rested, hugging her mother for saying, "Yes," and then putting the yoke across her shoulders and going off to do farm work.**
>
> You come to the center of the room and pantomime Pawlina giving milk to Freidza, telling Golda that she and her family cannot stay, taking and examining Golda's gold bracelet, and singing Mundek to sleep.

☙ Playing this exercise is recommended after students have read both *Remember My Name* and *Angel in the Night*. It is a role-playing improvisation designed to assist students in understanding the tormenting decisions required of some families during the Holocaust.

Role-Playing Improvisations

In both of these improvisations, the scenario should be played twice, with role reversal occurring for the second performance. Scene interpretation need not be similar. These improvisations are meant to reveal various points of view and to uncover thoughts and feelings; solutions are not required or, in some interpretations, even possible. After the improvisations have been performed, engage the class in a general discussion. Some possible probes are listed. At the conclusion of the exercise, compare/contrast the responses and reasons for them.

#1: Remember My Name

> *Who:* Rachel, Pauline, and Léon
>
> *Where:* The apartment in Marseilles
>
> *When:* Shortly before the train is to leave
>
> *What:* Léon wants to send Rachel away for her own safety; Pauline thinks the family should stay together.
>
> *Probes:* What arguments do Léon and Pauline present? What arguments does Rachel present? Do you believe that families are safer together or apart in times of trouble? Why?
>
> How would you feel if you, like Rachel, were to be separated from your parents? What might you say or do to convince them either to allow you to stay or to go?

#2: Angel in the Night

> *Who:* Domicela and Pawlina
>
> *Where:* Outside Domicela's thatched-roof farmhouse
>
> *When:* Twilight

What: Pawlina wants to persuade Domicela to let Golda and her children hide in the barn; Domicela wants them to leave.

Probes: How would you feel if you had an opportunity to protect someone from harm but knew that it would endanger your own family to do so?

What arguments do Domicela and Pawlina present to support their positions? Which of these arguments impressed you? Why?

Initially against her mother's wishes, Pawlina allows Golda and her family to remain in the barn. How do you feel about Pawlina's action? Do you think that there are times when a cause or situation justifies disobeying parents? Support your responses with examples.

"The Avenue of the Righteous was dedicated in 1987 as an avenue of flowering and coniferous trees with small bronze plaques recording the names of the righteous individuals who saved Jews during the Holocaust. Located on the grounds of the Evanston Civic Center, the Avenue is a small replica of the memorial grove at Yad Vashem in Jerusalem."

(The Honor of Humanity Project Under the Direction of National College of Education in Affiliation with The Avenue of the Righteous, news release.)

As noted above, the Avenue of the Righteous in Evanston, Illinois, is modeled upon a similar avenue at Yad Vashem in Jerusalem. Students should study the visual aspects of these sites in preparation for the following activity, as well as Polish farms like the one upon which Pawlina lived.

Scale Models of Special Places

Selecting either the avenue leading to the entrance of Yad Vashem, the Avenue of the Righteous in Evanston, Illinois, or the exterior of a Polish farmhouse such as Pawlina's and the grounds surrounding it, students should create a three-dimensional scale model of the location. Display completed models in the classroom.

Learning about ways in which righteous persons saved Jews is at the core of this activity. Upon completing the assignment, students are ready to play the *Righteous Persons Concentration Game.*

Righteous Persons Concentration Game

Students should research the life-saving actions of righteous persons such as Marysia Pawlina Szul. Following that, they sit in a circle. The first person begins with the phrase, "We are righteous persons. We saved Jews by ..." and states a life-saving action. Each student then repeats the phrase, the actions stated in the order given, and adds his or her own. An example shows how the game is played.

> *Student #1:* We are righteous persons. We saved Jews by hiding four people in my barn.

> *Student #2:* We are righteous persons. We saved Jews by hiding four people in my barn and by arranging for false identity papers.

> *Student #3:* We are righteous persons. We saved Jews by hiding four people in my barn, by arranging for false identity papers, and by claiming that a young

Jewish child was my visiting cousin who had come to stay with my family.

☙ Characters in *Angel in the Night* talk about things they and others did before being forced into hiding. Here, students can show these actions.

Life Before Hiding Pantomime Sentences

Invite students to pantomime the following sentences. After playing, ask for ideas of other things that these characters and their friends and family might have done prior to being cut off from the outside world. Form new pantomime sentences, always remembering to begin with, "You are..." or "Show me..." and to use active verbs. Provide an opportunity for students to pantomime these.

> You are Freidza planting a rose bush all by yourself.
>
> You are Freidza. Show me how you and your father hide your mother's jewelry in the garden and cover up the hole with grass and leaves.
>
> You are Mania's sister, Regina, showing your class the beads on your amber necklace and then telling them a story.
>
> You are Mania. Show me what you look like as you receive the amber ring as a gift and admire it.

☙ The idea of a scavenger hunt is adapted here as students take on the role of sound designer for *Angel in the Night*.

Sound Effects Scavenge

As a class, make a list of all of the sound effects required in the play. Note next to the effect where it is needed (act, scene, line) and its duration. Keep in mind the desire for historical and geographical accuracy. (A European police siren, circa 1942, would not, for example, sound like an American police siren, circa 1999.) Next, form teams and divide the items on the sound effects list so that each team is responsible for finding an equal number of aural segments. Each group will need a tape recorder and blank tape. Teams should find and record those effects which they, as sound designers, would use in a production of *Angel in the Night*. Listening to sound effects compact disks or to similar sources available in a library's media collection is recommended. When all teams have finished recording, they should play their tape for classmates and explain the rationale for each selection.

In the play, Mania talks about her sister's section of the ghetto being "liquidated" (p. 231). At the entrance to the notorious death camp, Auschwitz, were the words, "Work will make you free." These are examples of language the Nazis used to obscure the true meaning of their messages.

What Does It Really Mean?

In conjunction with studying the Holocaust and noting, in particular, examples found in this play, ask students to identify ways in which the Nazis manipulated language. Each student in the class should find an example of a euphemism used by the Nazis to obscure the real meaning of the words. Players then deliver the words, phrase, or sentence once in a way that disguises its true essence.

Next, delivery is repeated a second time, with the speaker conveying the true intentions found in the word(s). After all students have participated, as a class discuss how changes in delivery disguised or accurately conveyed meaning.

As a follow-up, students may wish to word-paint euphemisms. In word-painting, vocal delivery is used to enhance the mood or meaning of the word(s). In word-painting "liquidate," for example, a student might say, "Lickkkkk qui dddaaattteee."

In Act One, Scene Seven (p. 239), Tadeusz is captured during a search of the barn. The result, rather than the search itself, is reported onstage. Invite students to explore the script for this and other implied scenes and then to play the following activity.

The Scene Implied

Working in groups, invite students to create and to dramatize an implied scene such as Tadeusz's arrest. Dialogue can be used or the scene can be played in pantomime. This exercise can be repeated and various interpretations of implied scenes portrayed.

Statues is designed to create empathy for those hiding, day after day, in the bunker. When the exercise has been completed, ask students what it felt like not to be able to speak or to move. What were they thinking and feeling as they stood?

Statues

Working in teams of three people, students stand side-by-side with teammates and keep perfectly still. If any member of the team moves or makes a sound, that entire team is eliminated from the activity. Play this exercise for at least fifteen minutes. How many teams remain standing at the end of the designated time period? Now, ask players to describe how they think Mania, Golda, and Freidza felt as they hid in the bunker.

In the Epilogue (p. 258), the characters share memories of their time together during the Holocaust. In the following exercise, students apply research and imagination to the creation of memory.

Make a Memory

Recommend that students study the lives of children hidden during the Holocaust as well as the lives of those who rescued them. Next, invite players to adapt an experience they have learned about into a memory for Pawlina, Mania, or Freidza. Offer them opportunities to create and stage monologues in which, as the characters, they share these memories.

When characters, whether real or fictional, are as vividly drawn as they are in this play, readers or audience members sometimes speculate about what became of them after the final curtain. This exercise encourages students to give form to fancy.

Whatever Happened To...

Challenge students to think about what might have become of each of the following characters after his or her final appearance in the play. Did the character reunite with other characters and, if so, under what circumstances? Ask players to create a biography for the person of their choice. For Marysia, Pawlina, Mania, Freidza, and Golda, there are actual facts to glean from research. Conjecture will be necessary for Tadeusz, Domicela, Mundek, Bruno, and Ernst. Students should recount the character's life experiences, beginning with what happened to that person after his or her final exit. In role, they next should share their invented life story with classmates.

🔖 Poems, whether short or long, offer students an opportunity to express actions and emotions.

Under Arrest

After reviewing with them the final scenes of the play, encourage students to write a poem inspired by Pawlina's arrest. Students should write a poem telling how Pawlina's arrest effects them. They will want to review Act Two, Scene Four before writing. Poems that lend themselves to oral interpretation might be presented as choral readings and those that are suited to dramatization should be enacted. Actions, emotions, or themes in these poems should capture the audience's attention.

CHAPTER SIX

Sunday Gold

The Playwright Speaks

The goal of the commission was specific, but the subject was up to me. I had to write a one-hour school tour play for six actors based on North Carolina history. (In Chapter Seven of this anthology there's an article by Richard King on the unique partnership related to this commission. Institutions involved were The Raleigh Little Theatre, the North Carolina Museum of History, and the United Arts Council of Raleigh and Wake County with additional support from the North Carolina Department of Cultural Resources.)

Once the grant was approved and I signed a contract according to Dramatists Guild guidelines, my work began. What follows is the process I went through.

Personally, I wanted to focus on women's roles. However, aside from a portrait of Queen Elizabeth I and a few paragraphs about a female pirate, there was little mention of women in William Purcel's *North Carolina Through Four Centuries.*

My first two subject choices were vetoed. Eventually, we all agreed on the topic of the Gold Rush. I spent two weeks conducting preliminary research guided by the museum staff. This included work at the North Carolina Museum of History, state archives, and libraries at the University of North Carolina at Chapel Hill. At the Reed Gold Mine site, I went down into the mine shaft, panned for gold, and discovered the intensity of such a search and examined nineteenth-century mining artifacts (a whim, a kibble, a replica of a twenty-three pound nugget.) At Gold Hill, the old mining town and ultimately the setting for the play, I had interviews with the historical society and with elderly residents who remembered tales of the early days, searched the cemeteries for names, took photographs, and jotted down sounds and images. I collected books, newspaper, magazine, and journal articles, copies of visuals, theses, and a dissertation to examine later and started separate files, e.g., General Research, Reed Gold Mine, Gold Hill, characters.

There was all kinds of information about dimensions and weight of equipment, miners' wages, the assay office, minting coins. But I was having trouble finding what I was hunting for—women. Until recently, historians conspicuously ignored them. But one day I saw a woman's name on the wages earned list. I discovered that there had been rocker girls—and they'd been young, usually twelve to fifteen. Perfect!

Another day, while talking to the curator's assistant at Reed, she mentioned a visitor who said her grandmother got her first pair of shoes working in the mine. That was the trigger.

Then, at the museum at Gold Hill, I saw an old pair of ladies' boots. Lizzie's dream!

As I kept on with my research, I found two facts I wanted to include. Although miners came from all over the world, half the laborers down in the North Carolina mine shafts in the 1840s were hired-out slaves. The other fact was that free education was just beginning.

Originally, I'd thought about a play that traced what happened in a community when some struck it rich and others didn't. But I felt I could not, would not, avoid the above information. Annie jumped out. So did Lizzie's desire to know more than her ABC's. So did Dr. Thornton who radically believed Lizzie should go to a Common School.

Maybe it's my blunt Maine rearing, but later it occurred to me that some people use silence to avoid unpleasant issues. I kept writing and asking for an estimated amount to buy a girl's freedom. No answer. So I wrote a scene in which Lizzie sacrifices the nugget she's found to help Annie buy her freedom, and they hug goodbye knowing they will never see each other again.

Alarm bells sounded. Dead historians rolled in their graves. There were long letters. There were even longer telephone calls. In brief, what I'd written was impossible. I was angry, not at the museum staff, who were simply doing their job and trying to make the script accurate, I was angry at history. But some things I wouldn't give up. Lizzie and Annie are friends, I insisted. Maybe it was unlikely but it was not impossible. I asked what would make it plausible. I established an earlier relationship, when as children they could play freely. Years later, they meet again as teens. Also, I'd read that sometimes slaves bought their freedom with Sunday gold. Yes, the patient staff agreed, not knowing how to explain the facts of life to me, but never a young girl. So Annie doesn't buy her freedom. Instead, she attempts an escape. As for the hug, it was the director who argued, "It's emotionally right, artistically valid." The hug won, and judging from the faces in the audience it's a moving moment in the play.

In the spring, I did a residency. We had a workshop production with a sensitive and intelligent discussion led by Byron Woods, *News and Observer* journalist, who set the tone.

Then rewrites, rewrites, rewrites.

After the premiere, there were final revisions. At draft five, we reached a total agreement. We now had the script with which we were all satisfied. Or so I thought.

Since his initial vision, Richard and I had worked together with mutual respect, and I have great admiration for his abilities and confidence in his judgment. But he took another position at a New England professional theatre. An outside director was jobbed in and just before the opening, I was notified that a scene had been cut. Then the museum discovered that the ending had been altered, raising a question of historical accuracy. The disconcerting comment was, "I don't know why she's so upset. All we did was to cut a scene and change the ending."

At that point the museum director and the arts council representatives stepped in and fought to reinstate the fifth draft of the play. They were successful, but by then the tour was half over.

The theatre had been scheduled to tour the show a second season but would only do *their* shortened version. I thought it was better to lose income than integrity. Politely, we parted ways.

In spite of the disagreement, the commission provided me with a challenging opportunity to delve into a new part of the country and its history; and it was very exciting to see the workshop company's artistic effort evolve.

Throughout the story, both Lizzie and Annie display different kinds of courage. I hope many young people will meet them.

The Play

CHARACTERS

LIZZIE JOHNSON, rocker girl, strong-minded, impulsive, 12

ZEB JOHNSON, Lizzie's father, a laborer,
    focused on his own needs, 32.

MARY CATHARINE JOHNSON, Lizzie's mother,
    pragmatic, 28

ANNIE, a hired-out slave, feisty, resourceful, 12-15

DANIEL SCOTT,* owner of store, craftsman.
    Free African-American, 50s

DR. THORNTON, kindly, progressive, mid-30s

ADAM,* a hired-out slave, 30s

* Can be played by same actor.

TIME
Summer, late 1840s.

PLACE
The mining town of Gold Hill, North Carolina.

ACT ONE
Scene One

SCENE: *A unit set with levels and suggested set pieces to depict a mining town.*

AT RISE: *A dark stage. Shining, suspended in the air is a large rough-hewn gold nugget. Light comes up slowly, silhouetting "single jacks" [miners] at work, a kibble [large iron bucket], someone panning creekside, LIZZIE JOHNSON on a rocker. Sound: Sledge hammer of drills, ringing of pickaxes, rumble of explosions as ACTORS begin to move; Sound: A clanging of bell. Some ACTORS exit climbing up narrow shaft ladder. One comes up seated on the rim of a kibble. Light comes up on LIZZIE as she rocks one last time, checks the rocker and leaves. LIZZIE, barefoot, crosses down Main Street swinging a gray, tin round-lidded lunch pail by its wire handle. She stops transfixed outside Scott Shoe Company. She gazes at a magnificent pair of red leather ankle boots in the window. They are trimmed in black patent at the heel and toe and are fastened with round, black-domed buttons made of glass. She is mesmerized. DANIEL SCOTT crosses to doorway.*

DANIEL. Evenin', Miss Lizzie.

LIZZIE. Evenin', Daniel.

DANIEL. Just gettin' ready to close up. Something I can help you with?

LIZZIE. Them boots...are they for someone...in particular?

DANIEL. Made them for Mr. Coffin's daughter, Miss Victoria. *(Looks down the street.)* Supposed to show up and try them on.

LIZZIE. They're the most beautiful boots I ever saw!

DANIEL. Are they now? I don't mind telling you they're the finest pair of ladies' boots I ever made. Best kid leather I could find, and that's real patent leather on the heel and toe. And see those little black-domed buttons, Miss Lizzie? *(She nods, transfixed.)* They're glass. Glass from Bohemia. Bought them from a peddler passin' through. *(Takes one out of the window.)* Why these boots are so soft a kitten could curl up in 'em and sleep tight. *(Holds out the boot, LIZZIE touches it reverently.)*

LIZZIE. How much...does a pair...like them cost?

DANIEL. Mighty costly.

LIZZIE. I'm working now at the mine.

DANIEL. Aren't you too young to be doing that?

LIZZIE. I turned twelve last week. Pa got me the job.

DANIEL. Doing what?

LIZZIE. All those last specs of gold, I just rock 'em all out. Pa says it's important.

DANIEL. Your pa's right. No point in him and all the miners diggin' the gold out of the ground and then losing it. So you turned twelve. Reckon your feet done all the growin' they're going to do. You tell your pa I got some sturdy sensible shoes here if he's a mind to get you some. *(DANIEL points to ugly, graceless stout black shoes. LIZZIE focuses on the red boots.)*

LIZZIE. In all my life I ain't never seen anything like them boots!

DANIEL. Why's that, Miss Lizzie?

LIZZIE. Them boots, they could take you anywhere in the whole wide world. Anywhere.

DANIEL. Reckon you're right. After the weddin', Miss Victoria's travelin'.

LIZZIE. Travelin'? My pa said she just got back!

DANIEL. That was from the academy in Salisbury. Made all Miss Victoria's shoes while she was away at school. *(Looks down the street again.)* Been waitin' on her all afternoon.

LIZZIE *(sighs)*. It must be grand to read and write and wear boots like that. If'n she decides she don't want 'em—

DANIEL. The trouble with a gold mining town, Miss Lizzie, is some folks get rich and some folks don't. But everyone starts wantin' things they don't need and can't have.

LIZZIE. Can't, Daniel?

DANIEL. Now you think about them other shoes, Miss Lizzie. Just right for a rocker girl. *(DANIEL has returned boots to the window, locks his door, tips his hat.)* Evenin', Miss Lizzie.

LIZZIE. Evenin', Daniel. *(DANIEL exits. LIZZIE reluctantly leaves the unattainable boots, turning once to look back before she exits. Light fades on shoe store.)*

Scene Two

SCENE: *The Johnsons' rented one bedroom log cabin which rests on a stone foundation. The log cracks are sealed with mud. The home has an earthen floor, a log mantel over a stone fireplace and a wood-shingled roof.*

AT RISE: *Light comes up on MARY CATHARINE, practical, weary and expecting another child. She removes the bread that has been baking in a pan on a flat stone and stirs greens in a huge iron pot hanging near the stone hearth. Wiping her hands on her full apron, she goes to the door which is latched with a piece of rope.*

MARY *(calling into the darkness).* Lizzie. Lizzie. Elizabeth Anne Johnson. Girl, don't keep me callin' you.

(LIZZIE enters lugging two pails.)

LIZZIE. I'm here, Ma. Had to fill two buckets. Why do we need so much water?

MARY. Washin', cleanin', cookin'.

LIZZIE. Ma, you know the water that's at the bottom of the mine?

MARY. Your pa comes home with half of it in his clothes every night!

LIZZIE. Suppose they could send it right from the mine to our home. Like having a creek inside.

MARY. It would run over the floor.

LIZZIE. Make it easier.

MARY. Might as well get hot water without a fire while you're dreamin'. *(They laugh companionably as they prepare the evening meal.)* Lizzie, Lizzie, Lizzie! You always want to make things better than they are. It'd be better if you take things as they is.

LIZZIE. I just got to thinkin', Ma. I bet we both walk a few miles each day to get water.

MARY. Elizabeth Ann Johnson, life wasn't meant to be easy. Thank the Lord there's no drought. At least we don't have that to worry about.

LIZZIE. I ain't complainin', Ma. But it seems like the good things in this world ain't evenly divided.

MARY *(continues to work, looks up)*. Lizzie, mind the soup.

LIZZIE *(stirs soup)*. Ma, didn't you have dreams when you was young?

MARY. Ain't got no time for dreams. Your pa's the dreamer. A family can't take but more than one. *(Under the next few speeches, they finish the preparation of supper, set table, etc.)*

LIZZIE. Ma, did you ever see anything so beautiful it made you catch your breath?

MARY. Sunrise in the mountains. Lordy, I miss that. Gold Hill is sure one ugly place. Dead tree stumps. Broken rocks. Torn-up earth. Like we wasn't meant to be here at all.

LIZZIE. What else, Ma?

MARY. Your little brother. When he smiled I felt a bit of heaven in the room.

LIZZIE. Tell me about him. When I squeeze my eyes, I can't see his face no more. Is that what forgettin' means?

MARY. His hair was the color of corn silk, and his eyes, they was just like the sky. The sky come summer. Clear and blue. Oh, your pa loved him something fierce. When he died, something in your pa died too. And then the rains came that August, flood rains near to killed the few crops we had. One day he packed up the cart, and we came here. "A new start," your pa said. *(Smiles secretively.)* Now, don't you be tellin' everyone. Ain't even told your pa yet. But there'll be another little brother afore next year.

LIZZIE. Ma! How soon?

MARY. Sometime afore Christmas I 'spect.

LIZZIE. You gonna put a ribbon on him and give it to Pa as a present?

MARY *(laughs)*. Well now, I might just do that. Might just find some pretty blue ribbon.

LIZZIE. Ma, how do you know it'll be a brother?

MARY *(firmly)*. Your pa wants a boy. *(Affectionately.)* Now, what'd you see today that was so beautiful? *(Sound: ZEB coming up the path.)* Oh, there's your pa.

(LIZZIE scurries to get basin of warm water, soap and towel. ZEB JOHNSON, a self-centered dreamer, enters and sits down. MARY and LIZZIE remove his muddy miner's boots. MARY takes his jacket. LIZZIE gives him the basin of water, so he can wash.)

MARY. Tired, Zeb?

ZEB *(nods)*. My ears are still ringin' from the blastin'.

MARY. And your jacket's soaked through. Ain't there some way to get rid of all that water drippin' down?

ZEB. It's worse on the floor. Even with all this heat, my feet near froze today. But it's all gonna change, Mary Catharine. The owners are bringin' over a Cornish pump. Heard it cost a few thousand dollars. Said it's got a steam engine.

LIZZIE. A steam engine.

ZEB. They say we'll be as dry as toast, and they ought to know. They used it in Cornwall minin' copper.

LIZZIE. Pa, what's it look like?

ZEB. Don't rightly know, but they're buildin' an engine house for it right now. Probably has a whistle and smoke.

LIZZIE. What color will it be?

ZEB. Machine color. How do I know?

LIZZIE. Can I see it?

MARY. You stay away from the mine shaft, Lizzie. Zeb, it's hard enough raising a pretty girl in a mining town.

LIZZIE. Ma, you never said I was pretty. Am I?

ZEB. Pretty is as pretty does! You work hard all day, Lizzie?

LIZZIE. Yes, Pa. Well, it ain't too hard. I just stand on a board and rock. But the other girl was sick, so it was sorta lonely.

ZEB. Never you mind. Five dollars a month is nothing to sneeze at. High time you helped the family out.

LIZZIE. Pa, I was wonderin' if...if...could some of that money I earned...could some...go to me?

ZEB. It does go to you. You got a roof over your head, food on the table, clothes on your back. What more do you need?

LIZZIE. Shoes.

MARY. She's twelve now. Feet growed. Come December it'll be cold walkin' to work.

ZEB. I'll stop in at the store and find out what they cost.

LIZZIE. I'd like to pick them out myself, Pa.

ZEB. Seems to me you're gettin' pretty particular.

MARY. Lizzie, is that what made you catch your breath? A pair of shoes?

LIZZIE. Oh, Ma, they were the most beautiful boots I ever saw. For Miss Victoria. Red leather, trimmed with black patent at the heel and toe. With little black-domed buttons made of glass. And so soft...so soft a kitten could curl up in 'em.

ZEB *(laughing)*. Well, we ain't got any kittens or cats. And if we did, we'd eat 'em.

MARY *(laughing)*. And here I was afraid you'd taken a shine to a miner.

ZEB. The day you wear fancy boots, Lizzie, is the day I find a seventeen-pound gold nugget like that Reed fellow over in Cabarrus county.

LIZZIE. Pa, sometimes you want something just because it's beautiful.

ZEB. Rich folks can talk like that. Not poor folks.

LIZZIE. Pa, how did Mr. Reed find that gold nugget?

ZEB. He didn't find it. His son did. Just your age too. Huge rock sitting in a stream. That's an idea, Lizzie. You could go pan for gold Sunday afternoon.

MARY. What I never could understand is how they didn't know it was gold for three years. Used it as a doorstop.

ZEB. And then they swindled the guy.

LIZZIE. How, Pa?

ZEB. A jeweler paid him what he asked for, all right, three dollars and fifty cents, just what Reed reckoned he woulda earned in a week.

LIZZIE. Pa, that's more than I earn in two weeks.

ZEB. But then that Fayetteville jeweler turned around and sold that rock for three thousand, six hundred dollars.

LIZZIE. That's not fair!

ZEB. Reed made out all right in the end.

LIZZIE. Pa, if I found gold, could I keep it?

ZEB. Depends. Half goes to the property owner. But some mine owners let you take what you find in your free time. Heard tell about a slave way over in Burke County, went to the creek every Sunday huntin' for gold. Everyone thought it was a big joke. But finally he found enough to buy his freedom.

LIZZIE. Pa, why do there have to be slaves?

ZEB. Always have been. It's in the Bible. Mary Catharine, some of the miners below have bought pieces of placer[1] mines creekside. Workin' them in their free time. Found some gold nuggets too. Been thinkin' about that, Mary Catharine.

MARY. You're a farmer, Zeb. The sooner we leave the mines, the better.

ZEB. John Reed was a farmer too. Got himself a fortune. Heck, he started the gold rush. Just thinkin', Mary Catharine. A couple of nuggets could buy us a couple of dozen acres of good farmland. *(Excited.)* And if we really strike it rich, why maybe a couple of hundred acres. Maybe even head west—go out to Illinois. Start fresh.

MARY *(happy)*. Oh, Zeb!

ZEB. Just thinkin' on it.

(Sound: A knock at the door. LIZZIE crosses to door, opens it. DR. THORNTON enters.)

LIZZIE. Dr. Thornton!

MARY. Come in.

ZEB. Something wrong?

DR. THORNTON. Had a call nearby. Mrs. Chapman. She's got ague. Third case this week.

MARY. Oh, no. And another child on the way!

DR. THORNTON. If the fever yields, the baby will be all right. Otherwise— *(Shrugs helplessly.)* Have to wait to see now if the quinine I gave her helps. Don't like the way this summer is starting. Don't like it at all.

MARY. Lizzie, you best be takin' a basket over later.

---

1 Pronunciation: first syllable rhymes with glass

LIZZIE. Yes, ma'am.

DR. THORNTON. But I wanted to talk to Zeb while I was here.

ZEB. About what?

DR. THORNTON. About a school for Gold Hill. There's going to be a county vote in August.

ZEB. A school. For who?

LIZZIE. A school? Like the one Miss Victoria went to in Salisbury?

MARY. Lizzie, mind your tongue.

DR. THORNTON. No. That was a private academy. This would be a common school. Free.

MARY. Free?

ZEB. Ain't nothin' in this life that's free.

DR. THORNTON. Well, there'd be some costs. But not to the students.

ZEB. What students? Most everyone in Gold Hill works for the mine.

DR. THORNTON. Zeb, if they vote it in, I'm going to send my son.

ZEB. Son's different. Don't have a son.

LIZZIE. Pa—

MARY. Lizzie! Dr. Thornton, how about some sweet potato pie before you go?

DR. THORNTON. Thank you, Mary Catharine. I can't refuse the best pie in Rowan County.

MARY. Tell Zeb and me more about this here common school.

DR. THORNTON. Some states already have them. Like Massachusetts where I'm from. Zeb, remember when the North Carolina General Assembly passed a law giving all the voters a chance to decide?

ZEB. Nope. Nothin' to do with me.

MARY. Hear the doctor out.

DR. THORNTON. Now there's only two counties left in the whole state of North Carolina that don't have common schools. And Rowan County's one of them. The General Assembly wants us to reconsider.

ZEB. And where's the money comin' from for lumber and paint? Suppose they want a coal stove? Suppose they start wantin' books!

DR. THORNTON. The State Treasury has funds set aside for a common school. Of course, a small amount will have to be raised by taxation.

ZEB. Thought you said it was free. Now you're talkin' about raisin' my taxes.

DR. THORNTON. It figures out to be about twenty cents more a taxpayer, Zeb. A trifling amount.

ZEB. Twenty cents is twenty cents.

DR. THORNTON. I should think anyone would be ashamed to complain!

ZEB. Look here, Dr. Thornton, this here's a mine town. If you want to send your son to school, go ahead. You can afford it. But leave me alone.

LIZZIE. Pa, could you take part of what I earn?

ZEB. Miss High and Mighty! Workin' all of one week. Well, Missy, I been workin' my whole life.

DR. THORNTON. It would be for all the taxpayers' sons of this town. Daughters too, if they wanted to go.

LIZZIE. Daughters! Pa!

ZEB. Ain't no use for a girl to have book larnin'. ABC's is enough. And Mary Catharine's showin' her that. Mr. Coffin can waste his money if he wants to. One of the richest men in town. Owns the ore-grinding and the sand-washing company, and I don't know what all else. If he wants to send his only daughter to a fancy private school in Salisbury, no man's gonna say he's a fool to his face.

DR. THORNTON. Zeb, an education is a means to knowledge. She'll be a better wife and mother.

ZEB. My Mary Catharine never went to school, and there ain't nothin' wrong with her.

DR. THORNTON. I didn't say there was, Zeb.

ZEB. What's good enough for Mary Catharine is good enough for Lizzie. What use was Miss Victoria's piano lessons?

DR. THORNTON. Miss Victoria's musical. She'll be a happier person.

ZEB. Well, Mary Catharine's happy. Ain't ya, Mary Catharine! Ain't ya?

MARY. Yes, Zeb.

ZEB. SEE!!! And she don't play the pi-an-o neither.

MARY. Zeb, schoolin' ain't such a bad idea.

ZEB. Plain foolish for folks like us. Now, I'd like to finish my dinner in peace.

DR. THORNTON. As a free, male taxpayer, Zeb, you're entitled to vote. At least you could support the school for other families.

ZEB. Why should I care about them? They don't care about me.

DR. THORNTON *(carefully)*. You could let Lizzie go to school. *(LIZZIE looks at her father.)*

ZEB. That gal's a rocker, Dr. Thornton. So don't put ideas in her head. Family needs what she earns. Can't be sparin' her to go sit on a bench and be readin' all day long.

DR. THORNTON. It's an opportunity, Zeb. A door opening instead of closing.

ZEB. I'll thank you to mind your own business. And if you're done with your pie, I'll thank you to leave.

MARY. ZEB!

DR. THORNTON *(rises)*. I'm sorry to find you so intractable, Zeb. Evening, Mary Catharine. Lizzie. *(DR. THORNTON exits.)*

ZEB. What's "intractable"?

MARY. Maybe if either of us had schoolin', we'd know!

LIZZIE. A school, Pa! A school! *(Upset, LIZZIE runs out of the house.)*

ZEB *(reaching for a dogwood switch)*. That gal's got too much sauce in her.

MARY *(stops him)*. Zeb, let her sort it out herself. Didn't even finish her pie, and she loves it so. I gotta ask you somethin'.

ZEB. What!

MARY. If our John Henry hadn't died of the fever, would you have sent him to this school?

ZEB. Mebbe. Mebbe, I would have. Ain't no life bent over drillin' fifty feet underground all day for another man's happiness. I'm a farmer, Mary. And nothin' I do seems to work out right.

MARY *(close to him)*. Zeb, something's workin' out right. And I want you to be thinkin' about that vote some more.

ZEB *(looks at her)*. Mary Catharine?

MARY. Um-humm. *(MARY gently places ZEB's hand on her stomach.)*

ZEB. Are you sure?

MARY. Can you feel it kick? *(A look of wonder crosses ZEB's face.)*

ZEB. A son for sure! Hallelujah! *(ZEB lifts MARY from the floor, hugs her, dancing around the room. He stops *short.)* You better sit down. I'll call Lizzie to clean up in here.

MARY *(laughs happily)*. I will sit a spell.

ZEB *(crosses to door, calls)*. Lizzie! Come on back now, finish your pie and help your ma. *(ZEB looks at MARY.)* Mary Catharine, you ain't never looked prettier, includin' the day I first saw you.

Scene Three

SCENE: *Gold Hill mines. Sound: Grinding of the Chilean mill crushing ore, neighing of a horse, pulsation of the Cornish pump, a deep bass rhythmic beat that diminishes but underscores entire scene.*

AT RISE: *ADAM, a laborer with a limp, loads crushed ore into a wheelbarrow. ANNIE is with him, limited by circumstances but not by imagination.*

ADAM. Now just do what they tell you and don't talk back. Your momma don't want to lose any more children.

ANNIE. She didn't *lose* Willie.

ADAM. Won't never see him again.

ANNIE *(whispers)*. Do you reckon he's free by now?

ADAM *(looks around hastily)*. SH-HH! Annie, you is one lucky gal to be alive. You just count your blessings, y'hear. Count 'em.

ANNIE. They won't let me learn to *count* neither.

ADAM. Annie, that tongue of yours gonna get you in big trouble. You gotta learn, Annie. All them bright thoughts of yours—like little stars—you gotta hide 'em.

White folks don't want to see them stars shinin'. Now
try to be good, Annie. Try.

ANNIE. I'll try, Adam. I'll try. But I won't promise.

*(ADAM gestures to ANNIE to follow him. They cross to
rockers, where LIZZIE is at work.)*

ADAM. You be Miss Lizzie?

LIZZIE. Yes.

ADAM. This be Annie. Mr. Coffin says you show her
what to do. *(LIZZIE looks at ANNIE but isn't sure it's
the same person she remembers from her past.)*

LIZZIE. Are you the new rocker? *(ANNIE recognizes LIZ-
ZIE, but in front of ADAM, she doesn't indicate it.)*

ANNIE. Just fillin' in. *(ADAM looks at her warningly.)*
Yes, ma'am. *(ADAM delivers the ore and pours some
into the rocker trough.)* I learn fast, ma'am.

LIZZIE. Not much to learn. The hauler brings us the ore.
But we gotta keep the rockers filled and carry buckets
of water. Then you stand and you rock. Side to side.
End of the day we shovel the tailings into a pile. Sometimes we gotta sweep too. But with two of us, it won't
be too hard. Ever heard of quicksilver?

ANNIE. No, ma'am.

LIZZIE. Look here. They line the rockers with a cloth and
then add quicksilver. *(They peer into the bottom of the
hollowed-out log trough.)* See? *(ANNIE nods.)* All the
gold sticks to that. So while we're rockin' and the
water's washin' all the dirt and gravel and crushed
rock, all the earth they don't want, the gold gets stuck
to the bottom. Gold's what they're aimin' for. That's
why they crush the rock first in the Chilean mill. Don't
want to lose any of it.

ANNIE. What happens to the gold then?

LIZZIE. The foreman comes at the end of the day and takes the cloth away. They give us a new one to put down each mornin'. *(LIZZIE boards her rocker. ANNIE boards her set of rockers. They rock facing one another. LIZZIE watches her.)* You gotta rock hard. And quick. Like this. *(LIZZIE demonstrates. ANNIE imitates, then stops and wipes her brow.)*

ANNIE. Sure is a mean heat!

ADAM. You work hard now, Annie. *(He exits.)*

LIZZIE *(uncertain).* Are you from around here?

ANNIE. Same place you're from, Miss Lizzie.

LIZZIE *(stares at her, then grins).* Annie! I wasn't sure. Oh, Annie, is it really you? *(LIZZIE jumps off rocker, runs over as ANNIE climbs off also.)*

ANNIE. The same. *(LIZZIE starts to hug her, stops embarrassed. They aren't children any longer.)*

LIZZIE. How'd you know it was me?

ANNIE. I got a good memory. S'pose I gotta call you *Miss* Lizzie now.

LIZZIE *(uncomfortably).* I guess so. Annie, you look different.

ANNIE. Skinnier, that's all. There ain't no Aunt Evalina cookin' here.

LIZZIE. Aunt Evalina! Annie, I ain't heard that name in more'n three years. Wish I had a taste of her corn bread right now.

ANNIE. Me too, Miss Lizzie.

LIZZIE. She always saved some for us, when we come to deliver eggs.

ANNIE. We was real sorry to hear about your brother. Is that why you never came back?

LIZZIE. Annie, if I'da known he was sick, I never woulda hit him for droppin' the basket.

ANNIE. Sure was a mess to clean up, Miss Lizzie. Seemed like those eggs just kept multiplyin' all over Aunt Evalina's clean kitchen floor.

LIZZIE *(wistful)*. Wish we was back there—back then.

OFFSTAGE VOICE. LIZZIE!!! ANNIE!!!

LIZZIE. Annie, we gotta be careful talkin' together.

ANNIE. Yes, Miss Lizzie. *(They scurry back to work.)*

LIZZIE. But I sure am glad to see you.

ANNIE. You are, Miss Lizzie?

LIZZIE. How come you ain't still workin' in that hotel kitchen?

ANNIE. Owner hired me out. Caught me lookin' at a book. Said he never wanted to see my face again at the hotel.

LIZZIE. Can you read?

ANNIE. Slaves ain't allowed to read. He had me whipped so I couldn't walk for a week, couldn't sit for two. Still have the scars.

LIZZIE. That's one mean man!

ANNIE. Nearly killed me, Miss Lizzie. And he made my momma watch. Her cryin' hurt near as much as the beatin'.

LIZZIE *(shudders)*. I woulda cried too. Annie, how come you're workin' here today?

ANNIE. Owner hired me out to the Coffins. Me and Adam. Mostly been doin' things for Miss Victoria. But she's gone over to Charlotte shoppin' for her wedding, so they sent me here for a couple of days.

LIZZIE. Miss Victoria! Is she as beautiful as everyone says?

ANNIE *(studies LIZZIE)*. No prettier than you are, Miss Lizzie.

LIZZIE. You tellin' the truth, Annie?

ANNIE. I be tellin' the truth, Miss Lizzie. She's just got fancier dresses.

LIZZIE *(sighs)*. And she reads. Annie, I want to learn how to read books. My mama's taught me my ABC's. I can write some. But I want to do more than that.

ANNIE. Miss Victoria, she writes long letters to her school friends. Almost every day. I gotta mail 'em.

LIZZIE. Annie, if we could read and write, we could send letters too!

ANNIE. When the rooster crows at midnight!

LIZZIE. Annie, I saw the boots Miss Victoria's gonna have.

ANNIE. I saw 'em too. Had to fetch 'em and bring 'em back.

LIZZIE. Back! Why?

ANNIE. She's gonna buy some English boots in Charlotte. They're gonna send me back after the wedding.

LIZZIE. Back where they whipped you!

ANNIE. Yes.

LIZZIE. Can't you stay here?

ANNIE. Can't do as I like.

LIZZIE. Me neither, Annie.

ANNIE. It ain't the same, Miss Lizzie.

LIZZIE. Annie, remember how we all used to play in the orchard, when we was little? Reckon I was eight.

ANNIE. Remember John Henry hollerin' at the apples to make 'em come down off the tree.

LIZZIE. And you climbin' up and shakin' the branch so he'd think he'd done it all by himself. Then my pa said we was gettin too big to play together. Annie, we was barefoot then, and we're barefoot now.

ANNIE. You don't have no shoes at all?

LIZZIE. My pa's gonna get me some. Before winter. And someday, someday, Annie, those shoes gonna take me someplace special.

ANNIE. Where?

LIZZIE. School!

ANNIE. You're jokin' me, Miss Lizzie.

LIZZIE. Am not. I mean to go. I just don't know how yet. Annie, you got a dream?

ANNIE. Sure.

LIZZIE. Tell me?

ANNIE. Can't. Not now.

LIZZIE. Never?

ANNIE. Didn't say never. Just said not now. *(Sound: Cornish pump gets louder.)* What's that sound? Why don't it stop?

LIZZIE. That's the new pump. Annie, want to go see it? It was made in England. Pa said it came clear across the ocean to Charleston, and then they brung it by wagon to Columbia, and then on to Charlotte. It was so heavy, they had to build a special road to get it to Gold Hill. Twice it got stuck in the mud comin' here, and it took twenty mules and fifteen men to get it out.

ANNIE. Sure is a shivery sound, Miss Lizzie. Like somethin' bad's gonna happen.

LIZZIE. Un—unh. Just gonna take the water out of the mine, Annie. C'mon, let's sneak over when we're done.

ANNIE. I don't want to get any closer, Miss Lizzie.

LIZZIE. What was that song Aunt Evalina used to sing every time we came?

ANNIE. You mean— *(ANNIE starts to sing a folk song appropriate to the period.[2] LIZZIE joins in. As the song gets livelier, ANNIE jumps around on the rocker and does a tricky turn.)*

LIZZIE. Show me how you did that. *(ANNIE does it again. LIZZIE follows. They snap and clap their hands to the beat, as they jump about on the rocker boards.)*

ANNIE. That shuts the sound out good!

LIZZIE *(jumps off and inspects the trough)*. Gotta make sure we're still shakin' out the gold.

ANNIE. We gonna get in trouble for singin'?

LIZZIE. Not so long as we keep on rockin'. But we better do some regular rockin' when the foreman comes by. Oh, Annie, I feel just like we was eight years old all over again!

ANNIE. But we ain't, Miss Lizzie. We ain't.

Scene Four

SCENE: *The mine shaft area. A head frame towers above the mine shaft. Nearby is a horse-drawn whim and pulley arrangement that raises and lowers the kibble. There is a small loading platform.*

AT RISE: *ADAM enters leading a horse, Star. [This should be presented theatrically. Possibly an abstract wooden structure that represents the horse's head. The structure has a horse collar with an iron ring at the top]. Sound: The neigh of the horse. ADAM attaches*

---

2 See p. 322 for suggested song: " 'Tain't Gonna Rain No More."

the ring to the whim. Sound: The loud boom of the Cornish pump. Star neighs.

ADAM (*talks to Star, patting her head and stroking her flank*). EASY! I'm gonna get you a lump of sugar.

(*ADAM exits. LIZZIE and ANNIE sneak on. Sound: The loud boom of the Cornish pump. Star neighs again.*)

ANNIE. Thought you said you ain't supposed to go near the mine, Miss Lizzie.

LIZZIE. Sh—h. Just wanted to see the pump they're all talkin' about.

ANNIE. Where is it?

LIZZIE. Not exactly sure.

ANNIE. Ask someone, Miss Lizzie.

LIZZIE. Annie, how can we sneak up, if we ask someone! (*Sound: Violent crashing.*)

ANNIE (*scared*). Is that the blasting?

LIZZIE. Only heard it once before. But it didn't sound like that.

ANNIE (*wants to leave*). Let's go! (*Sound: A voice is calling from the mine shaft, but the crashing sound is so loud they can't understand. LIZZIE creeps closer.*)

LIZZIE. That's my pa's voice! That's my pa!

ANNIE. Now you're gonna get in trouble for sure.

ZEB (*calling from below*). —UMP!!

LIZZIE. Annie, it's something about the pump! (*LIZZIE and ANNIE run over to the shaft and peer down but dart back as the kibble slowly begins to rise.*)

ZEB (*calling from below*). STOP THE PUMP!

LIZZIE (*runs, calling*). STOP THE PUMP! SOMEBODY STOP THE PUMP!

ANNIE *(calls)*. Stop the pump! Stop the pump!

ZEB *(calling from below)*. STOP!

ADAM *(offstage)*. WHOA!! WHOA there, Star!!!

(ADAM enters and as fast as possible limps over to pull a signal rope that is connected to the engine house. It is nowhere near the horse. Before ADAM gets there, the pump makes an agonizing sound. Suddenly Star goes berserk disregarding the order to stop. Agitated by the confusion and noise, Star keeps on going, and the kibble continues to rise above the ground. LIZZIE and AN-NIE, huddled together, watch horrified.)

LIZZIE. Annie, I'm scared!

ANNIE. Me too, Miss Lizzie. Me too.

ZEB. STOP THE HORSE! FOR GOD'S SAKE, STOP THE HORSE! *(To avoid getting his hand crushed, ZEB lets go of the kibble rope and throws his arm across a wooden beam of the whim, hanging on for dear life.)*

ADAM *(running the best he can)*. WHOA THERE, STAR! WHOA!

ANNIE. Miss Lizzie, grab the mane. *(LIZZIE does. AN-NIE, who is closer, seizes the horse's head and stops Star in her tracks. ZEB lets go of the beam and holds on to the kibble again. ADAM reaches Star's side.)*

ADAM. I've got her, Mr. Johnson. *(ADAM backs Star up until the kibble reaches the platform, where ZEB descends. To GIRLS.)* Thank you! Miss Lizzie. Annie. Thank you!!

ZEB. One minute more, and I could have been tossed right back down there. Where were you, Adam?

ADAM. I had to stop the pump, Mr. Johnson.

ZEB. What's wrong with that dang-blamed horse? Didn't even know I was up here.

ADAM. The noise scared her. That's all, Mr. Johnson. The noise scared her.

ANNIE. And the horse is blind.

LIZZIE. Blind!

ADAM. So it won't run away, Miss Lizzie. (*ZEB is safely on the ground.*)

ZEB. What you doin' here, Lizzie? And who's this?

LIZZIE. This is Annie. She used to work at the mountain hotel, where me and John Henry delivered eggs. Now she's a rocker like me.

ZEB. Why ain't you two rockin' then?

LIZZIE. It's Saturday, Pa. Nine hours, not twelve.

ZEB. Annie, is it? Well, reckon you two just saved one man's life and I be thankful to you.

LIZZIE. Pa, are you all right? What happened down there?

ZEB. Pump's not workin' right. About one hundred and fifty feet from the bottom it started crashin' through all the timber linin' the shaft. Wood flyin' everywhere. Sent me up to get help. Can't do any more work today till that's fixed.

ANNIE. Was anybody hurt?

ZEB. Find out soon enough. You got kinfolk down there?

ANNIE. No, sir.

ZEB. Then you gals run along now. A coupla dozen miners be comin' up soon. There's them that says a woman in a mine is bad luck. And, Lizzie, don't you worry your mother about all this neither, y'hear? (*They start to go.*) Annie, Lizzie, never expected I'd be thankin' two little girls for savin' my life. But don't you go tryin' it again. You coulda got hurt. (*Light fades on whim.*)

LIZZIE. Annie, how'd you know what to do?

ANNIE. My big brother Willie took care of the horses. Sometimes I watched.

LIZZIE. Is he still back at the hotel with your momma? *(Pause.)*

ANNIE. No, ma'am.

LIZZIE. Annie, we's alone now. Told you you don't have to say "ma'am" or "miss" when we's all alone. Ain't we still friends?

ANNIE *(nods)*. But I'm feared I be forgettin' one day and somebody'll hear.

LIZZIE. So what?

ANNIE. So what for you. But not for me. *(Blurts out.)* Miss Lizzie, it ain't right to blind a horse. Never to see the sunlight come mornin'.

LIZZIE *(thoughtfully)*. Never to see the sunlight come mornin'.

ANNIE. Never to run free.

LIZZIE *(stares at her, shocked)*. Is that what you want, Annie? Is it? I won't tell on you, Annie. Is that your dream?

ANNIE. I don't want to run or sneak or hide, Miss Lizzie. I just want to walk proud like I had a right to.

LIZZIE. Like Miss Victoria.

ANNIE. Like you do. All the time. Without even thinkin' about it.

LIZZIE *(pained)*. Annie, Annie, you think that will ever happen?

ANNIE. The day dogs dance, Miss Lizzie. The day dogs dance. *(Pause.)* Or maybe...a little bit sooner.

ACT TWO
Scene One

SCENE: *Lizzie's home.*

AT RISE: *ZEB, MARY and LIZZIE are scrutinizing a legal paper.*

ZEB. See that twelve, Mary Catharine? Means twelve square yards of a placer mine. This paper means we own it. *(He tries to dance MARY CATHARINE around the room, but she stands still, shocked.)*

MARY. But gamblin', Zeb! You never done nothin' like that before. A month's wages. What if— *(A sob escapes.)*

ZEB. What's all this caterwaulin' about? I won, woman, I won.

LIZZIE *(distraught)*. Pa, are you sayin' you took a chance on what I earned too?

ZEB. A man's got to take some risks in his life, don't he? Mine's closed. How long they gonna keep me dippin' candles?

MARY. Where this placer mine be?

ZEB. Good location, Mary Catharine. One hundred and thirty paces from the Randolph head frame. Come Sunday we're all gonna see it. Gotta clear the land afore we start diggin'. You shoulda seen the nugget that this fella Martin pulled out of his pocket. Shined brighter than a candle. Heck, brighter than a star.

MARY. Who's this fella, Martin?

ZEB. Told ya. A travelin' man. Talked real fancy-like. Like he'd gone to school or somethin'.

LIZZIE. Where'd you meet him, Pa?

ZEB. At the tavern. All the miners were there. No place else to go.

MARY. You got a home, Zeb.

ZEB. Can't stay there all day waitin' for that pump to be fixed. Besides, I went to get my wages.

LIZZIE. And mine! Pa, you said you'd get me my shoes today.

ZEB. Got somethin' better, Lizzie.

MARY. Zeb, ain't we gonna need tools?

ZEB. Sure, some. But I got me an ax. And I'm gonna build my own rocker. Gonna let Lizzie run it.

MARY. How we gonna buy them tools, Zeb? Barely enough food as it is. And Lord knows when the mine will start up again.

ZEB. I got just enough for what we need.

MARY. Zeb, some of that money's gotta go for flour and sugar and molasses and corn meal and some shoes for Lizzie and... and the doctor.

ZEB. All right, all right! Gotta eat, I grant you. But it's still summer. Lizzie's shoes can wait. Plenty of time afore winter. And if you do need a doctor, Mary Catharine, it wouldn't be for months. *(Excited.)* Wanna get me a pickax, shovel, mebbe two, and a wheelbarrow, some metal pans and scales to weigh up the gold. If the three of us work clearin' the land—

MARY. Zeb, I'm not sure I can be doin' all that. Not right now. I ain't been feelin' quite myself.

ZEB. It's for him we're doin' it! Mary, you be sick or somethin'?

MARY. No. Not sick. But Zeb I went to see Dr. Thornton.

ZEB. Doc Thornton! What you goin' to him for?

MARY. A few pains.

ZEB. Ain't that natural? In your condition?

MARY. Ye..ess. It's just...well, he's worried about the marsh fever goin' around. It's mighty bad this summer.

ZEB. Why, bet the fresh air do you a world of good. Lizzie and I'll do the real heavy work.

LIZZIE. Pa, there's still ore to wash. If I leave my job, what if you don't find nothin'?

ZEB. Girl, you're enough to try the patience of a saint. No one said nothin' about you stoppin' work. 'Course you gotta work. But Sundays—Sundays the Johnson family's gonna be findin' themselves some gold.

LIZZIE *(mutters)*. The day dogs dance.

ZEB. What'd you say, girl?

LIZZIE. Just somethin' Annie says.

ZEB. Don't like you bein' so friendly with a slave.

LIZZIE. Pa, she saved your life!

MARY *(startled)*. When was that?

ZEB. Told you not to go worryin' your mother.

MARY. Zeb, what's this all about? *(ZEB is silent.)* Lizzie? Lizzie!

ZEB. Go ahead.

LIZZIE. The day the pump broke, Pa came up on the kibble. But the horse went crazy and nearly dumped the kibble over back into the pit.

MARY. Zeb!

LIZZIE. Annie grabbed the horse's head, and I grabbed the mane.

MARY. You nearly got killed.

LIZZIE. Adam was yellin', "Whoa!" But it was Annie and me who stopped the horse.

MARY. Why didn't you tell me about this?

ZEB. Not important.

MARY. Dr. Thornton said there were accidents, but I didn't know— Zeb, are you all right?

ZEB. Not a scratch. But got me to be thinkin' about my life.

MARY *(to LIZZIE)*. How'd you know what to do?

LIZZIE. Annie told me.

MARY. The same Annie from the mountains?

LIZZIE. Yes, ma'am.

MARY. That was right smart of her.

LIZZIE. Annie's real smart.

MARY. I woulda been scared to death, if I'd been there.

LIZZIE. I was.

MARY. But you went ahead anyway. That takes grit, Lizzie. Grit. *(LIZZIE grins.)*

ZEB. Johnson folk are full of grit. Grit and gumption.

MARY. Now, Lizzie, ain't I told you never to go near the mine shaft?

LIZZIE. Yes, ma'am.

MARY. You helped save your pa, so we'll say no more. But don't be goin' over there again, y'hear?

LIZZIE. Yes, ma'am.

MARY. And somethin' else.

LIZZIE. Yes, ma'am?

MARY. I saw you writing' Annie's name, when I set you to practicin' your letters. Didn't pay no heed at the time. But don't you go gettin' Annie into any trouble.

LIZZIE. Trouble?

MARY. Teachin' her writin' and such. Won't do her a lick of good, and it could lose you your job.

ZEB. And a lot worse could happen to Annie, so mind what your ma says.

LIZZIE. Yes, Pa.

ZEB. Bet you never thought about that, did ya, Lizzie?

LIZZIE. No, Pa.

ZEB. That's why it just don't do for you to get too friendly.

MARY *(to ZEB)*. Did you remember to go to that votin' on the school?

ZEB. Mary Catharine, I plumb forgot!

LIZZIE *(devastated)*. Pa, you said you was gonna vote for it. You said you'd changed your mind.

ZEB. What's more important, winning a placer mine or votin' for a school? Anyway, what's one vote?

MARY. One vote can be the decidin' vote.

LIZZIE. Pa, don't you care at all about me?

ZEB. Why do you think we're here at Gold Hill? For you and your ma. Why do you think I've been doin' all that extra work, breakin' up ore, diggin' an engine pit, dippin' candles? For you and your ma. Now for the first time I got a chance to get us our own gold. I'm that close to findin' a fortune. And all you be doin' is whinin' about a pair of shoes and a vote for a school you won't even go to. Don't you be carin' about your family, girl? The kin that is and the kin that's comin'? Lizzie, this family's got to stick together!

Scene Two

SCENE: *The edge of a creek.*

AT RISE: *LIZZIE and ANNIE, equipped with pie pans, are panning for gold. ANNIE looks around, crosses to LIZZIE, leans over.*

ANNIE. Miss Lizzie, I been practicin'.

LIZZIE *(intent on panning).* Practicin' what?

ANNIE. You know.

LIZZIE. Oh, Lordy, don't let anyone see you. And don't say I taught you.

ANNIE. I won't. Wanna see?

LIZZIE *(looks around hastily).* All right. Now. While no one's here. *(ANNIE picks up a stick and laboriously writes her name in the sandy creek bank. LIZZIE studies it.)* Sure do spell "Annie"!

ANNIE. I done it! I done it, Miss Lizzie! *(Sound: Indistinguishable voices.)*

LIZZIE. Quick! Rub it out! Someone's comin' on the path. *(ANNIE does. LIZZIE and ANNIE now pretend all that they have been doing is panning for gold.)*

ANNIE *(laughing as she watches LIZZIE).* You ain't never gonna get nothin' that way, Miss Lizzie. *(Under next few speeches, ANNIE demonstrates.)*

LIZZIE. You said to scoop up the dirt from the creek bed and swirl it.

ANNIE. Didn't say to make an earthquake! All you want to do is loosen the sand. *(Demonstrates.)* Like this.

LIZZIE *(copies her).* Like this?

ANNIE. Better. Tilt the pan forward and down, Miss Lizzie, so the water washes over the edge.

LIZZIE. But then the gold will wash out too.

ANNIE. Gold's heavy, Miss Lizzie. Goes to the bottom. *(ANNIE peers in.)* Gotta move it side to side till the water's gone and there's nothin' left but little bits of sand and gold. *(LIZZIE shakes pan.)* Easy, Miss Lizzie. Easy.

LIZZIE *(listens).* They've gone. *(Suddenly sees something shining in her pan.)* Annie! Look! I think I got somethin'.

ANNIE (*picks up LIZZIE's pan and inspects*). Unh—unh, Miss Lizzie. That ain't gold.

LIZZIE. It's yellow, and it's shinin'.

ANNIE. So's the sun! Don't mean it's gold. That's what Adam called "fool's gold."

LIZZIE. How can you tell?

ANNIE (*breaks it apart*). See how hard it is. Breaks easy. Gold's soft. You can shape it anyway you like. Miss Victoria's got a gold pen she writes with.

LIZZIE. A gold pen!

ANNIE. Mr. Coffin had it made for her. It writes nice and easy.

LIZZIE. How do you know that?

ANNIE. On account of I watched her.

LIZZIE. For all I'm findin', I might as well have helped my pa!

ANNIE. How come he let you come to the creek today?

LIZZIE. He's got this friend from Cornwall. Told him a woman's bad luck, when you're huntin' for gold. 'Course, he didn't say nothin' about me and my ma clearin' the land all month. Didn't say nothin' about that! (*Worried.*) My momma shouldn't have been workin' outside. Not with all this heat. I told her to stop, but she said she had to help Pa finish. Never saw her so tuckered out. Off her food. Headaches. Must be the baby comin'.

ANNIE. Sorry she's feelin' so poorly. But I like hearin' you talk about your momma, Miss Lizzie. Wish I had mine.

LIZZIE. Everybody's got a momma.

ANNIE. I mean one I could see, one I could touch. I seen Miss Victoria's momma's face, when she came home from school. Oh, they was smilin' and huggin' and kissin'—and cryin' too. Near had a brass band, there was so much commotion just seein' each other.

LIZZIE. I see my momma every day, but she don't carry on like that.

ANNIE. That's 'cause it's every day. *(Softly.)* I ain't seen my momma in a whole year. *(Blurts out.)* And now... now they're fixin' to send me to South Carolina. To the meanest man there ever was. Right after the wedding on Saturday.

LIZZIE. Wish you could stay here. Bein' a rocker.

ANNIE. Owner won't let me.

LIZZIE. If you could stay, and if I ever get to go to school, I could teach you.

ANNIE. A lot of "ifs," Miss Lizzie. A lot of ifs.

LIZZIE *(upset)*. Annie...there ain't nothin' I can do! *(More positive.)* But listen, Annie, now that you know some letters, why you just keep practicin', when no one's lookin', mind. No tellin' what'll happen. Maybe one day you'll even send me a letter!

ANNIE *(brave)*. Miss Lizzie! Miss Lizzie...will you help me write a letter...to my momma?

LIZZIE. But, Annie, how she ever gonna read it?

ANNIE. She'll find a way. My momma will find a way. Please, Miss Lizzie. *(From her pocket, ANNIE removes a carefully folded piece of paper.)* I got some paper.

LIZZIE. You didn't take it, Annie, did you?

ANNIE. No, ma'am. Found it on the floor. Miss Victoria threw it out.

LIZZIE. That's all right then. But I ain't got no gold pen like Miss Victoria. *(LIZZIE hunts and finds a piece of charred wood.)* This might work. *(LIZZIE writes the date at the top of the paper.)* It's not too good, Annie.

ANNIE *(looks at it)*. Good enough.

LIZZIE. What do you want to say?

ANNIE *(ponders over words as she dictates)*. You gotta say "Dear" first. That's how letters start. I hear Miss Victoria read 'em aloud. "Dear Mama. I'm going...far away. Hope I'll see you...and Willie again...sometime. Love, Annie." *(ANNIE peers over LIZZIE's shoulder.)* You write nice, Miss Lizzie. If you had a gold pen, it'd look just as nice as Miss Victoria's writing.

LIZZIE. Now you sign it, Annie.

ANNIE. No, I can't.

LIZZIE. Sure you can. Same as you just wrote in the sand—only smaller. *(LIZZIE spreads paper out.)* Right here. *(ANNIE slowly signs. LIZZIE swiftly looks around and then watches ANNIE work.)* Annie, that's perfect!

ANNIE. There's still half a page left.

LIZZIE. Put it away, quick. Before someone catches us.

ANNIE. You be a good teacher, Miss Lizzie.

LIZZIE. I want to go to school so bad, it hurts. But my pa don't see no need. That's what he said. No need. I was thinkin' if I could just find a chunk of gold, I'd put it on his dinner plate and say, "Pa, I'm goin' to school."

ANNIE. Sun's gettin' ready to set, Miss Lizzie.

LIZZIE. I'm gonna go get some dirt from up there. There's still some time before dark.

ANNIE. There just ain't any gold in the creek today, Miss Lizzie. Not even a flake.

LIZZIE *(stubborn)*. I want to do one last panful.

ANNIE. All right. *(LIZZIE and ANNIE go separate ways to collect more dirt from the creek bottom. LIZZIE stops short, stares and digs out a small nugget about the size of a peanut. She carries it back.)*

LIZZIE. Annie! Look! *(She crosses with the shining gold nugget in her hand.)*

ANNIE. What's that you got, Miss Lizzie?

LIZZIE. What I got? I got boots, that's what! I can feel them on my feet, soft as a quilt. And maybe somethin' to give my pa for schoolin'. Well, probably not enough for that. But I got gold this time, Annie, sure as I'm standin' here. I got gold. That's what I got. (*ANNIE crosses and inspects. She lifts it, examines it and chips at a flake that she holds on her fingertip.*)

ANNIE. Miss Lizzie, you done found yourself a nugget! That's gold, Miss Lizzie. Real gold. (*ANNIE returns nugget to LIZZIE.*)

LIZZIE. On my first Sunday! (*LIZZIE puts nugget in her pocket.*)

ANNIE (*dejected*). It's my last Sunday.

LIZZIE. How do you know that South Carolina man's so mean?

ANNIE. Every slave knows his name. I even heard Mr. Coffin say he was meaner than a mad hornet. Some slaves rather die than go there. (*ANNIE shivers. For the rest of the scene they constantly check to make sure that no one is there. They speak in hushed voices until the last exchange.*)

LIZZIE. Annie, you ain't thinkin' of...runnin' away, are you?

ANNIE. No, ma'am.

LIZZIE. When you say "ma'am" that way I know somethin' else's spinnin' in your mind. But, Annie, if'n they catch you, why, you be no better than dog meat.

ANNIE. I gotta be gettin' back now, Miss Lizzie. After dark a slave without a pass can get into big trouble.

LIZZIE. Annie, you ain't even hearin' me proper. (*Stops short.*) What kind of pass you talkin' about?

ANNIE. Sayin' it's all right for you to be out. There's men on the road, pattyrollers, always checkin'. Especially at night.

LIZZIE. What do they do to you?

ANNIE. Think of the worst thing you can.

LIZZIE *(shudders)*. I did.

ANNIE. Then they do worse.

LIZZIE. Annie, who writes this pass?

ANNIE. People you work for.

LIZZIE. What does it say?

ANNIE. Somethin' like... "permission to travel."

LIZZIE. Annie, lemme see that letter again.

ANNIE. Why?

LIZZIE. Just give it here. *(ANNIE hands it to her.)* There's a whole half sheet left. *(LIZZIE tears the sheet in half.)*

ANNIE. Miss Lizzie! *(LIZZIE returns letter, which ANNIE pockets. LIZZIE picks up charred stick.)*

LIZZIE. Wish I knew how to spell permission. *(Ponders, then writes.)* "All right to leave Gold Hill." How does that sound?

ANNIE. Sounds beautiful, Miss Lizzie. *(A tear rolls down ANNIE's face.)*

LIZZIE. Don't cry, Annie. Friends supposed to help each other.

ANNIE. Adam said we shouldn't be friends. Said I'd get hurt. Said you could too. *(LIZZIE hands her the pass, which ANNIE puts away.)*

LIZZIE. Some things you just gotta do! Annie, ain't you scared? *(ANNIE nods.)* What you gonna eat... later on?

ANNIE *(casually)*. Berries, acorns, hickory nuts. I'll find somethin'.

LIZZIE. Wish I had some food to give you. I'm worried, Annie.

ANNIE *(quoting)*. Miss Lizzie, "some things you just gotta do." Like you said. *(LIZZIE puts her hand in her pocket and feels the nugget. Very slowly she puts it in her palm and holds it out to ANNIE.)*

LIZZIE. Here.

ANNIE *(looks longingly, then shakes her head)*. No, Miss Lizzie. It's yours. You found it.

LIZZIE. Wouldn't have known how to pan if you hadn't showed me.

ANNIE. No, Miss Lizzie, I can't. You found that nugget all by yourself. And I been hearin' about them boots and that school since June!

LIZZIE. Annie, I want somethin' to walk in. You want somethin' to walk to. But dreams gotta come true else they die. And I been thinkin' how maybe your dream's gotta come first—else those boots gonna pinch my toes! Besides they ain't even built the school yet. *(LIZZIE puts the nugget in ANNIE's hand.)* Take it, Annie. You ain't got another Sunday. I do.

ANNIE. Ain't no one...no one, y'hear...ever been...a...a friend...like you.

LIZZIE. Annie, be careful.

ANNIE. I will.

LIZZIE. If'n...you can...will you write me? Just put "Lizzie Johnson, Gold Hill" on the outside and "Annie" on the inside...so's I know...you're safe.

ANNIE. If I make it.

LIZZIE. You're gonna make it. I just knows. And you're gonna walk proud. The way you wants.

ANNIE. Miss Lizzie, I won't ever forget you. EVER.

LIZZIE *(trying not to cry)*. Remember I'm hopin' for you. Hopin' hard. *(LIZZIE looks around hastily. Despite all the prejudice surrounding them, LIZZIE and ANNIE hug a brief goodbye. As they separate, LIZZIE attempts to camouflage ANNIE's escape. In a loud commanding voice.)* See you tomorrow, Annie. Be on time, y'hear!

ANNIE *(understands, in a loud, forced, cheerful voice).* I will, Miss Lizzie! I will! See you tomorrow! *(ANNIE darts off, but just before she exits, she waves a last goodbye. LIZZIE waves, watches. ANNIE exits. LIZZIE turns, wiping her eyes, grabs her pan and runs off.)*

Scene Three

SCENE: *Lizzie's home.*

AT RISE: *MARY CATHARINE lies in bed, ill. LIZZIE sits anxiously beside her. DR. THORNTON is mixing a tablespoon of quinine powder with four ounces of water. He stirs the mixture and then pours the medicine into a small wine glass, crosses to MARY, lifts the glass to her lips to drink. The taste is horribly bitter.*

MARY *(exhausted).* Water. Lizzie...some water.

LIZZIE *(takes a pottery mug and lifts it to her lips).* Here you are, Ma. *(MARY takes a sip. LIZZIE adjusts the quilt.)* Dr. Thornton, why is she so pale?

DR. THORNTON *(feels MARY's forehead).* The end of the fever, Lizzie. I don't know what I would have done without enough quinine this summer. Don't try to talk, Mary Catharine. Just rest.

MARY. My baby? Is...it...a boy?

DR. THORNTON *(grimly).* Yes, Mary, a boy. *(MARY sinks into a sleep.)*

LIZZIE. Ain't ya gonna tell her?

DR. THORNTON. She needs the sleep. Time enough when she wakes.

LIZZIE. If only I got back sooner. All she had was a headache when I left. And she didn't want no breakfast.

DR. THORNTON. You've been a good nurse, Lizzie.

LIZZIE. Just kept bringin' a cool cloth for Momma, and made her some fresh mint tea.

DR. THORNTON (*feels MARY's forehead again, checks her pulse, checks her ankles for swelling*). We're out of the woods, Lizzie. Out of the woods. But you're going to have to watch her now. There could be a relapse. Just keep her warm, if she gets a chill, and apply cool cloths, if she's hot. And she has to stay in bed until she's stronger. That's important. No carrying water.

LIZZIE. I do that.

DR. THORNTON. And no lifting rocks!

LIZZIE. Land's cleared out. Dr. Thornton, is that what killed my brother?

DR. THORNTON. I wouldn't say that. But it probably didn't help. Ague always breaks out in the summer. I reckon it's all the heat and standing water. All the bad air. But for a woman expecting a baby, intermittent fever's a lot more dangerous. I tried to warn her.

LIZZIE. I knew she shouldn't have been outside so much. Hottest summer I can ever remember. I told her that, Dr. Thornton.

DR. THORNTON. Gold does strange things to people, Lizzie. I've seen it before, and I'll see it again. (*Passionately.*) I wish to heaven there were no gold left in Gold Hill.

LIZZIE. But that's why we came.

DR. THORNTON. Not all gold's in the ground. You get yourself an education, Lizzie. No telling then what you

can do. That vote passed. We're going to be building a
schoolhouse.

LIZZIE. But, Dr. Thornton, you heard my pa 'bout school.

DR. THORNTON. I heard him. But I've got a few things
to say to your pa.

*(ZEB comes up the path singing, swinging a pair of
boots and carrying an eight-pound nugget.)*

ZEB *(calling).* Lizzie! Mary Catharine! *(LIZZIE runs outside. As she does, MARY wakes. DR. THORNTON talks
to her; but the audience does not hear what is said.
Expansively.)* Try these on for size, little Lizzie. Try
these on for size.

LIZZIE. Boots! Pa! How did you get them boots? They're
the ones I wanted.

ZEB. Whole town knows that. You been pressin' your
nose against the glass so hard, there's a Lizzie smudge
right in front of the boots.

LIZZIE. Pa... Pa...listen—

ZEB. Hadn't been diggin' but three feet down, and there it
was just settin' and shinin'. *(Calls.)* Mary Catharine!

LIZZIE. Pa, the doctor's here. You gotta be quiet.

ZEB. It ain't her time yet. *(ZEB strides in followed by
LIZZIE.)* What you doin' here, Dr. Thornton? *(ZEB
crosses to MARY.)*

MARY. Zeb...Zeb... *(Cries.)* I'm sorry. I'm sorry. *(ZEB
crosses to DR. THORNTON.)*

ZEB. What happened, Dr. Thornton?

DR. THORNTON *(aside to ZEB).* It was the fever. She's
still pretty sick, Zeb. So don't upset her. The baby was
born dead. A boy.

ZEB. A son! *(ZEB sinks into a chair, dropping his precious rock on the floor.)* What good is Sunday gold now? What good is it?

DR. THORNTON. Your wife will be needing a lot of extra care right now. *(LIZZIE crosses to ZEB.)*

ZEB *(lashes out)*. Why didn't you help your ma more? I told you to make sure she—

DR. THORNTON *(interrupts)*. Lizzie's done all she could. And she's been a big help to me. You've got a fine daughter, Zeb. Couldn't ask for a better one.

ZEB *(distraught, crosses to MARY)*. Mary Catharine, listen! *(MARY tries to sit up, but worn out, her head sinks back down on the pillow. She looks at ZEB.)* Mary Catharine, I found gold today. Listen. Gold. For all of us. It's for all of us. You'll get well. We'll have another son, you'll see. Mary Catharine, you gotta get better! *(DR. THORNTON gently pulls ZEB away.)*

DR. THORNTON. Let her be, Zeb. She has to rest. *(Aside to ZEB.)* But, Zeb, there'll be no more children.

ZEB. No. She'll get stronger. My family's tough.

DR. THORNTON. I'm a doctor, Zeb. We nearly lost her.

ZEB. And I suppose you want to get paid for killing my dreams! All my dreams. All my dreams. What good are they without a son?

DR. THORNTON. You have a daughter, Zeb, bright as the gold you carried in that door. A daughter you can be proud of. A daughter who's aching to go to the new school when it starts. Think about that, Zeb, will you? *(DR. THORNTON prepares to leave.)* I'll be leaving now. Just keep her still and comfortable, Lizzie. I'll stop by later to see how she is. *(He exits.)*

ZEB. What you want to go to school for, Lizzie?

LIZZIE. I want to learn things, Pa. Why the sun comes up each day. Why babies get born and then hafta die. Why some people are free—and others ain't.

MARY *(calls)*. Zeb. Lizzie. *(They rush to her.)*

ZEB. All the gold in Gold Hill ain't nothin' without you.

MARY. Help me sit up.

LIZZIE. Ma, you shouldn't.

MARY. Just for a minute, Lizzie. I gotta say somethin'. *(They help MARY sit up. MARY points.)* It's about those boots.

ZEB. Now, don't you worry about payin' for them, Mary. That rock there is gonna get us a lot of things we ain't never had before. Anything you want.

MARY *(looks at LIZZIE)*. I want to see you wearin' those boots.

LIZZIE. Now?

MARY. Now. It'll rest my mind, Lizzie.

LIZZIE *(holds MARY's hand)*. I'm sorry, Ma...about the baby.

MARY. Me too, Lizzie. Powerful sorry. Now put on those boots, so I got somethin' more cheerful to think on.

ZEB. Go ahead. *(LIZZIE puts them on while MARY and ZEB watch.)*

LIZZIE. Pa, they're beautiful! *(LIZZIE walks about.)* They fit perfect!

MARY. Mighty fine for takin' Lizzie where she's goin'.

ZEB. Kind of fancy for goin' to work.

MARY. Just right for the first day of school at Gold Hill. *(They look at ZEB. He struggles with his thoughts. Abruptly, MARY cries out and starts to shake with a teeth-rattling chill.)*

ZEB *(beside himself, rushes to her)*. Mary Catharine!

LIZZIE. Quick, Pa. Get the quilt.

ZEB *(argues)*. But it's hot in here.

LIZZIE. Pa, the quilt. The chill's come back. *(MARY clutches LIZZIE's hand, scared. ZEB grabs the quilt and rushes over with it attempting to cover MARY. LIZZIE smooths the quilt and speaks soothingly.)* It's all right, Ma. You'll be all right. I'm here. Pa's here. Dr. Thornton said you might feel cold again. *(MARY clutches at her throat, tries to sit up, but she is too weak. Her breathing is difficult and labored.)*

ZEB *(terrified)*. Lizzie, I don't know what to do. Her face's gone blue.

LIZZIE *(quickly, lifts MARY's head)*. Pa, get me a pillow to prop her head up. *(ZEB finds a cushion and rushes to put it under her head.)* Just ease it under. Pa, I need somethin' else. *(ZEB grabs his jacket and rolls it into a ball.)* She'll breathe easier if her head's up higher. Hold her head a minute, Pa. *(LIZZIE adjusts the "pillows.")* Now, lower it. Slow and easy. *(ZEB does.)* There now. *(MARY is half sitting up, leaning on the "pillows." The shaking has nearly stopped and her breathing is easier. She tries to smile.)*

ZEB. Mary Catharine, don't scare me like that!

LIZZIE *(strokes MARY's hand)*. Don't talk, Ma. Just rest. You're gonna be all right. You'll be fine soon. Real soon. *(The shaking stops. MARY gestures and gently LIZZIE folds down the quilt. LIZZIE feels MARY's forehead.)* Better now, Ma? *(MARY nods. ZEB looks at his daughter with a brand new admiration.)*

ZEB. You gone and growed up, Lizzie. You gone and growed up! *(LIZZIE looks at ZEB, smiles radiantly and crosses to him.)* She gonna get well?

LIZZIE. Yes, Pa. Dr. Thornton said this could happen.

ZEB *(slowly)*. Lizzie, them questions you be askin'. They're mighty big.

LIZZIE. I know, Pa.

ZEB. Reckon you're fixin' to go to that school no matter what.

LIZZIE. I wanna go, Pa. Just like you wanted that gold nugget. *(Looking at it.)* Can it really buy us anything we want?

ZEB *(realizing as he looks at MARY)*. There be some things it can't buy. *(ZEB crosses to MARY. She opens her eyes.)* Lizzie ... I be thinkin' mebbe your ma's right. *(MARY smiles up at him. ZEB decides.)* Gonna let you go!

LIZZIE *(excited)*. To school? *(ZEB nods. Elated, LIZZIE rushes over and hugs him. MARY raises herself up slightly, and they support her. The three are together now.)*

MARY. You're a good girl, Lizzie. Do us proud.

ZEB. You're a true Johnson, Lizzie. Don't give up till you gets what you want!

THE END

'Tain't Gonna Rain No More

Chorus

'Tain't gon-na rain, 'Tain't gon-na snow, 'Tain't gon-na rain no more.

Steal up ev-'ry bod-y. 'Tain't gon-na rain no more.

Verse

Old sow died at the mouth of the branch. 'Tain't gon-na rain no more The

buz-zards had a pub-lic dance. 'Tain't gon-na rain no more.

2. What did the blackbird say to the crow?
   'Tain't gonna rain no more.
   'Tain't gonna hail and it 'tain't gonna snow,
   'Tain't gonna rain no more.

Chorus

3. Two and two and round up four,
   'Tain't gonna rain no more.
   Six, two and round up four,
   'Tain't gonna rain no more.

Chorus

4. Gather corn in a beegum hat,
   'Tain't gonna rain no more.
   Ol' Massa he mad if you eat much of that,
   'Tain't gonna rain no more.

Chorus

The Frank C. Brown Collection of North Carolina Folklore. Durham, North Carolina: Duke University Press, 1962, Vol.V (Negro Secular Songs), pp.288-289 has this song as sung by H.H. Hanchey, Durham in 1919.

The song dates back to slavery days and is in public domain. The above piano arrangement is by Dr. William Hullfish, State University of New York College at Brockport. According to Hullfish," It has a verse-chorus format, so that the first two lines (chorus) should be sung after each new verse. It's perfectly acceptable and quite usual to start with the chorus as this version does."

The playwright suggests using verses 2 & 3 only with the chorus as indicated above.

Classroom Concepts

⌐℘⌐ The use of recall, or remembering something in detail, helps an actor to relate truthfully to objects on stage. In the following activity, encourage students to take their time and see the object clearly and in detail in the mind's eye. Sharing aloud the directions below is advised.

Recalling Something Special

In Act One, Scene One, Lizzie first sees the red boots and immediately wants them very much. Have you ever coveted a material object that much? Close your eyes and recall the object of your desire in as much detail as you can. Think about its size, shape, texture, weight, sensory properties, and so forth. With your eyes remaining closed, describe the object for classmates. Next, open your eyes and reveal (1) whether or not you received the object and how that made you feel and (2) how your emotions were like or unlike how you think Lizzie felt about the boots.

⌐℘⌐ Several machines and tools specific to mining in the 1840s are mentioned in *Sunday Gold*. Both teacher and students will need to research what these looked and sounded like so that participants in the activity can recreate them[3].

Machines and Tools

In this activity, students use body and voice to create the following tools or machines: Chilean mill, Cornish

---

3 Please note that pictures of some of these may be difficult to find. Reference librarians and staff at historical museums may be able to assist the teacher in preparing for this exercise.

pump, kibble, and rocker. This can be done with the entire class building each object or by dividing the class into four groups and assigning one machine to each team. One person begins by doing a motion and, if appropriate, making a sound befitting the object. Others join with their own motions and sounds until the machine or tool has been completely depicted through physical and oral means.

⌐♫ In Act One, Scene Three, Lizzie shows Annie how to do the job of a rocker girl. Imagining that they are Lizzie, students should play the following pantomime paragraph. The teacher narrates.

Rocker Girl

You are Lizzie and you must show the new rocker girl, Annie, how to do her job. First, show her how a new cloth is laid at the start of the day and how the hauler brings ore to the rocker girls. Remember to show her how heavy the ore is. Next, demonstrate for her how you keep the rockers filled. You also have to carry buckets of water and you teach her how to do this. You are now ready to show her the proper way to rock. You move side to side, rocking hard and quickly while carefully maintaining your balance. At the end of the day, rocker girls have to sweep up pilings. Show Annie how this is done.

⌐♫ Found sounds are musical sounds made by manipulating common objects. Purposefully jangling car keys, running a pencil against the spiral of a notebook, or clicking the top of a pen are examples of found sounds. Body sounds are musical sounds made with the body such as clapping, stomping feet, or popping fingers in the mouth. Two ways to use found and body sounds can be applied to the song (p. 322) "'Tain't Gonna Rain No More."

"'Tain't Gonna Rain No More"

After experimenting with a variety of found and body sounds, invite students to accompany the song, "'Tain't Gonna Rain No More." Encourage them to compose accompaniment which supports the lyrics and mood of the piece.

Next, ask them to substitute found or body sounds for the words "rain," "snow," "sow," "buzzards," and "dance." Follow this by singing the song as a group and, when coming to one of these words, inserting the sound instead of singing the word.

🎜 In a mirroring exercise, one partner tries to precisely and simultaneously replicate the actions of another partner. In *Panning for Gold*, students have an opportunity to use this technique.

Panning for Gold

Pair the students and ask one to assume the role of Lizzie while the other plays Annie. In Act Two, Scene Two, Annie shows Lizzie how to pan for gold. The student playing Annie should initiate these actions while the one playing Lizzie mirrors them. Remind players to keep precision as the goal and to remember that, when mirroring is most successfully done, onlookers cannot tell who is initiating the action and who is reflecting it.

Scoop up the dirt from the creek bed and then swirl it around in the pan.

Tilt the pan forward and down so that water rushes over the edge.

Move the water around in the pan from side to side until it is gone and only sand and gold remain.

Inspect Lizzie's pan and determine that she has found "fool's gold."

Break apart the "fool's gold" to show Lizzie how hard it is.

In the play, Lizzie writes a letter for Annie. One at a time and in pantomime, students also should write a letter. After each has finished, classmates should be asked to determine the content they observed being penned.

Writing a Letter

Just as Lizzie did for Annie, each student will write a letter, determining to whom he or she is writing as well as what is being said. Is the student corresponding to a business associate? a significant other? a friend? What is the content? Sitting where all classmates can see, each person should pantomime writing a letter. When finished, observers should identify behaviors, facial expressions, and gestures that gave clues about the letter's content.

Both Annie and Lizzie have been told by others that they shouldn't be friends. Issues of race and societal norms are expected to keep them apart. Zeb rationalizes that his failure to vote is without consequence. Although *Sunday Gold* is set in the late 1840s, these examples remind us of the expression, "The more things change, the more they remain the same."

The More Things Change, the More They Remain the Same

Students should improvise the following scenarios twice, setting the first playing in the late 1840s and the second in the present. In the contemporary interpretation, Lizzie and her father should be played as modern-day characters. The same cast can be used for both playings, or the scenarios can be recast if desired. When the improvisations have been completed, as a class discuss the arguments offered each time. How did the characters' positions on the issues and persuasive techniques change or remain the same given the difference of a century and a half?

Who: Lizzie, Zeb

What: Lizzie wants her father to accept Annie as her friend; Zeb wants Lizzie to stop seeing Annie

Where: The Johnson home

Who: Lizzie, Zeb

What: Lizzie wants her father to promise to vote for the school; her father doesn't want to waste time voting

Where: The Johnson home

In Act Two, Scene Three, Lizzie talks about what she wants to learn in school. This is the basis for the following activity. Students should sit in a circle for this concentration game.

In School I Want to Learn

Players begin with the phrase, "I'm Lizzie. In school, I want to learn..." and identify something found in the script or something each speculates might be of interest to Lizzie. Every person must begin with this opening phrase and name all of the items stated before adding his or her own. An example is given to show how the game is played.

> *Student #1:* I'm Lizzie. In school, I want to learn why the sun comes up each day.

> *Student #2:* I'm Lizzie. In school, I want to learn why the sun comes up each day and why babies get born and then have to die.

> *Student #3:* I'm Lizzie. In school, I want to learn why the sun comes up each day, why babies get born and then have to die, and why some people are free— and others ain't.

Students will need to research what life was like in a mining town such as Gold Hill in the late 1840s. What was a typical day like for those who worked in the mine? for family members who tended to the home? for merchants, doctors, and other service providers? Allow adequate time for this project. Videotaping is suggested for preserving this journey back in time.

Life in Gold Hill

After they complete their research, divide students into two groups. Group #1 will represent those characters associated with the mine. Group #2 will portray those who maintain homes, shops, and services. Each group is responsible for creating a typical working day in Gold Hill at the time of the play, showing how their characters spend their time from sunrise to sunset. What do they do? Who do they see? With whom do they interact? What actions and dialogue are essential to performing tasks and maintaining relationships? The following will be helpful.

Gold Hill

1848	1850	1851
5 stores 1 tavern 4 doctors professions represented included mechanics, carriage makers, blacksmiths, boot makers, harness makers, brick layers, and stonemasons	125 dwellings a boarding-house and hotel were among these buildings	cabins and cottages for housing cheap, one-story houses pump engine from the mine could be readily heard crooked streets piles of ore visible businesses included a hotel, carriage making, and a general store

(James S. Brawley, *Rowan County ... a brief history.* Raleigh: North Carolina Division of Archives and History, 1974. Brent D. Glass, "The Miner's World: Life and Labor at Gold Hill." North Carolina Historical Review, October 1985, 420-447.)

After improvisationally developing satisfactory dramatizations, group members should script the action and dialogue. Scenes then should be rehearsed and, if possible, memorized.

A day should be designated for performances of *Life in Gold Hill*. If desired, scenery can be created and props and costumes used to enhance the scenes. Other classes can be invited to view the performances or groups may simply elect to share work with each other.

⋙ Using biographies, historical novels, journals, diaries, periodicals, and similar sources of the period, students should investigate the realities associated with each character's dream(s).

The Dream versus the Reality

After completing the necessary research, direct students to write a monologue in which, as the character, they describe how they imagined their dream coming true and if, in actuality, the dream was realized. Why or why not? Monologues should describe what was involved in bringing the dream to fruition. These dramatic pieces are then delivered in character by the student actors.

Annie dreams of freedom and of learning to read and write.

Lizzie dreams of getting an education and owning the leather boots.

Zeb dreams of a better life for his family, moving west to Illinois, and having his own farm.

Mary Catharine dreams of making a home for her family on a farm.

Dr. Thornton dreams of establishing a common school in Gold Hill.

⋙ For an activity related to the oral interpretation of literature, encourage the class to use published diaries and letters written by women during the period of the North Carolina Gold Rush, as well as slave narratives, to script a dramatic reading. Content should reflect what Annie and Lizzie would say to each other if they had authored such personal documents. One student should play Lizzie and the other should play Annie in performance. Share the following directions with students to help them get started.

A Woman's Role

Lizzie and Annie are the characters here. Using content from sources of the period, imagine that you and a partner are these young friends writing to each other after Annie leaves Gold Hill. If possible, your letters should communicate how you see your respective roles as a young white and a young African-American female affecting your destiny. These letters also describe your life since last seeing the other person.

The subject matter of *Sunday Gold* is specific to North Carolina history. In staging local history, students can learn more about their own area's past.

Staging Local History

Ask students to identify an event of historical importance in their state or local region for this activity. They should gather relevant data and then craft a story to dramatize inspired by the episode or occurrence. Written stories can be displayed in the classroom or compiled in a class book. Actual story dramatizations can be performed for classmates or for an invited audience.

Some students may wish to take this activity one step further by adapting the stories into scripts. Just as the play

Sunday Gold was workshopped in preparation for its premiere, these scripts can be developed through workshops and, ultimately, staged for an audience.

❧ In the study of U.S. history, students should be able to "Compare and contrast differing sets of ideas, values, personalities, behaviors, and institutions." Divide students into small groups whose assignment is to imagine that they are historians researching the North Carolina Gold Rush period. Give them the following instructions.

Historical Analysis

As a team of historians, analyze *Sunday Gold*. For the characters below, describe personality, ideas, values, and behaviors attributable to each. Next, determine if and how these are in keeping with the cultural norms of the period. As historians, be able to support ideas and answers. Report findings to a hypothetical group of fellow historians.

Characters: Annie, Lizzie, Zeb, Mary Catharine,
Dr. Thornton

❧ Joanna H. Kraus has been described as a playwright whose "plays focus on realistic people facing major choices in historically significant times." (Woods, Byron. "The 'Gold' standard." *The News & Observer* June 9, 1996, sec. G:1 & 3.) This exercise looks at serious issues and choices characters make in *Sunday Gold*.

Choices Over Time

Students should work in groups of five for this activity. Ask them to identify the choices facing Annie and Lizzie. In each group, cast two students as the Lizzie and Annie of the late 1840s, two as the twelve year olds in the late 1990s, and one as a reporter from the future, circa 2040. The reporter should interview both sets of characters for their perspectives of their circumstances and the issues influencing them in their respective centuries. How are their choices the same or different given the temporal worlds in which they live? How do issues of slavery and racism affect them? How do their actions bear out the concept that not all gold is of the material kind? After interviews are presented for classmates, each group should create a visual image (i.e., time line, chart) in which information gathered during the interviews is used to compare and contrast the girls' circumstances and responses to them.

A Unique Collaboration Between a History Museum and Community Theatre Strikes Gold in "Sunday Gold"

Richard King

In 1799, the son of a farmer discovered a seventeen-pound gold nugget alongside a creek bed in central North Carolina. Not until years later did he and his family realize its immense value. Similarly, when the youth education program at Raleigh Little Theatre decided in 1994 to commission a new play for young audiences, we had no idea that the end results would be so rewarding. *Sunday Gold* is now an award-winning, published play for young audiences worthy of inclusion in this anthology of playwright Joanna H. Kraus' significant contributions to youth theatre.

In most cases, the commission of a new work is related to professional theatres and university theatre programs. Raleigh Little Theatre is a community theatre serving over 500 volunteers annually, many of whom participate in theatre just as an enjoyable activity. However, the youth education program, staffed in 1994 by a Youth Theatre Director, Jennifer Scott McNair, and myself as Youth Education Director, was committed to providing educational theatre activities that would expose young people to respected professionals in the field. We wanted a project that gave us an opportunity to invest the youth education program in an activity that would provide our students insights into the professional process of creating theatre while at the same time making a significant contribution to our field. In the previous year, we had received our first education project grant from the North Carolina Arts Council. The project was a moderate success and now we wanted to set our sights on something more in-depth.

While sitting at our favorite coffee shop evaluating our education programs and discussing ideas for a second education project grant, Jennifer and I agreed that the idea of a new work commission seemed an appropriately ambitious project.

The notion that a community theatre would engage in the commission of a new play for young audiences posed many challenges. First, we had to consider the trends in arts funding, realizing that there is strength in numbers and that funding agencies like to see how far their dollars can be stretched to serve the needs of many. Second, we knew that the subject matter needed to be relevant to the criteria of funding agencies and of interest to our primary audience. Third, we needed to find subject matter about which we, as artists/educators, could get excited. Fourth, we needed to gain support from our staff, board of directors, and volunteers in order to sustain the momentum that developing a new work requires. Over the course of the next three years, the new work project had its share of ups and downs. It persevered to meet the goals of the project's mission and contributed to the canon of original scripts for young audiences.

To get the ball rolling, we needed funding. The project simply could never be given an appropriation of funds from the operating budget of the non-profit community theatre. It was an advantage to have an established relationship with two primary funding sources in the county and state, the North Carolina Arts Council and the United Arts Council of Raleigh and Wake County. Both agencies offered funds for arts education initiatives. Before we could seek funds, however, we needed to clarify our project goals. What would be the topic of this new play commission? Who would be our partner? What was of interest in North Carolina to us? To help us shape the goals of this project, we approached the North Carolina Museum of

History. We had established a relationship with the museum a year earlier when we brought the production *Talking Leaves*, a play about the life of the Cherokee Indian chief, Seqoyah, to the museum for free programming. Essentially, we asked them if they wanted to join forces to commission a new play based on a significant event or individual in North Carolina's history. They said yes. It was truly that simple. We had our partner and we were giving them the opportunity to guide us toward the topic.

At the same time, I also realized that the grant proposal would be stronger if a playwright was committed to the project. I contacted Dorothy Webb of the IUPPI playwriting symposium. I first came to know Dorothy several years earlier, while in graduate school at Arizona State University. I was soliciting new scripts for a directing project. She had been a tremendous resource then. After I explained that I wanted to contract a playwright for a new work commission, she gave me the names of several playwrights and described their individual attributes. Our first and only conversation was brief. She assured me that there were other playwrights I should consider and that she would get back to me with more names. About thirty minutes later, I received a phone call from Joanna Kraus. I was somewhat taken aback by her call. Joanna is required reading for theatre for youth graduate students and I was well aware of her work dramatizing history. After discussing the goals of the project with her, I secured our playwright and the strength of the grant proposal increased significantly.

At this point, Jennifer and I realized that the new work commission would be an opportunity to explore a new education program—that of a professional touring company performing for school systems and communities. We outlined a two-phase project. Phase I would be the commission of a new play resulting in a workshop production and a world premiere in Raleigh Little Theatre's Youth Series. Phase II would consist of a statewide tour to schools and extension sites for the North Carolina Museum of History. In addition, the United Arts Council wanted to insure that students would be afforded participatory activities to extend the learning value of the theatre experience. To that end, Phase I of the project would include an intensive playwriting residency with theatre students at a local performing arts high school, and Phase II would offer a variety of theatre workshops to accompany performances in schools. In addition, a comprehensive teacher's guide would be developed with cross-curricular activities relevant to the topic of the play.

It is important to consider how crucial the pre-planning process is when preparing grants. After several meetings with the program directors at both funding agencies and several rewrites of grant narratives, the project began to take shape and proposals were submitted. After several months of anticipation, nail biting, and second guessing, funds were secured for Phase I.

Back to the topic of the new work. The basis of our partnership with the museum was that the theatre would control the artistic process and the museum would approve the topic, facilitate research, and authorize acceptance of the playwright's concept. Because North Carolina is so rich in significant history, we asked the museum to prepare a list of topics that would be appropriate for the target audience of grades four through eight. State history is almost always a required social studies topic and the subject matter needed to be fresh material. The Wright Brothers had been thoroughly covered, the textile mill history was considered too controversial for the target audience, finding redeemable qualities for Blackbeard and pirate lore was too difficult, and so on. The North Carolina Gold Rush, however, seemed fascinating. Several people we spoke to about the subject didn't even know North Carolina had a gold rush. We found our topic. We struck gold of our own.

Joanna immediately began her research. She came to Raleigh and spent hours poring through museum archives and visiting historic gold-rush sites in search of a compelling character, story, or incident that would serve as an appropriate hook. She also wanted to remain true to her commitment to bring significant women to the forefront as she has done in so many of her plays. It was nearly impossible to find an historic female who had contributed to the North Carolina gold rush. However, she gained a lot of insight into the gold-rush era and what it meant for farmers whose farms were failing, and why they were drawn to the promise of gold in central North Carolina. She also became aware of the social issues surrounding the use of slaves and children, particularly girls, who worked in mining operations. She proposed the idea of a fictionalized history about a family who moved to Gold Hill, North Carolina, to take up mining with the hope of striking it rich. The museum approved this suggestion and, armed with a wealth of historic references, Joanna went to work.

Soon, we all were introduced to our protagonist, Lizzie Johnson, a twelve-year-old girl who was sent to work in the mining camp as a rocker girl (a rocker was a device used to sift gold dust from dirt excavated from the mines). Like many young girls today, Lizzie was a dreamer who wanted a better life for herself and her family. She wanted happiness for her family, boots for her feet and, most of all, an education, all of which were hard to come by for a poor mining family in the 1840s. An important subplot to this story involved the plight of slaves and their universal desire for freedom. Lizzie befriended a slave girl named Annie who also worked the rockers and, through their brief friendship, learned that the material possessions gold can buy are not as important as human dignity.

The museum had accepted this scenario and, after several drafts, the museum and the playwright were in agreement on the script. There were challenges however and, respecting the museum's role of authorizing historical accuracy and plausibility, Joanna was able to craft a play that accurately portrayed circumstances of the gold-rush era. Between the rewrites, I had an opportunity to work with actors and get the script on its feet for the first time. As a director working with a playwright's new material, my responsibility was to do just that—to get the play on its feet so the playwright can view the storyworld created in her mind in real time.

Joanna returned to Raleigh for an extended period of six weeks for additional rewrites leading up to the workshop production. While here, she conducted a playwrighting residency at a local performing arts high school and taught a professional development workshop for teachers. All of this activity kept Joanna quite busy but the impact on the theatre community was significant. Our students at Raleigh Little Theatre, teachers in the school system, officials at the North Carolina Museum of History, and members of the community saw the development of something new.

The workshop production was simply staged in a small black box theatre and was seen by a disparate group of supporters whose theatre experiences ranged from a child's first play to veteran theatre professionals with extensive attendance records. Most had never witnessed the creation of a new play and a tremendous sense of pride coursed through our relatively small community. After some minor rewrites, which included the cutting of a very popular "poker scene" (the play had to be no longer than sixty minutes to be viable for touring to schools), *Sunday Gold* received its world premiere in Raleigh Little Theatre's 1996 youth series. Again, Joanna and her family were in attendance and Phase I came to a successful completion.

There was added excitement to the completion of Phase I because grants had been submitted in the previous spring for Phase II of the project, a tour to schools and North Carolina History Museum sites throughout the state. We had learned at the end of the summer that our grants were funded and so prior to the world premiere, we were making preparations to bring *Sunday Gold* to an estimated 20,000 school children in the spring of 1997.

Although I left the Raleigh Little Theatre prior to the school shows, I was able to secure a sold-out tour of *Sunday Gold* and oversee the development of a cross-curricular teacher's guide to accompany the production. Raleigh Little Theatre had never produced a touring production and there were some mistakes made in the preparations. However, *Sunday Gold* made its way across the state and the response from students and teachers was tremendous. The students were engaged, challenged, and through this production, learned an important aspect of their state's history. More than learning just historical facts, young audiences gained insights into how citizens and slaves felt during the trying times of the gold-rush era.

Our ultimate goal had been achieved. We wanted to contribute to the education of North Carolina's students and entertain them with a glimpse into their state's past. We wanted to contribute to the field of theatre for young audiences. We wanted to grow as artists. We struck gold with Joanna H. Kraus and *Sunday Gold*.

Permissions Acknowledgments

Bibliography

Academic Affairs Library, University of North Carolina at Chapel Hill. "Documenting the American South: Harriet Tubman." http://www.sunsite.unc.edu/docsouth/harriet/about.html, 1998.

————. "First-Person Narratives of the American South, Beginnings to 1920." http://www.sunsite.unc.edu/docsouth/fpn.html, 1998.

————. "North American Slave Narratives, Beginnings to 1920." http://www.sunsite.unc.edu/docsouth/specialneh.html, 1998.

Brawley, James S. *Rowan County...a brief history.* Raleigh: North Carolina Division of Archives and History, 1974.

Corey, Orlin. "Presentation of the 1971 Chorpenning Cup at the CTC Awards Luncheon." Art Institute of Chicago. Chicago, August 16, 1971. Courtesy of Special Collections, Arizona State University.

Glass, Brent D. "The Miner's World: Life and Labor at Gold Hill." *North Carolina Historical Review,* October 1985, 420–447.

Honor of Humanity Project Education Committee. *Study Guide for "Angel in the Night": A Play by Joanna H. Kraus.* Woodstock, Ill.: Dramatic, 1999.

Kraus, Joanna H. Papers. Special Collections. Arizona State University Library.

————. *Angel in the Night.* Woodstock, Ill.: Dramatic Publishing Co., 1995.

————. *The Ice Wolf.* Charlottesville, Va.: New Plays Inc., 1967.

————. *Mean to be Free.* Charlottesville, Va.: New Plays Inc., 1968.

————. *Remember My Name.* New York: Samuel French, Inc., 1989.

————. *Sunday Gold.* Woodstock, Ill.: Dramatic Publishing Co., 1998.

Swortzell, Lowell. Director, Program in Education Theatre, New York University, 1996. Courtesy of Special Collections, Arizona State University.

UCLA National Center for History in the Schools. "Chapter 2—Overview of Standards in Historical Thinking." http://www. sscnet.ucla.edu/nchs/uschap2.htm#overview, 1995.

————. "Era 4 Expansion and Reform (1801-1861)." http:// www.sscnet.ucla.edu/nchs/us3era4.htm, 1995.